VICTORIOUS CHRISTIAN LIVING CONFERENCE

U.S. HEADQUARTERS
VCL International
14819 N. Cave Creek Rd.
Phoenix, AZ 85032
(602) 482-2164

ISBN: 0-7392-0015-1

VCLI is a nonprofit ministry. By your purchase of materials, you are helping to provide FREE services to hurting people. Thank you for being a part of the team.

Printed in the USA by

MORRIS PUBLISHING

3212 East Highway 30 • Kearney, NE 68847 • 1-800-650-7888

THIS CONFERENCE IS A MINISTRY OUTREACH OF
VCL INTERNATIONAL
Formerly Neues Leben International

VCL International is a nondenominational biblical-discipleship training ministry. It is committed to renewal and discipleship in the body of Christ. VCL International is a total-life ministry. Our purpose is to see new life in Christ become the daily living experience of each individual and family to whom we minister. Our source book is the Bible, the Word of the living God, in which knowledge of God, salvation in Jesus Christ, and directions for effective living are found.

VCL International:
1. Provides biblical discipleship.
2. Trains Christians to be biblical disciplers.
3. Helps churches start discipleship ministries in their churches funded by their people for their people.

VCL International believes only Christ's life produces genuine renewal for the individual and the church.

MAXIMIZING YOUR CONFERENCE EXPERIENCE

▶ Ask the Lord to teach you how to personally apply the principles taught in the VCL lessons.

▶ Don't spend time thinking about other people who need this message.

▶ After each lesson, listen to the corresponding audiotape and read the transcript.

▶ Be diligent to complete your study guides.

▶ Be prepared to participate in group discussion.

▶ Plan to share what the Lord has shown you with someone He brings to your mind.

HOW TO COMMIT YOUR LIFE TO CHRIST

The beginning of victorious Christian living has to be an intimate, personal relationship with the Lord Jesus Christ. Without that relationship, you have no power or ability on your own to live victoriously.

What God's Word says about committing your life to Christ:

◆ **"For all have sinned and fall short of the glory of God" (Romans 3:23).**
  Has the Holy Spirit shown you the truth of your sinful choices?

◆ **"The wages of sin is death" (Romans 6:23).**
  Have you realized you are without hope, facing death—eternally separated from God because of your sin?

◆ **"He Himself bore our sins in His body on the cross" (1 Peter 2:24).**
  Do you understand that Jesus came to die on the cross to bear the penalty for your sin—that only His shed blood is sufficient to meet God's requirements for eternal life?"

◆ **"He who has the Son has the life" (1 John 5:12).**
  Do you see that eternal life is in the person of Jesus?

◆ **"As many as received Him, to them He gave the right to become children of God, even to those who believe in His name" (1 John 1:12).**
  You may believe Jesus lived and died for you, but have you received Him into your life as your Savior and Lord?

◆ **"Behold, I stand at the door and knock; if anyone hears My voice and opens the door, I will come into him" (Revelation 3:20).**
  Have you opened the door to your heart and life and invited Him to come into you? If you have you can rejoice and thank Jesus for His free gift of eternal life!

  If you have not, now would be a wonderful time to simply pray and admit you have sinned, thank Him for dying for your sins, and then open the door to your heart and life and ask Him to come into you and be your Savior and Lord.

VICTORIOUS CHRISTIAN LIVING Conference
Copyright © 1999 Victorious Christian Living International, Inc.

GODSHIP ⟶

GODSHIP

REJECT

EXT/INT

PROBLEMS

FLESH

REPENT

WHAT'S NEW

ACCEPT RIGHT

EXTEND FORGIVE

SEEK FORGIVE

REST

LOVE

GODSHIP

> . . . your eyes will
> be opened, and you
> will be like God . . .
>
> Genesis 3:5

This lesson pinpoints the beginning of man's original rebellion against God and the results. Ever since Eve's conversation with Satan, man has sought to be like God. We coined the term "godship" for this basic problem of mankind. Godship (sin) is the term used to identify: **(1) an individual functioning as his or her own god, (2) the self-life or walking after the flesh, (3) an individual living without considering what God has to say, or (4) allowing circumstances or feelings to rule instead of God.**

This lesson has often been used by God to change people's lives. Ask the Lord to open your heart to His truth.

EXERCISING GODSHIP

☐ Determining standards of conduct for myself, others, and God.

☐ Demanding absolute obedience to those standards.

☐ Judging God, others, and my life, attitudes, and actions by those standards.

☐ Seeking revenge.

☐ Selfishly endeavoring to control circumstances and people.

☐ Exercising "sovereign" independence, doing whatever I please.

☐ Seeking praise, approval, & acceptance from others and not from God.

☐ Asking no help or guidance from anyone, not even God.

100-A

NOTES

VCL
VICTORIOUS CHRISTIAN LIVING Conference
Copyright © 1999 Victorious Christian Living International, Inc.

Godship
STUDY GUIDE

PURPOSE for Diagram **100-A:**

To show how people try to be like God.

1. What is godship? _____
_____

2. Study Genesis 3:1-7.

3. Whose idea was it to be like God? _____

4. What actions of godship do you see in verses 6-7? _____
_____
_____

5. Which of these eight expressions of godship are most common in your life?
_____
_____
_____
_____

> *. . . your eyes will be opened, and you will be like God . . . .*
> Gen. 3:5

6. Have you said, "I wish people would just do things right!" Right according to whom— you? Who made you the standard setter for others to follow? _____
_____

7. Have you judged yourself and condemned yourself recently? Why? Whose standards did you break? _____
_____

8. Have you ever tried to control people by silence, yelling, intimidation, or kindness? Do you see your use of alcohol, drugs, food, or sleep as an attempt to control your life? _____

9. Do you try hard to please people? _____

10. Do you see these actions as sin? _____

"It will wear me out to try to be like God. I am not equipped to be God."

GOD BEING GOD:

- **Determines standards of conduct for mankind**—*Ex. 20:1-17*

- **Demands absolute obedience to those standards**—*Gen. 22:1-12*

- **Judges the lives, actions, and attitudes of man**—*Gen. 18:25; Acts 17:31*

- **Takes vengeance**—*Ps. 94:1; Rom. 12:17-19*

- **Controls all of life**—*Job 12:13-25; Acts 17:24-28a*

- **Exercises sovereign independence,
  doing whatever He pleases**—*Ps. 135:5-6; Dan. 4:35*

- **Seeks the praise, worship, and
  acceptance of mankind**—*Isa. 42:8; John 4:23*

- **Asks help and guidance from no one**—*Isa. 40:13-14; Rom. 11:33-34*

100-B

NOTES

VCL
VICTORIOUS CHRISTIAN LIVING Conference
Copyright © 1999 Victorious Christian Living International, Inc.

PURPOSE for Diagram **100-B:**

To illustrate the "rights" of God.

? 1. Why is it God's right to perform all these actions? _____

_____

📖 2. Study Job 12:13-25.

? 3. How much of life does God control? _____

_____

? 4. Why is it foolish for us to try to play god in our lives or someone else's life? _____

_____

_____

_____

> *I am the Lord, and there is no other . . . .* Isa. 45:5

📖 5. Study Isaiah 42:8.

? 6. What is God's attitude toward someone who would usurp His place?

_____

_____

? 7. How do you know when you are exercising godship? _____

_____

_____

God is God and I am not!

JUDGING GOOD AND EVIL

	GOOD		EVIL
GOD'S LAWS *(Absolute)*	Whatever God, out of His infinite goodness, justice, and love, states to be ultimately for man's blessing and God's own glory	**GOD**	Whatever God rejects as being inconsistent with His perfect righteousness and therefore against His good purposes in the world
MAN'S LAWS *(Relative)*	Whatever is personally thought at present to be beneficial to the greatest number of persons or to the persons of greatest importance	**SELF**	Whatever is rejected by the present consensus and therefore is perceived as being bad for society

Judges 21:25

100-C

VCL
VICTORIOUS CHRISTIAN LIVING Conference
Copyright © 1999 Victorious Christian Living International, Inc.

PURPOSE for Diagram **100-C**:

To distinguish between God's absolute law and man's relative law.

1. What things have society decided are good based on the beliefs of the majority of the people? _____ _____

2. What things have you decided are good based on your own benefit without considering what God says? _____ _____

3. Study John 7:24

4. What determines good or evil? _____ _____ _____

5. How do God's values differ from society's values? _____ _____ _____ _____

6. Study Proverbs 16:25.

7. How does that passage apply to you? _____ _____ _____ _____ _____

> *There is a way which seems right to a man, But its end is the way of death.* Prov. 16:25
> (NKJV)

8. Study the last verse in the book of Judges. How does that apply to today?

"Everybody could be wrong."

THREE KINGDOMS

Ephesians 4:1-6

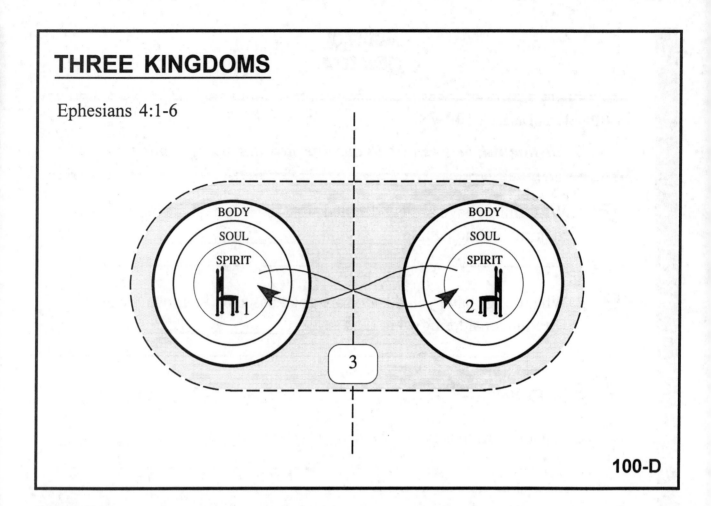

VCL
VICTORIOUS CHRISTIAN LIVING Conference
Copyright © 1999 Victorious Christian Living International, Inc.

NOTES

PURPOSE for Diagram **100-D**:

*To illustrate conflict between two parties
when either or both are functioning in godship.*

1. Are you in a relationship where there is a conflict? _____

2. Study Matthew 7:1-5.

3. Have you been judging another person?
_____

> *For where you have
> . . . selfish ambition,
> there you find
> disorder . . . .* James 3:16
> (NIV)

4. Have you been trying to change the
person in the other kingdom?
_____

5. How's it going? Do you find yourself feeling frustrated or angry?
_____
_____

6. What areas of godship (Diagram 100-A) does your frustration or anger
reveal? _____
_____

7. Have you thought about or talked about ending the relationship?
_____
_____

8. Are you ready to yield yourself to the Lord to rule your kingdom?
_____

*If I play god of my own kingdom,
I shouldn't expect another person to
be my subject.*

"GOOD" TAKEN BEYOND THE BOUNDS—IS *SIN*

Gen. 2:17; 3:6

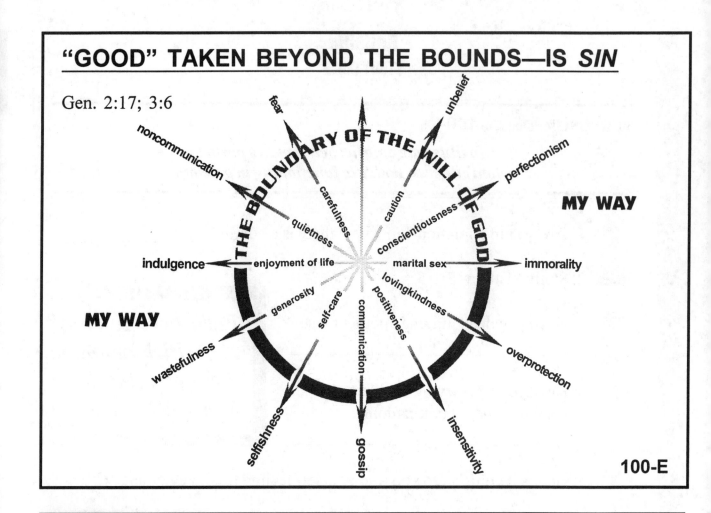

100-E

VCL

VICTORIOUS CHRISTIAN LIVING Conference
Copyright © 1999 Victorious Christian Living International, Inc.

PURPOSE for Diagram **100-E:**

> *To illustrate that what God created as good*
> *can be pushed beyond the boundaries of His will.*

? 1. In the Garden of Eden, did God make fruit of the trees for Adam and Eve's enjoyment?   YES   NO

? 2. In Genesis 2:17, what did God say would happen if Adam and Eve ate of the tree of the knowledge of good and evil?_____

_____

? 3. Did God put a boundary on what was good?   YES   NO

> *. . . do not turn your freedom into*
> *an opportunity for the flesh . . . .*
> Gal. 5:13a

📖 4. Read Genesis 3:6. Is sin often appealing to us as humans?

_____

? 5. Which of those attributes in Diagram 100-E cross over the boundary of God's will in your life? _____

? 6. How did the boundary get crossed? _____

_____

? 7. Do you agree that crossing these boundaries is deciding for yourself what is good and evil?   YES   NO   (If yes, that is godship.)

My way is not God's will.

GOD'S WAY

Gal. 5:22-23

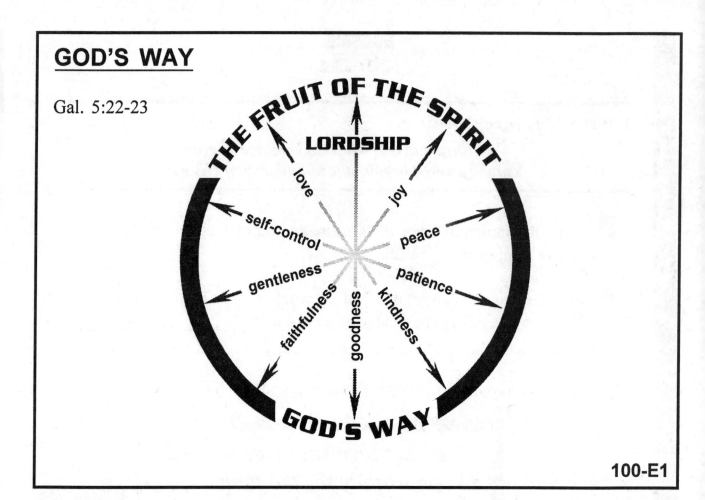

NOTES

VCL

VICTORIOUS CHRISTIAN LIVING Conference

Godship
STUDY GUIDE

PURPOSE for Diagram **100-E1:**

*To demonstrate that the fruit of the Spirit will be evident
in our lives when we abstain from walking in godship.*

? 1. What is the difference between godship and Lordship? _____

_____

? 2. Where do you see yourself—in godship
or Lordship? _____

_____

against such things there is no law.
Gal. 5:23b

📖 3. Study Galatians 5:16-23.

? 4. What do you see in your life—the fruit of the Spirit or the deeds of the
flesh? _____

_____

📖 5. Study Romans 10:9.

? 6. What position is Jesus to have in our lives? _____

_____

_____

? 7. Are you ready to admit exercising godship in your life? _____

_____

🙏 8. Admit your sin of trying to be god.

🙏 9. Receive His forgiveness and cleansing.

🙏 10. Reject the actions of godship in your life!

🙏 11. Yield yourself to Christ and let Jesus reign as LORD!

Jesus—Lord of all or not Lord at all.

REVIEW

- God is God and I am not.

- God is God and only He has the right to set standards, judge, and demand absolute obedience of people.

- There is something within me that desires to be like God.

- Godship is sin and leads to withdrawal from God and others and doubting instead of trusting.

- Only when God rules over our relationships with others will we experience relationships that bring glory to His kingdom.

- Good taken beyond God's boundaries leads to sin.

NOTES

VCL
VICTORIOUS CHRISTIAN LIVING Conference
Copyright © 1999 Victorious Christian Living International, Inc.

GODSHIP

Lesson Transcript by David Ritzenthaler

Have you ever wondered why there is so much conflict in the world—nations fighting nations, husbands and wives wanting to murder each other, children angry with their parents? Someone sent me this article about a man by the name of Marty Course. "Marty tried unsuccessfully to ease his tow truck into the jammed Los Angeles freeway traffic. A Datsun pickup moved forward to block him from merging, so he slowed down. But the occupants of the pickup weren't satisfied with the fact that he slowed down. In fact, they slowed down to match Marty's speed. Then the passenger in the pickup pulled out a hand gun, aimed it at Marty's truck, and fired." These kinds of terrifying incidents happen constantly on the freeways across our country. What is it that makes man who is supposedly innately good, so ugly in his actions and his attitudes?

This session is entitled "Godship." Turn to the front page and there is a box in the center where Genesis 3:5 is quoted. It says, ". . . your eyes will be opened, and you will be like God . . . " What I want to help you see in the next few minutes is that there is a major malady that has existed from the beginning of the human race, and this malady is the cause of all these conflicts. On the front page, you'll notice some numbers 1, 2, 3, and 4 that are highlighted. You might even want to underline them. These various definitions are to define a little word that's the title of this lesson on godship. Godship is simply a little word that I thought of as I was reading Genesis 3:5 ". . . and they shall become as gods . . . ." I thought, "There is a problem of godship. These people are wanting to try to be God." I want to give you four definitions that will help you grasp

this concept so we're thinking together whenever I use that term "godship."

The first one says, "an individual functioning as his or her own god." I think most of us when we think of that, think of other people's names regarding this problem of godship.

Secondly, it says, "the self-life or walking after the flesh." Now we have an entire session on the flesh-life and self-life and walking after the flesh, but godship is expressed in walking after the flesh.

The third one is "an individual living without considering what God has to say." You say, "What do you mean by that?" Let me give you some examples of that. Most of us are very desirous of having financial success. Yet, how many of us have ever taken the time to take God's Word and find out what God has to say about spending money. Spending money is a major issue that I have dealt with for years with people who are in trouble financially. Very few of them have any understanding of what they should be spending their money for, much less know what God says with regard to spending money. There are six things that God says with regard to spending money and seven if you need to get out of debt, but most people don't know that. People get married and have children and they are wondering why they have terrible two's or why they have troubled teenagers and they've never taken the time to find out the seven things God has to say with regard to parenting children. God has delineated the details of how to live successfully in a marriage, yet how many people have taken the time to really thoroughly study and then begin to act on the things that God has to say? Well, that's what I mean when I say people are living without considering what God has to say. That's what we call godship.

Maybe you are thinking, "Well you didn't get me yet." Hopefully, this fourth one will collect the rest of you. These are the people "allowing circumstances or feelings to rule instead of God." They do what they do based on how they feel. They base what they do on their circumstances. You might even ask one of them, "How are you doing?" "Well , under the circumstances . . . ." God never intended a believer to live "under the circumstances" and let circumstances control the believer's life. That is not God's design for a person who is supposed to be allowing God to rule his or her life.

EXERCISING GODSHIP
(Diagram 100-A)
When we talk about godship, it's simply this little word that I began to see back in Genesis 3:5 when Adam and Eve did what God said not to do. They began to decide for themselves how life should work and that's godship. When we see the problems that exist in society, we're seeing this issue of godship. In fact, if you'd turn to your first diagram, 100-A, you'll notice various things that you and I might do in exercising godship. On the left hand side you'll notice a bunch of little boxes. The reason those boxes are there is because I want you to think personally, do any of these apply to me? Is any one of these an issue of godship in my own life that I need to face and deal with so that I don't create all kinds of unwanted problems?

Notice the first one: I determine standards of conduct for myself, others, and God. You say, "What do you mean I determine standards of conduct?" Well, let's think about some of those things. We just talked about the freeway and Marty and his truck. How many of you have found yourselves on the street driving your car and suddenly someone is reacting to you be-

cause you pulled in front of that person or you came up on that person too fast and the driver is all upset with you? The driver may even be giving certain motions to you, because he or she considers you are not driving in the certain space and place where you should be. That person is setting the standard for how you should drive.

Look at the next one. Not only do people set standards, but then they demand absolute obedience of those standards. In fact, you probably thought about this when growing up. I don't think there are any children that haven't been upset with their parents' standards and decided that their parents aren't fair with them. They demand their parents to function according to the values or the standards that *they think their parents should have*. The same thing is true in marriages. Over and over we have people come for help and the husband and the wife have both come into the marriage with various baggage— their value systems, their ideas, their opinions, their standards—and expect the other person to meet those same conditions and standards.

Third one. People judge God, others, and their own lives, attitudes, and actions by those standards. How much of our society today is judged on standards like the size of a lapel or the size of the tie or the way a dress or haircut looks? How many times do we look at other people and we make a judgment about them because we have certain standards and we use those standards to judge others? In fact, many times we have probably missed out on meeting and knowing a most incredible person. We never got the privilege, because we already had set a standard that the way the person looked or dressed or talked didn't meet the conditions of somebody with whom we wanted to have a relationship. In fact, maybe at some point you have broken through the barrier of your judgments against some person and found out this is an incredible person.

Look at the next one, seeking revenge. I think of one couple we ministered to here that had al-

VCL
VICTORIOUS CHRISTIAN LIVING Conference
Copyright © 1998 Victorious Christian Living International, Inc.

ready been divorced when they came to the center. They came for counseling because at the time they were in court fighting over the children. In the process of getting them reconciled, the gentleman revealed the fight over the children in divorce court was so severe that he had actually gone to a store and put a deposit on a gun. In his view, in the next few days, he was going to have to eliminate her. He thought, "If I can't control her and I can't get her to do it the way I want to do it, I'll just eliminate her completely." As we talked with him, one of the things he said was, "You've got to understand, in my family we don't get mad—we get even!" And so, in his mind, he wasn't just going to get mad over this situation, he was going to get even. In fact, he was going to get more than even, he was going to eliminate her. So, seeking revenge is one of the expressions of godship. It is the way people express their commitment to being god.

Look at the next one: I selfishly endeavor to control circumstances and people. This is one I see often when people come in and they're depressed or anxious. It's over this issue of godship. This might be one you'd check if you're an anxious or depressed person. Almost always, people who are anxious or depressed are people who are upset with either the circumstances not working the way they want them to or the people around them not functioning the way they want them to function. They're frustrated. They're angry because they can't control. In fact, to think about it, being god is really a difficult project, and yet, that is what godship is all about. It's an individual trying to be god in other people's lives and in every area of the person's own life and circumstances. Usually when somebody does that, the individual is a frustrated, angry person, maybe depressed, or anxious.

Next one: I exercise "sovereign" independence, doing whatever I please. In fact, just as an illustration of that, someone gave me an article

out of the Phoenix paper some time ago. It's about a woman by the name of Carrie Munson. I want to just read to you what it says here. This is a woman who is terminally ill, a victim of cancer. The title of the article says, "She Will Attend Her Own Funeral." This caught my attention and I began to read it. She scheduled her funeral early, so that she could attend it alive. "Carrie Munson, 62 years of age, from Milwaukee sent invitations to her friends, associates, enemies, and three sons for the next Saturday service. Munson, who has pancreatic cancer, had been told by her doctor she didn't have long to live. She had a 25-year addiction to heroin, attended the university, and acted as a hostess on a radio jazz show. The heroin habit led her to prison terms for crimes committed to get drugs including theft, prostitution, forgery, and mailbox fraud. As she considered this funeral in planning it ahead of time, she decided that one of the things she wanted was to inform everybody that she had achieved all of her goals." Now those sound like quite worthy goals but, also as a part of the funeral, she decided that the only music she was going to have was "My Way" by Frank Sinatra. This is an illustration of a person who has decided to live a life of sovereign independence. The sad part about it is, though she was acting as if she was god and she was living this life of independence, she had no power over when the day was that she was going to die. Because you see, ultimately, no one as a person exercising godship truly has the power to be god. Nobody has the resources to control everything, only God does. So, we consistently see in ministry to people, people trying to be god, exercising godship in the area of sovereign independence.

Look at the next one: Seeking praise, approval, and acceptance from others and not from God. One illustration of this is people who have grown up convinced that the only way they can have value and the only way they can be important is to perform. So, what they do is spend their whole life trying to be perfect. They become perfectionists and, in their perfectionism, they just become filled with anxiety and trials and tribulations with many physical maladies as a part of it. As we help them understand this issue of trying to be god, trying to control everything, trying to be perfect, they release this godship, and they begin to let God be God of their lives. As they begin to entrust themselves to Him and they begin to rest in Him, many of the physical maladies just disappear because they are the effects of this issue of godship. In seeking praise and worship, the perfectionist says, "Well that's not me. I'm a Christian. I don't do that kind of thing." Well, let's think about that for a minute. Here's an illustration of godship—of seeking praise and worship. How many have spent their lives buying new cars every year or every couple of years, when the cars they had were still fine? How many have found themselves wanting to buy a bigger, fancier house when the one they've got is actually fine; it's perfectly sufficient for their family? How many get caught up with the fads because they want to look good and they want people to see them? Or, how many adorn themselves with jewelry and various things to give evidence that they're really successful? What's that all about? Are they seeking God's praise and worship or are they seeking the praise of men because they want to be viewed as really important? That's godship.

The last one: Asking no help or guidance from anyone, not even God. I see this especially with men, but it's not limited to men. I don't know if you've had a little child that you've raised, maybe your own or you've been dealing with another one, and you observe that something is wrong and so you ask the child, "What's wrong?" He answers, "Nothing." Well, it's kind of a laughable thing when you see him in your office, he's 50 or 55 years of age, his wife has filed for divorce, and she has come in for counseling. As a part of the counseling process, you've invited him to come in to get his perspective of things. You ask him a question, "Well, how are things going?" and he answers, "Every-

thing is fine, there is nothing wrong." You say, "What about the divorce papers?"

"Oh, that's no problem. I'm sure we'll work that out."

He has no idea of the desperate state he's in and his need for help. He has no idea that he should ever ask for help because he thinks he's self-sufficient.

I remember particularly my brother Richard sharing this with me at one point in time. When he was first in the process of divorce, we tried to help him. He assured us that he didn't need any help. Well, to appreciate this you'd have to know that my brother is really a genius. In fact, he owns the patents of things that have never existed before. He has a very creative, brilliant mind. His view was he could do anything. He didn't need anyone's help. He could just think it out with his brain, and he could solve it. Well, he ended up divorced.

Years went by and at one point in time when I went to see him, he was living in a corncrib in the middle of January, in Illinois, with a little light bulb that was basically a heating system and the light for the facility. His two children were sleeping in sleeping bags. There was no heating system. He didn't have a job. He didn't have a car. In fact, he didn't even have any food. He was at the end of things. I remember as we sat there and he asked me if I would help, I said "Well, you'd have to be willing to let me open my Bible and read to you what God has to say." You see, he also didn't see that the Word of God had anything to do with life. He had been given a brain and his brain was quite brilliant. The only problem was that night he said to me, "You know, I don't know if I'll ever even be able to think again." I realized at that moment the most precious thing he had, which was his ability to think, which was his god, when he realized that didn't work anymore he had nothing left. He had nowhere to go, and he was

VCL
VICTORIOUS CHRISTIAN LIVING Conference
Copyright © 1998 Victorious Christian Living International, Inc.

willing to then listen to what God had to say. I answered his questions that night, and God began to do a supernatural thing, because God's supernaturally capable. Because Richard realized he needed help, he wasn't God, he wasn't capable, and that only God was capable.

I have to tell you that today my brother takes the Word of God and helps other people transform their lives to the wholeness and healing that only God can do supernaturally. So today it's just fun to watch, to see his children living and walking with Christ. Then 18 years later, for him to remarry his wife, for them to be a family again, and for them together to be seeking God's will to do things God's way. God's capable of doing what none of us could think or imagine could ever happen because He's God and we are not.

GOD BEING GOD (Diagram 100-B)

In fact, look at your next diagram, 100-B. You'll notice there the same things that we just described in 100-A. The only difference is that next to each of those is a verse which I'm not going to take the time to read. You can read these verses later. The first one is that God determines standards of conduct for mankind. You see because God is God, because He created mankind, because He owns everything including us, God has the right to set standards. We're in a society where everybody is talking about rights. It's an interesting thing that we're all caught up with what our rights are. Yet, we're these puny little human beings under the control and authority of the One who created everything and owns everything. He's the one that has the rights. We don't have any, ultimately; but God, because he is God has the right to determine standards of conduct for people. If we don't want to be little gods exercising godship, then we're going to have to go back and find out what His standards are and operate according to His standards. If we don't, then we're acting as god ourselves.

Notice the second one. He demands absolute obedience of those standards. He has the right to demand absolute obedience. The wonderful thing is when you get to know who God is, He doesn't demand absolute obedience for anything that He doesn't empower to make possible. So for every one of these standards that He demands, He has provided all the resources to make it possible for us to obey them.

Thirdly, He judges the lives and actions and attitudes of the human race. He has the right to do that because of who He is.

He takes vengeance. In fact, He says no person has the right to ever exercise vengeance. He says vengeance is His and His alone. Does He have the right to do that? Well, if He owns everything, created everything, He's God, therefore He has the right to do whatever He wants, including vengeance.

Controls all of life. Well this is an interesting one. He happens to be the only One, the only Person who actually has all the resources necessary to control life. He truly can. That's because He's God and we aren't.

Exercises sovereign independence, does whatever He pleases.

You see because of who He is, He has the right to seek the praise and the worship and the acceptance of mankind. He created us for the purposes of worshiping and praising Him; that was His whole purpose for creation.

Asking help and guidance from no one. Who is He that He would need to ask us how things should work? You see, the problem is we need to ask Him how things work. Otherwise, we're living a life without considering what God has to say, and we're exercising godship.

JUDGING GOOD AND EVIL
(Diagram 100-C)

Notice your next diagram, 100-C. When Genesis 3:5 took place and Adam and Eve ate of the fruit that God told them not to eat, they became as gods to decide what was right and wrong. You see, when God is the standard as to what is good, whatever out of God's infinite goodness ultimately blesses man is what is good. When God is the standard as to how you judge what's evil, whatever God rejects as being inconsistent with His perfect character and against His good purposes in the world is what is evil. When that is true all of us live under the same absolute standard. There are no differences. The standard is the same for every human being.

But an interesting thing happens when godship goes into motion. Every human being who is exercising godship is now deciding what personally seems to be most beneficial for "me"; or if you get the greatest number of people together, because they have the greatest power through numbers, then that's what is good. Good changes from generation to generation, from society to society, from person to person and, pretty soon, you've got millions of gods all deciding what is right and wrong. You've got incredible confusion; and that's exactly what is happening to society, because we have so many gods deciding what is right and what is wrong.

THREE KINGDOMS (Diagram 100-D)

Turn to your next diagram, 100-D. This is just simply another illustration to help you and me understand this idea of godship, to realize the gravity of it, and what happens when we exercise godship. You see, godship really is just sin. We're just describing to you a way that sin evidences itself in what we call godship. This little diagram has three kingdoms. You'll notice that kingdom number one on the left-hand side is a circle that represents a person. On the right side there is another circle and that is another person. In the center of each of those is a little throne or chair. That little chair just represents that in each of these people there is a control center. There is a king or queen that is in charge of that center of control. Anytime you put two people together, you have not only kingdom

number one and kingdom number two, but you create a third kingdom called a relationship.

Let me illustrate that. When you put a man and a woman together in marriage, you call it a marriage relationship. When you put together two guys in business, you call it a partnership relationship. When you put two friends together, you call it a friendship relationship. Now here is the interesting phenomenon. You notice on your diagram, you have a dotted line going down through the center and a little arrow line going from each of the circles to the other circle. What that represents is a relationship. A man and a woman commit to each other in marriage. They're convinced that when they met each other they had just met "Mr. or Mrs. Right." I mean, they'll be happy forever, because this person is everything they ever thought they wanted to marry. Now a little program starts when they come home after the honeymoon. Because they made a commitment that they would stay married to each other for the rest of their lives, they now feel free to really be who they actually are. So, they start opening the baggage they brought into the relationship. Person number one (the husband) starts seeing in person number two (the wife) things that he didn't realize he got as part of the deal. Person number two starts seeing in person number one things that she didn't realize she got as part of the deal. And so, all of a sudden, there begins to be a war, back and forth with these arrows—a conflict of whose standards and opinions are going to be the rule for this marriage relationship.

This war begins to be one where person number one decides, as the head of this home, he is going to take control and he's going to dominate person number two. He begins to actually suppress person number two because she wants her standards. He knows if his standards rule the marriage they rule the kingdom that is inside of that marriage, and that's what he wants. He wants to be able to rule their marriage. That's

VCL
VICTORIOUS CHRISTIAN LIVING Conference
Copyright © 1998 Victorious Christian Living International, Inc.

called godship. Person number two, maybe growing up in a Christian home, thinks, "Well, I don't want to rock the boat here, I want to be a nice Christian wife." She wrongfully decides not to express any thoughts or feelings and pretty soon begins to be a "nonperson." She begins to repress herself to where she's actually sick emotionally and eventually goes in for psychiatric help. She feels a nonperson, wrongfully thinking the way to live is to not be a person, not express her feelings. If she expressed anything, he would get angry and mad and blow up and they would be divorced. Again, that is a very subtle example of godship.

The interesting thing is that not only is suppression going on by person number one and repression is going on by person number two, but what is happening is that person number two is probably becoming depressed in the middle of the whole process. So there begins to be a conclusion by both parties. We see this happen over and over. In fact, I actually have people come in and say, "Well, God wouldn't want me to be unhappy, so I think the best thing is to end this relationship kingdom, and divide the third kingdom. Let's get separated from each other so we can each rule our own kingdoms and be happy again [god again of our own lives]." It's called divorce and it's called godship.

The same thing happens when two guys get into business. They begin to think: "Hey, I don't like his standards, opinions, and ideas. I want to do it my way. Let's dissolve this partnership, so that I can be king of my kingdom again." It's called godship.

The interesting and exciting thing is that even though we have this terrible malady of the human race—mankind committed to being gods of their own lives—God designed the system so that this problem would drive us to our knees and we would recognize that we need somebody bigger than we are—God to be God, instead of us exercising godship. We need God to be the

Lord and the Ruler and the Controller of our lives in these two kingdoms down here. If person number one and person number two began to let the One Person with the one standard rule both their kingdoms, guess what, those two kingdoms could function effectively in a third kingdom. In fact, in the 30 years I have been counseling, I've never seen any two people who couldn't be successfully married if they got off the throne of their lives and they began to let the same God rule both of their kingdoms by His standards.

"GOOD" TAKEN BEYOND THE BOUNDS—IS SIN (Diagram 100-E)

Turn to your next diagram, 100-E. This is just another way of showing you the same problem, the problem of godship. These are just illustrations of it and, hopefully, make it easier to see something that you and I have to face if we're ever going to live a victorious Christian life. I will tell you that in all the years that I have been counseling, I have never yet seen a counseling case or a situation in ministry to people that hasn't included serious issues of godship as to the reason why a person is not living effectively.

"'Good' Taken Beyond the Bounds—Is Sin." When we do things our way, it isn't because we're doing something that isn't good, it's just we're doing something good that's out of God's boundaries. You see, some people think that Satan is a creator and he created sin. Let me tell you, sin is not something new or unique that is created by Satan. It's something good that God created that is being used outside of God's design and outside of His boundaries.

Look on the list here. For example, on the right-hand side, right across it says marital sex. Do you know that God designed sex? He designed all the instruments for it. He said it was good. He thinks it is wonderful. But you notice around the outside it says, "The Boundary of the Will of God." Whenever anything that is good is taken outside the boundary, that's when it becomes sin. That's all Satan does. Sin is simply Satan wanting you to move outside of God's boundaries to do something according to your own will, your own way. That is sin and that is godship. And you'll notice here in this particular one, marital sex, when it is outside of God's design which is only in marriage, the sin is immorality. In other words, if you are single and you have sex, it's called fornication and is outside of God's boundary. If you're married and you have sex with someone other than the person to whom you're married, it's called adultery. It's sin and it's godship and it's outside of God's bounds.

It is all the same in every one of these things. In the circle, on the inside, are good things, but when taken outside of the boundary of God's design, they are issues of godship and that results in sin because it is our way. It's using the good things that God created, on our own terms, in our own way, and in our own time frame—it is godship.

GOD'S WAY (Diagram 100-E1)

Notice 100-E1, "The Fruit of the Spirit." This is simply showing you the positive picture. When you and I face this issue of godship that causes most of the problems that exist in the human race today, when we face this problem that started back in Genesis 3:5 at the fall of the human race, and we face it for ourselves, personally, that's the beginning of us doing what's necessary to be able to have God be God in our lives. We looked at the little boxes in 100-A and we checked our checks in that column to evidence what are the real, obvious, continuous issues of godship in our lives. When that happened, we faced that, and we saw God's way. Whenever you and I begin to allow the Lord to be Lord of our lives, letting Him be in charge with His ways, and letting His standards be the rule, we begin to experience the fruit of His Holy Spirit.

Notice the fruit of the Spirit are all inside the boundaries. I can tell you as I've been ministering to people all these years, I have never found anybody, Christian or non-Christian, who isn't desirous of experiencing all of these things— love, joy, peace, patience, kindness, goodness, faithfulness, gentleness, and self-control. Everybody I have ever met wants to experience these. In fact, I can tell you having met with very, very wealthy people, wealth, money, material things don't begin to match having your life filled with these ingredients of joy, peace, love, and patience. These are the things that I find people are really searching for. In fact, I find that people who have what would be considered everything that would make them happy in this world—have everything, can do anything, and can buy anything—and they're still miserable inside. That is a worse misery than the people who are anticipating maybe something else that they could get or have that will finally make them happy. The worst misery is to have everything and know that there isn't anything that makes you happy; because, at that point, life is hopeless. There's no answer, there's no possibility of something that might make you happy. But God's way— allowing the Spirit of God to rule, letting God be God, letting Him determine the standards, letting Him determine how marriage should work, letting Him be the guide as to how we should raise our children, letting Him be the ruler and the authority as to how we spend our money— when we begin to let God be God, we begin to experience a life on the inside that every human being is searching for.

REVIEW

Let's review. "God is God and I am not." If you can see that one lesson, that the problem is a problem of you and me trying to be god or acting as god when God is the only God and we're not, then we're halfway there, beginning to learn what it takes to let Him be God.

The second thing it says is, "God is God and only He has the right to set standards, judge, and demand absolute obedience of people." Only God has that right. I don't know if you've

VCL

VICTORIOUS CHRISTIAN LIVING Conference
Copyright © 1998 Victorious Christian Living International, Inc.

experienced it, but every time you and I take any of those rights, it usually ends up in difficulty in relationships with other people.

The next thing is, "There is something within me that desires to be like God." In creation, God created the human being in His image. He created within us the desire to actually be like Him. The only problem is that instead of truly being like Him because we're letting His Spirit produce Him in us and through us, it is us exercising godship in our own power, on our own initiative, our own ways, with our own ideas. We're trying to copy Him. We're going to try to do what we want to do for ourselves with all the resources He gave us, instead of using them for God. You see, God didn't create us for ourselves, for our own benefit. He created us for Himself and for His benefit. Until you and I begin to understand what it is to be like God because we're doing it for Him, because He's producing it in us, only then, will we experience the Lordship of Christ.

The next one, "Godship is sin and leads to withdrawal from God and others and doubting instead of trusting."

Next one, "Only when God rules over our relationships with others will we experience relationships that bring glory to His kingdom."

And then lastly, "Good taken beyond God's boundaries leads to sin." It's an expression of godship anytime we do something outside the boundaries.

You have been listening and thinking about this issue of godship. Would you join me right now, and instead of you and I digging around and trying to find things that might be issues of godship in our lives, would you join me as we bow our heads. We'll ask God who says He convicts of sin, of righteousness, of judgment. He's the one that knows because He knows the thoughts and the intents of our hearts. Would you bow your head with me and as we let God show us that. "Heavenly Father, as we come before Your presence, I pray right now as we've considered this issue of godship, that You by Your Spirit, at this very moment, would begin to reveal to each of us what You want us to see as areas of godship in our lives. And then, Lord, I pray that You would create within each of us a desire to begin to enjoy the fullness of Your presence and the joy and the peace that comes as a part of You being God in our lives. We thank You that You have given us Your Word, You've given us Your Holy Spirit, You have given us everything necessary to be able to deal with this issue of godship in our lives. Thank You for what You are going to do. In the great name of our Savior, the Lord Jesus, we pray, amen."

GODSHIP ——————————————————————————————

REJECTION ➤

EXTERNAL/INTERNAL ——————————————————————

PROBLEMS, PROBLEMS, WHY PROBLEMS? ——————

MY FLESH—GOD'S ENEMY ——————————————————

REPENTANCE ————————————————————————————

WHAT'S NEW ABOUT YOU? ———————————————————

ACCEPTING YOUR RIGHTEOUSNESS ————————————

EXTENDING FORGIVENESS ——————————————————

SEEKING FORGIVENESS ————————————————————

REST, ABIDE, WALK ——————————————————————

LOVE ——————————————————————————————————

GODSHIP

REJECT

EXT/INT

PROBLEMS

FLESH

REPENT

WHAT'S NEW

ACCEPT RIGHT

EXTEND FORGIVE

SEEK FORGIVE

REST

LOVE

REJECTION

> ### There is therefore now no condemnation for those who are in Christ Jesus.
> Romans 8:1

Rejection is one of the most common reactions when another person does something that doesn't please you or you do something that doesn't please some other person. If your parents didn't reject you, your peers, or the public probably did. You may have even personally rejected yourself.

Those who feel rejection tend to reject the "rejecter" setting up a cycle of hurt and retaliation. This lesson shows the trauma of rejection in a person's life, its transferal from the rejected person to others, even God, and how the rejection cycle can be broken. We believe that rejection is a consequence of man playing god in his own life or the lives of others—what we call godship.

THE REJECTION CYCLE

Jonah 1:6-15;
3:10-4:3

①
I
THINK or FEEL
I'm rejected or unloved

①

**LIVING
DEATH**

③

②

I
REACT ③
by
rejecting
others and/or
myself, or seeking
acceptance (godship)
(see Diagram 110-C)

②

**I CHOOSE to
ALLOW** those
thoughts and feelings
to control me
(see Diagram 110-B)

110-A

NOTES

VCL
VICTORIOUS CHRISTIAN LIVING Conference
Copyright © 1999 Victorious Christian Living International, Inc.

PURPOSE for Diagram **110-A**:

To show the three steps of the rejection cycle and how they are repeated.

---

1. Study Genesis 4:1-16.

2. When was a time you were rejected? _____
   _____
   _____

3. Who overtly rejected you? _____ Who covertly rejected
   you? _____ How? _____
   _____

4. How did you feel? _____
   _____
   _____

5. What did you think? _____
   _____
   _____
   _____

   > *So Cain became very angry and his countenance fell.* Gen. 4:5b

6. How did you choose to allow those thoughts and feelings to control you?
   _____
   _____
   _____

7. What did you do: reject others, reject yourself, seek acceptance from others? Circle those that apply.

8. Do you see your reaction was godship?   Yes   No

I own my feelings.
My feelings don't own me!

FEELING REJECTED . . .

John 12:25a

- [ ] 1. I AM FILLED WITH SELF-PITY.
- [ ] 2. I FEEL THAT LIFE "ISN'T WORTH IT."
- [ ] 3. I AM SELF-OCCUPIED.
- [ ] 4. I AM UNABLE TO EXPRESS MY FEELINGS.
- [ ] 5. I AM EASILY DEPRESSED.
- [ ] 6. I INSULATE MYSELF EMOTIONALLY.
- [ ] 7. I AM FOCUSED ON MY FEELINGS.
- [ ] 8. I AM CONTINUALLY EXAMINING MYSELF.
- [ ] 9. I AM PERFECTIONISTIC.
- [ ] 10. I AM LACKING IN SELF-DISCIPLINE.
- [ ] 11. I AM IRRESPONSIBLE.
- [ ] 12. I AM FILLED WITH WORRIES, DOUBTS, & FEARS.
- [ ] 13. I AM SELF-CONDEMNING.
- [ ] 14. I FEEL GUILTY.
- [ ] 15. I TRY TOO HARD TO PLEASE.
- [ ] 16. I ANSWER ONLY WHAT I THINK OTHERS WANT TO HEAR.
- [ ] 17. I FEEL EVERY CONVERSATION RELATES TO ME AND TAKE IT PERSONALLY.
- [ ] 18. I CLING LIKE A LEECH TO ANYONE WHO FINALLY ACCEPTS ME.

110-B

NOTES

VCL

VICTORIOUS CHRISTIAN LIVING Conference
Copyright © 1999 Victorious Christian Living International, Inc.

Rejection
STUDY GUIDE

PURPOSE for Diagram **110-B:**

To illustrate how a rejected person's thoughts and feelings control the person. (See step two of the rejection Diagram 110-A.)

✔ 1. Look down the list and check the numbers that apply to you.

❓ 2. Are you being controlled by your thoughts or feelings of rejection?
_____
_____

📖 3. Study John 12:25. If you love your life, are you more or less likely to experience rejection? How? _____
_____

❓ 4. Who or what is responsible for you feeling this way?
   a. others
   b. myself
   c. circumstances

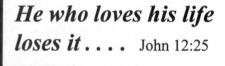

He who loves his life loses it . . . . John 12:25

You can't blame others for your thoughts and feelings.

❓ 5. If you are controlled by those thoughts and feelings, is it because you love your life?   Yes   No

Loving myself is destructive!

VCL _____
VICTORIOUS CHRISTIAN LIVING Conference
Copyright © 1999 Victorious Christian Living International, Inc.

REJECTION, Page 3B

REACTING *TOWARD OTHERS* . . .

1 Thessalonians 5:15

☐ 1. I AM RESENTFUL.

☐ 2. I AM BITTER.

☐ 3. I REBEL AGAINST AUTHORITY.

☐ 4. I HAVE CONFLICTING FEELINGS OF LOVE AND HATE.

☐ 5. I AM DISTRUSTFUL.

☐ 6. I AM UNABLE TO ACCEPT OR EXPRESS LOVE.

☐ 7. I HAVE DIFFICULTY TOLERATING OTHERS.

☐ 8. I SPEND LITTLE TIME WITH THEM.

☐ 9. I VENT HOSTILITY IN PUNITIVE WAYS.

☐ 10. I MAKE OPEN STATEMENTS OF REJECTION.

☐ 11. I GIVE VERBAL ACCEPTANCE WITH EMOTIONAL REJECTION.

☐ 12. I MAKE TOO MANY DECISIONS FOR THEM.

☐ 13. I GIVE TOO LITTLE GUIDANCE.

☐ 14. I MAY ABUSE THEM PHYSICALLY.

☐ 15. I REFUSE TO COMMUNICATE.

☐ 16. I GIVE MORE IMPORTANCE TO OTHER PEOPLE OR THINGS.

☐ 17. I INTENSELY REJECT ANYONE WHO REMINDS ME OF SOMEONE WHO HAS REJECTED ME.

SUMMARY: *"You reject me; I'll reject you!"*

110-C

PURPOSE for Diagram **110-C**:

> *To show the reactions (step three of the rejection cycle) toward others when a person is being controlled by thoughts and feelings of rejection.*

✔ 1. Go through this list asking, "Am I resentful? Am I bitter? Do I rebel against authority?" Check those that apply.

> *See to it . . . that no root of bitterness springing up . . . defiles;*   Heb. 12:15

❓ 2. Who are you currently rejecting or who feels rejected by you? _____
_____

❓ 3. Has that person rejected you? _____
_____

❓ 4. How have your reactions brought about more rejection? _____
_____
_____

📖 5. Study Matthew 5:11-12, 39-42.

❓ 6. What is to be our attitude toward someone who rejects us? _____
_____
_____

This is impossible apart from Christ!!
2 Corinthians 3:5

Reacting by rejecting is revenge.
"You hurt me, I'll hurt you!"

REACTING *TOWARD GOD*...

☐   1.   I RESIST GOD'S AUTHORITY.

☐   2.   I AM UNABLE TO TRUST GOD.

☐   3.   I VIEW GOD AS A TYRANT.

☐   4.   I AM ANGRY AT GOD.

☐   5.   I REJECT GOD.

☐   6.   I HAVE LITTLE REAL FELLOWSHIP OR COMMUNION
WITH GOD.

☐   7.   I AM UNABLE TO RECEIVE GOD'S LOVE.

Job 40:1, 4-8
Romans 9:20-21

110-D

NOTES

VCL
VICTORIOUS CHRISTIAN LIVING Conference
Copyright © 1999 Victorious Christian Living International, Inc.

PURPOSE for Diagram **110-D:**

To show how a person's reaction to rejection affects the person's relationship with God.

✔ 1. Check any of the statements that apply to you.

❓ 2. Why have you rejected God? _____
_____
_____
_____
_____
_____

> *You shall not curse God . . . .*
> Ex. 22:28

❓ 3. Do you see how being "stuck" in the rejection cycle affects your walk with God? Explain. _____
_____
_____

📖 4. Study 1 John 4:20-21.

❓ 5. How has your relationship with God been affected by your negative feelings toward another person who has rejected you? _____
_____
_____

📖 6. Study Isaiah 65:2.

❓ 7. What is preventing you from receiving God's love? _____
_____
_____

❓ 8. Would you like to admit to God the statements you checked and receive both His forgiveness and His love? _____
_____

Being angry at God is judging God!

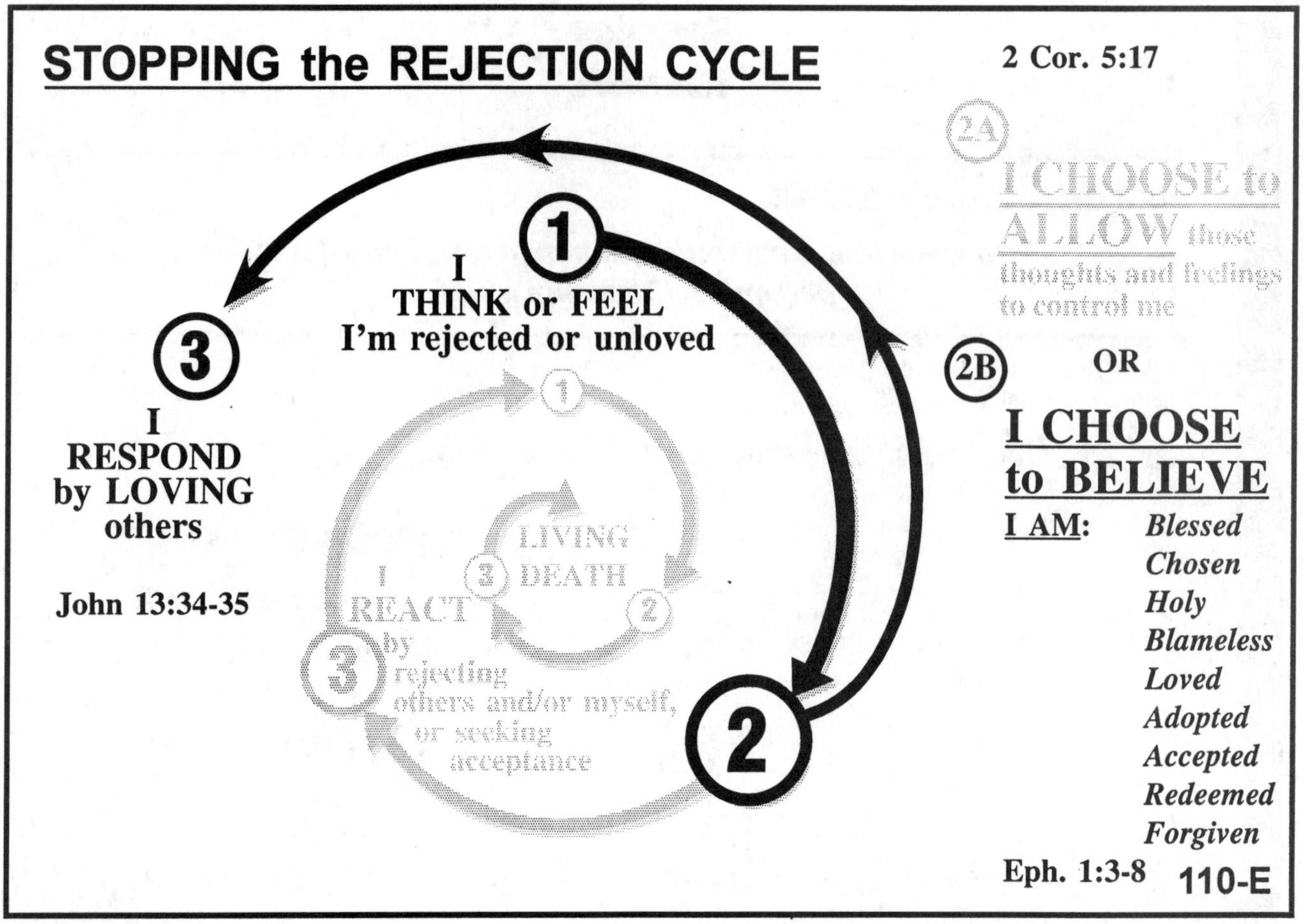
STOPPING the REJECTION CYCLE
2 Cor. 5:17
1
I
THINK or FEEL
I'm rejected or unloved
3
I
RESPOND
by LOVING
others
John 13:34-35
1
LIVING
DEATH
3
2
I
REACT
3
by
rejecting
others and/or myself,
or seeking
acceptance
2
2A
I CHOOSE to
ALLOW those
thoughts and feelings
to control me
2B
OR
I CHOOSE
to BELIEVE
I AM:
Blessed
Chosen
Holy
Blameless
Loved
Adopted
Accepted
Redeemed
Forgiven
Eph. 1:3-8
110-E

NOTES

Copyright © 1999 Victorious Christian Living International, Inc.

PURPOSE for Diagram **110-E:**

> *To explain how to break the rejection cycle by*
> *choosing to believe our true identity in Christ.*

1. When you last experienced rejection, which choice did you make—2A or 2B? _____

2. Study Ephesians 1:3-8.

3. Do you believe all these statements are really true about you, even if you don't feel all these things? _____
   _____

4. Study 2 Corinthians. 5:17.

5. How does God see you? _____
   _____
   _____
   _____

> *Bless those who*
> *curse you . . . .*
> Luke 6:28

6. What speaks louder to you, the voice of your rejecter or what God says? _____

7. Study Acts 7:54-60. Stephen was being rejected—unto death.

8. Where was Stephen's focus (verses 55-56)? _____

9. When you choose to allow rejection to control you, where is your focus? _____ Where should you focus be? _____

10. Can you pray and ask God to fill your heart with love for your rejecter? Will you do that now? _____
    _____

Choose truth!

REVIEW

- Rejection happens to everyone.

- A rejection cycle begins when we allow thoughts and feelings of rejection to control us.

- The person who believes he or she is rejectable and unlovable makes a number of decisions that reinforce his or her view of being rejectable. These decisions create a lifestyle consistent with that point of view, bringing more rejection upon the person.

- People who live in a rejection cycle react by becoming self-centered. They also react by rejecting others, even God.

- Choosing to believe who I am in Christ will stop the rejection cycle.

NOTES

VCL
VICTORIOUS CHRISTIAN LIVING Conference
Copyright © 1999 Victorious Christian Living International, Inc.

VCL International

VICTORIOUS CHRISTIAN LIVING CONFERENCE

REJECTION

Lesson Transcript by Steve Phinney

This is probably one of the messages that is a little difficult to get through because many people have the tendency to be a little rough on themselves. As we go through it, we're going to be talking about some things that are very difficult to hear. Oftentimes we do a little too much self-examination which causes us to reject ourselves.

Rejection is one of the most common consequences of man trying to be like God, playing God's role. In fact, as I was maturing as a Christian, I thought the way to grow was to understand the subject of rejection. I thought rejection was the core reason for the things people do. I believed that helping people understand how to deal with rejection would help them deal with life and become more mature Christians. This is not the case. Rejection is simply the most common consequence of man trying to play god.

I came into this world rejected. In fact, when I was born, I was put into a bubble. I was allergic to the air, all forms of food, and I could barely breathe on my own. I stayed in this bubble on and off for about five years. While in the bubble, I remember certain people visiting me, particularly my mother. As she would touch me, she had to wear rubber gloves. That's how we would bond, through rubber gloves. I could not remember the feelings of rejection during that time, but I certainly began to experience rejection by the environment, by my family, by doctors, by whoever was in the world. I developed a little bubble of my own in my heart. I didn't want anyone to get too close to me. As I was going through life, if someone started to get

too close to me, I would do things to keep them away. In fact, I believe I became a master at rejecting people. I kept them away from me. I didn't care if they rejected me or not.

Rejecting people was not my initial goal like it is for some. Some reject others first, so they will not be rejected. They are accustomed to it. That became my practice in junior high or high school. Prior to that I simply didn't want people around me. I felt safe in my bubble. That little bubble began as my bedroom and became my home. When I went to school, I would sometimes play hooky or get sick, so I could come home again. Home was my safe little fortress.

As I was approached by friends in the neighborhood or at school, I would continue to do and say things that would definitely communicate the message, "stay away from me, leave me alone." Today I understand what I was doing. I see how the enemy used rejection in my life to actually stop me from being able to enjoy and experience the body of Christ. God wanted to use friendships in my life to mature me as a believer. As I began to discover the truth behind rejection, I began to experience freedom. Rejection is not the root problem. The problem was my effort to try to be as God, or do God's job.

Jesus was rejected—excessively rejected. In fact, I just want to share with you a couple passages to help you see that rejection is really not the key issue. All of us will experience rejection, some more than others. Jesus said if we choose to walk after the Spirit, we are going to be rejected.

Turn to Matthew 27:27-31. Here is what the Word says, "Then the soldiers of the governor took Jesus into the Praetorium and gathered the whole Roman cohort around Him. And they stripped Him, and put a scarlet robe on Him. And after weaving a crown of thorns, they put it on His head, and a reed in His right hand; and they kneeled down before Him and mocked Him, saying, 'Hail, King of the Jews!' And they spat on Him, and took the reed and began to beat Him on the head. And after they had mocked Him, they took His robe off and put His garments on Him, and led Him away to crucify Him." That's just some of it. Jesus experienced a great deal of rejection, but there was no sin in Jesus.

You see, spending time talking about how you have been rejected is not the solution. There is something else going on and that's what we have to look at. I want you to write down this definition that I'm about to give you. This is the definition of *rejection*: "Knowingly or unknowingly withholding love from another person." You see, when I was a baby, I was not in touch with the fact that there was love being withheld from me. My medical condition put my mother and family in a position that they had to withhold love from me. This is called "covert rejection." There are two kinds of rejection and I want you to write definitions for them. The first type is "overt rejection." It is obvious rejection that is known by both parties. Most of us are pretty good at overt rejection. The second kind is "covert rejection." Covert rejection is only known by one party. I was covertly rejected by my family and the environment when I was born.

Others were put in the position of rejecting me. For example, my brothers and sisters didn't know how to deal with this sick kid, so they stayed away from me. They didn't mean to, but they were rejecting me. They were withholding love from me. I noted that and as I grew older I held it against them. Over the years we have

talked and reconciled a lot of the issues. You see, that was covert rejection.

Let's consider overt rejection. Belittling or name calling would be examples. Suppose you are going about your day and someone decides to reject you by calling you "stupid." That's pretty obvious. The one doing the name calling deliberately rejects you. You know you are being rejected. Because it is easily identified, it is easier to deal with overt rejection.

Covert rejection is more dangerous. Many people who experience covert rejection often can't identify it. This makes dealing with covert rejection more difficult. I want to give you the example of my wife Jane. She gave me permission to share this with you. When she was tall enough to see what was on the kitchen table, one day she spotted a soda on it. Her mom was doing the dishes. She turned around and saw that Jane was about to grab this soda. Mom said, "Please do not touch Dad's soda." Now, Jane was spanked twice in her whole life. Once she was punished for something she didn't do. The other time both Jane and her mom were laughing while she was being spanked. It wasn't a very good education on the elements of discipline. She learned nothing of proper training through discipline. Here is an example: Jane heard her mom regarding Dad's soda and put her hand right on the pop bottle. Mom turned around, saw Jane touching the bottle, but didn't say anything. She turned around and continued washing the dishes. What do you think little Jane did? She slid that bottle of pop to the edge of the table and she waited for Mom's response.

Now, meanwhile, covert rejection is kicking in high gear. Withholding discipline from a child is covert rejection. Jane had her hand on the bottle and waited for Mom's response. Mom turned and saw, but returned to the dishes. Jane slid the bottle off the table and took her first drink of the soda. Mom saw her take the first drink of the soda but said nothing. I personally believe

VCL
VICTORIOUS CHRISTIAN LIVING Conference
Copyright © 1999 Victorious Christian Living International, Inc.

the most severe form of rejection is the lack of discipline. It "trains people up in the way that they should **not** go" and then when someone does step into their life to disciple them, they start bucking against it. They are not used to being corrected. It creates very sensitive, but yet big problems in people's lives when they become adults. Those who have experienced a great deal of overt rejection have a better chance of dealing with it than those who suffer covert rejection. They know they were rejected and who there is to forgive. They clearly have a choice to forgive or not to forgive. However, people who experience covert rejection often do not know they are being rejected. In fact, my wife shared with me the first year we were married that she did not ever remember being rejected by her parents—not once. It was obvious to me, but she did not see it. That is covert rejection. It is typically identified by only one party, but sometimes, believe it or not, it is not recognized by either party. You can covertly reject others and not even know you are rejecting them.

Overprotecting a child is an example of covert rejection. Most overprotective parents believe they are helping their child. They do not understand they are rejecting the child. The child actually believes he or she is being protected, but the child is not. Both parties are unaware that rejection is going on.

It is so very important for us to understand these two kinds of rejection. God wants us to deal with them through Christ. We need to know what to lay at the feet of Jesus. If we do not understand what or whom we resent, we will just carry it and live in misery. God wants us to understand rejection.

God gave me a great illustration while counseling a young man. I held an empty pop can and read through a list of rejection incidents I had been recording in our conversation. For each incident I would put a new dent in the can with my pencil. He saw graphically how each rejection incident affected him. By the time I was done this poor can was mashed up. I asked him, "Is this how you feel?" He responded, "Yeah." I said, "I want to show you something." I walked with him over to a sink and put as much water into the can as it would hold. I poured the water into a cup, but there was only a little bit. Then I started pushing out the dents from the inside, explaining that God wanted to change his life from the inside out. God wanted to change his life by giving him what is true about him. I started quoting what was true about him: he's a child of God, he has been redeemed, he's been sanctified, he's been made whole, he is complete. I tried to get that pop can as close as I could to its original shape. It still had some scars. It was still beat up a little bit. We walked to the sink and again filled the can with water. I poured it into the cup and guess what happened—more water. I helped this young man understand that the same thing is true of our spiritual life. If we allow the life of Christ to pound out "our dents," the areas we have not reconciled, we have more room for the filling of the Lord in our lives. The presence of the Lord will inhabit every corner of our lives available to Him.

We do not live in perfect environments. We're going to experience dents and bruises through life. Rejection will happen, but God works from the inside through the identity truths. I wonder if the word "identity" comes from "I-DENT-ity"? I think so. What we accept as our identity has a great impact on our lives. By the time I was 16 years old, I felt like that smashed up can. I had long hair; I was into drugs and theft. I was a mess because I believed I was rejectable. I thought it, felt it, and believed it. After getting saved at 16 years of age, I still struggled with rejection because there was no overflow in my life. Why? It was because I continued the same godship pattern. I was trying to do God's job in my life. God had to reveal to me what was going on behind all of the rejection.

Here are three sources of rejection. The first one is parental rejection. Parents can reject by overcorrection and undercorrection. Examples of overcorrection are: belittling, criticizing, or constantly hounding a child to do something. Undercorrection is what I described to you in regard to my wife. Sometimes parents think it is too painful to discipline their child. They don't want to hurt the child, but by not disciplining him or her, they actually reject the child. This is parental rejection.

The second is peer rejection. When I was a teenager I dressed in ways to draw rejection. I let my hair grow and painted my face. I wanted peer rejection. I felt rejected and I wanted to be rejected. I was rejected by my peers for the way I looked and acted. I did not measure up to their standards.

The third one is public rejection. A great example of that is traffic. You can be driving down the road, life is good, you're singing to the Lord having a good time. Maybe you veer off a little bit over the white line and the guy in the car next to you shakes his fist and yells at you. You didn't really do anything. That's public rejection. There are many forms of public rejection. What I read to you out of Matthew about Jesus was public rejection. You can even be rejected for doing what is right.

THE REJECTION CYCLE
(Diagram 110-A)
Turn with me to Diagram 110-A, "The Rejection Cycle." When rejection comes crashing in, makes its first dent, suddenly you may begin thinking and feeling rejectable. That suggestion starts going around in your mind. "Why did they do this? Should I have done . . . ? Maybe it's because I'm . . . ." I come around to point number 2 on the diagram. "I decide I'm rejectable." Notice that number 2 is a lot bigger than the other numbers. We did that because this is the most important point. It is the time to

make a decision. Am I going to choose to allow these thoughts and feelings to control me? If I do, I proceed to point 3. "I do or say things that bring more rejection," which is godship. I react by rejecting others or the person who just rejected me. I was a shotgun rejecter. I would load my rejection shotgun and blow away anyone standing by. I didn't care who they were. I didn't care what they looked like. I would blow away innocent people. I didn't care. Others are a little more selective, they'll only reject those who have rejected them.

Some people search for acceptance. Notice the word "godship" under point three on the diagram. Remember, godship is man trying to be like God, taking God's job. When we try to seek acceptance and approval from others, that is godship. God is the only one entitled to praise, honor, and worship. When we start seeking it from others, it sets us up for rejection.

Perhaps you are looking at point three on the diagram, but you don't desire to reject others. Your desire might be to keep people happy. This is still a reaction built on the feelings, thoughts, and fears of being rejected. This can control you. It then moves deeper in the cycle to the smaller point 1. "I think or feel even more rejected or unloved." Let's suppose you send back a rejecting comment. The person responds in kind. As you progress in the cycle, you yield more and more control of your life to people and circumstances. The cycle continues, 1-2-3, 1-2-3, 1-2-3, etc. I explain it this way. If you draw this diagram three dimensionally and pull the spiral up, what do you have? You have a tornado. This tornado is going through life destroying everything in its path. That is what I was like and likewise anyone who gets stuck in the rejection cycle. It's a living death. Even if they are trying to please people, it's still a living death. For me, when I started thinking and feeling rejected and unlovable, I started to choose to believe that must be true.

VCL

VICTORIOUS CHRISTIAN LIVING Conference
Copyright © 1999 Victorious Christian Living International, Inc.

Let's take a look at Jonah. Turn to Jonah, Chapter 1. I want you to understand the picture of Jonah. He was asked by God to go to Nineveh, which was a great city. But this city was very wicked. In fact, it was so wicked the Word says they did not know the difference between their right and left hand. They did whatever they wanted to do. God wanted to save this city. He called Jonah to ministry, but Jonah didn't like the people of Nineveh. Verse 2 says, "Arise, go to Nineveh the great city, and cry against it, for their wickedness has come up before Me." Next, Jonah rejects God. Verse 3 says, "But Jonah rose up to flee to Tarshish from the presence of the Lord. So he went down to Joppa, found a ship which was going to Tarshish, paid the fare, and went down into it to go with them to Tarshish from the presence of the Lord." Jonah thought, "I am going to reject the Lord." He had already rejected Nineveh.

The rejection cycle has already started and now he is rejecting God's plan for him. God rejects Jonah's plan. Here's what Jonah 1:4 says, "And the Lord hurled a great wind on the sea and there was a great storm on the sea so that the ship was about to break up." God is the only one who has the prerogative to reject people. God causes everything in Jonah's life at this point to bring him to the end of himself. It was very important for Jonah to hear God's voice. Jonah could have avoided this whole thing by hearing God's voice, but Jonah would have none of it. God had to speak to Jonah through his circumstances. God creates a great storm and the boat starts falling apart. Jonah makes a choice. Verse 1:5 says, "Then the sailors became afraid, and every man cried to his god, and they threw the cargo which was in the ship into the sea to lighten it for them. But Jonah had gone below into the hold of the ship, lain down, and fallen sound asleep." We have this great storm busting up the ship and Jonah is down in the hold of the ship sound asleep. There are some people who actually sleep through rejection. That's their number 3. They just try to

sleep it off and escape reality. It is impossible.

The story goes on. Jonah gets rejected again. Verse 1:7 says, "And each man said to his mate, 'Come, let us cast lots so we may learn on whose account this calamity has struck us.' So they cast lots and the lot fell on Jonah." God is even in control of the lot. You cannot escape God with your number 3, your reactions to rejection. Jonah's rejection tornado continued. The men became extremely frightened and they said to him in verse 10, "How could you do this?" They knew he was fleeing from the presence of the Lord because of what he told them. Verse 1:11 says, "So they said to him, 'What should we do to you that the sea may become calm for us?'—for the sea was becoming increasingly stormy."

Jonah rejects himself now. Verse 1:12 says, "And he said to them, 'Pick me up and throw me into the sea. Then the sea will become calm for you, for I know that on account of me this great storm has come upon you.'" Self-rejection is now kicking in full force. Jonah gets rejected again. Verse 1:15 says, "So they picked up Jonah, threw him into the sea, and the sea stopped its raging." As you know, Jonah was swallowed up by a great fish. While in the belly of that fish for 3 days, Jonah repents. There's a beautiful repentance prayer in this book. He was spit out on the shore. He goes to Nineveh and preaches the gospel and 120,000 people in that great city came to know God.

That's quite a successful day of evangelism. Strange, but Jonah wasn't happy. The rejection cycle kicked in again, even after repentance and obedience. What happened? He went to the edge of the city and he sat down. God raises up a plant so he has some cool shade to sit under. Jonah begins to whine and complain, "Oh God, how come you were so tough on me and you showed such grace to this city." God and Jonah had a discussion. Here is what Jonah concluded. Verse 4:3 says, "Therefore now, O Lord, please take my life from me, for death is better to me than life." Jonah was stuck in the rejection cycle. Who was Jonah thinking about the whole time? Himself. The end result of the rejection cycle is self-love.

FEELING REJECTED . . .
(Diagram 110-B)

Turn to Diagram 110-B, "Feeling Rejected . . . I am filled with self-pity. I feel that life 'isn't worth it.'" Did Jonah think these things? Yes. There are 3 times in the book of Jonah that Jonah tried to end his life in some way. That is what the rejection cycle will do. The focus is constantly the big "I." In reality the goal is to avoid more "dents," but they keep coming. You cannot avoid dents by avoiding rejection. Why is that? It is because rejection is a consequence of man playing god.

Let's consider a few others on our diagram. Number 5 says, "I am easily depressed." One of my friends defines depression as "an internal temper tantrum." When depressed people become upset that things aren't going their way, they often turn inward and engage in internal temper tantrums. They don't talk to others. They close themselves off and sink into a dark hole in their minds. It is allowing rejection to be in control.

Look at number 9, "I am perfectionistic." It is putting things in order externally in order to feel emotionally in order. That's perfectionism. The perfectionist likes to straighten things up just a bit. They are continually adjusting things. Why? Because they feel emotionally out of order. It's another fleshly way of choosing to allow rejection to be in control. Consider number 12, "I am filled with worries, doubts, and fears," or number 15, "I try too hard to please."

I became the biggest people pleaser. Someone told me, "Phinney, you need a degree before you can help someone." I went out and got a degree. Then someone told me, "You know, if you had a masters degree you could have a better outreach." I went and got a masters degree. "Phinney, if you had a Ph.D., you could become a licensed psychologist and you could really be effective." You see, I was driven every day to please someone. Why? I didn't want rejection anymore. I labored to please people in order to avoid being crushed. I was tired. I kept dishing out what I thought people wanted to hear or doing what they wanted me to do. It stressed me out so much that it brought me to a Victorious Christian Living Conference.

The first lesson was called "Godship." I wrestled with that one. The second lesson was "Rejection." I knew that life. "Want me to teach it?" That was my attitude. It was godship, trying to be as God. That one was the one that took me down. God said, "Oh Steve, you're just trying to do my job. Let go."

Turn to Matthew 15:11 and 18. These 2 verses I'm going to read to you were 2 verses that God used to transform my life. Matthew 15:11 says, "Not what enters into the mouth defiles the man, but what proceeds out of the mouth, this defiles the man." Verse 18 says, "But the things that proceed out of the mouth come from the heart, and those defile the man." What I learned was that it is not the rejection that comes to the man that defiles him, it is the rejection in the heart that defiles that man. That totally changed me. God started using that in my life and set me free. I used the excuse myself, "If you reject me, I have no choice but to act the way that I am acting." God said, "Not true. You are acting the way that you are acting because of the defilement and godship in your heart. You're being defiled by your own rejection." That was a tough one for me to swallow, but once I swallowed it, I was set free.

REACTING TOWARD OTHERS . . .
(Diagram 110-C)

This list is a further description of the kinds of reactions we might experience from point 3 on

VICTORIOUS CHRISTIAN LIVING Conference
Copyright © 1999 Victorious Christian Living International, Inc.

Diagram 110-A. This list shows how you might dish it out to others. In Matthew 12:35 it says this, "The good man out of his good treasure brings forth what is good; and the evil man out of his evil treasure brings forth what is evil." If I draw from my righteous treasure box in my life, I am going to give out righteousness. If I draw from the evil treasure box in my life, the flesh, I am going to exhibit what you see on this list. The treasure box is in our heart. Perhaps you pull out "people pleaser." You will then work at pleasing people so they won't reject you. Even after all that work, sooner or later you are still going to be rejected by the person you long to please. When that happens, you might reach into the evil treasure box and pull out "name calling." He or she responds in kind and you are rejected again. Again you reach into that treasure box and pull out "refuse to communicate with him." If you don't talk, he won't reject you. This doesn't work either. He continues to reject you. You can continue to pull out destructive choices from the evil treasure box. That's what this list is for. Take a few minutes and check the boxes that you know are in your life. God does not want you drawing from this list. He wants something else. But I'm afraid it doesn't stop there.

REACTING TOWARD GOD . . .
(Diagram 110-D)
Turn to Diagram 110-D. This is Satan's number one goal. He wants us to reject ourselves and others, but he really wants us to reject God. He wants you to resist God's authority. He wants you to be unable to trust God. He wants you to view God as a tyrant like your dad or your mom or whoever it was that really was beating up on you through life. He wants you to be angry with God and reject Him and His sovereign hand. He wants you to have little fellowship or communion with Him. Satan definitely does not want you to be able to receive God's love. Second Corinthians 5:17 says "Therefore if any man is in Christ, he is a new creature; the old things passed away; behold, new things have come."

God wants us as believers to understand that all the old has passed away. It is not your life anymore. He says, "Behold I have done something new. I have given you a new treasure box and I want you to draw from this new treasure box, so reach down inside and draw from this treasure box. Out of this treasure box, when you are slapped on one cheek turn the other cheek, and while you're turning the other cheek, give love. When they slap you again, reach into that treasure box. Realize that you are holy. Don't concern yourself with what they say about you. I say that you are holy." God says you are holy. When you are rejected again, you reach into that treasure box. "You're blessed." You may not feel blessed, but you are blessed.

STOPPING THE REJECTION CYCLE
(Diagram 110-E)
When we feel rejected, number 2 needs to become our focus. It is the fork in the road. I can choose to believe I am blessed, chosen, holy, blameless, loved, adopted, accepted, redeemed, forgiven, and the list goes on and on. We have a list of 100 that we cover with people who come for discipleship, but even that doesn't scratch the surface. They go on and on about who we are in Christ. Notice the new number 3. "I respond by loving others." I am redeemed. I will deal with this person in such a way as to help the person understand his or her redemption.

Do you see the difference? It abandons worrying about self to helping others be set free. That's why I can stand up here today, having gone through what I went through, with a passion to show you how God's way functions. It is not Steve Phinney's way, not your way, but God's way. If God has brought some conviction in your life going through this lesson, I want to just take a moment and pray. I call it the rejection prayer, and if these words speak what you are experiencing right now, just in your heart quietly pray this prayer with me. Let's bow our heads.

"Dear Lord, I agree that I have been stuck in the rejection cycle, thinking and feeling rejected by myself and others. I have been wrong for choosing to allow these thoughts and feelings to control me. It is wrong for me to reject others and myself by hurting them and seeking acceptance from them. I choose now to accept your forgiveness for all these wrong choices. I now choose to believe what you say is true about me, that I am blessed, chosen, holy, blameless, loved, adopted, accepted, redeemed, and forgiven. I thank you, Lord, for allowing me to go through being rejected, and I thank you for your promise that all things work together for good. Amen."

REVIEW

Consider our review. "Rejection happens to everyone." It does happen. "The rejection cycle begins when we allow thoughts and feelings of rejection to control us." Point 3, "The person who believes that he or she is rejectable and unlovable makes a number of decisions that reinforce his or her view of being rejectable. These decisions create a lifestyle consistent with that point of view, bringing more rejection upon the person." "People who live in a rejection cycle react by becoming self-centered. They also react by rejecting others, even God." And finally, the rejection cycle can be stopped by making the choice to accept who you are in Christ.

VCL
VICTORIOUS CHRISTIAN LIVING Conference
Copyright © 1999 Victorious Christian Living International, Inc.

GODSHIP

REJECTION

EXTERNAL/INTERNAL ➤

PROBLEMS, PROBLEMS, WHY PROBLEMS?

MY FLESH—GOD'S ENEMY

REPENTANCE

WHAT'S NEW ABOUT YOU?

ACCEPTING YOUR RIGHTEOUSNESS

EXTENDING FORGIVENESS

SEEKING FORGIVENESS

REST, ABIDE, WALK

LOVE

GODSHIP

REJECT

EXT/INT

PROBLEMS

FLESH

REPENT

WHAT'S NEW

ACCEPT RIGHT

EXTEND FORGIVE

SEEK FORGIVE

REST

LOVE

EXTERNAL/INTERNAL

> *We look not at the things which are seen, but at the things which are not seen . . .*
>
> 2 Corinthians 4:18

How have you been pursuing happiness? Jesus said that life does not consist in the abundance of the things that man possesses (Luke 12:15). Rather, life is to be found INternally, not EXternally. Yet we are tremendously influenced by what the world tells us is important. Most Christians easily stand against the idea that fulfillment is found in drugs or alcohol or illicit sex—and yet, more often succumb to the seductive idea that education determines success or that financial security assures happiness or that psychological understanding provides satisfying answers to life's problems. This lesson will uncover the deceptions of the world. Where is *life*? Could Jesus say of us that we are unwilling to come to Him to have *life*? (John 5:40).

THE DECEPTION OF EXTERNAL FULFILLMENT

Eccl. 2:1-11

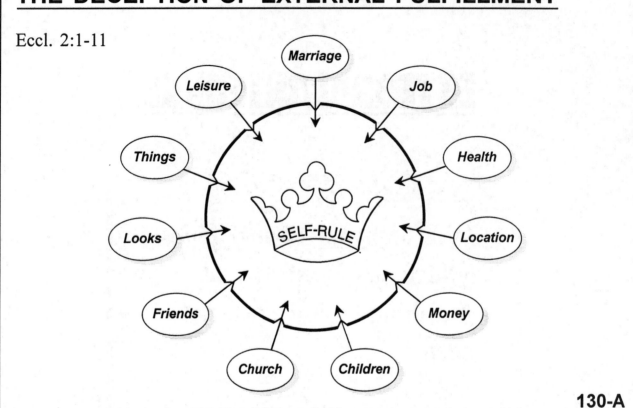

130-A

VCL

VICTORIOUS CHRISTIAN LIVING Conference
Copyright © 1999 Victorious Christian Living International, Inc.

NOTES

PURPOSE for Diagram **130-A:**

*To show that happiness and fulfillment
cannot be attained through external things.*

? 1. Have you tried to find happiness in any of these areas? Describe.

_____

_____

? 2. Which of these areas would you consider to be a negative in your life?

_____

_____

? 3. Have you pursued fulfillment through
turning the negatives into positives?
How? _____

_____

_____

> *. . . everything is
> futility . . . .* Eccl. 2:17

? 4. Which ones are you currently pursuing to change into a positive?

_____

_____

📖 5. Study Ecclesiastes 2:1-11. Notice how many times the pronouns "I",
"my", or "myself" are used.

? 6. Did the positives in Solomon's life bring contentment?   Yes   No

📖 7. Study Luke 12:15. Where does Jesus say life is not found?

_____

? 8. Do you see how you have been deceived into believing that life is
found in any of these areas? _____

External fulfillment is a lie!

THE CHRISTIAN'S DECEPTION OF EXTERNAL FULFILLMENT

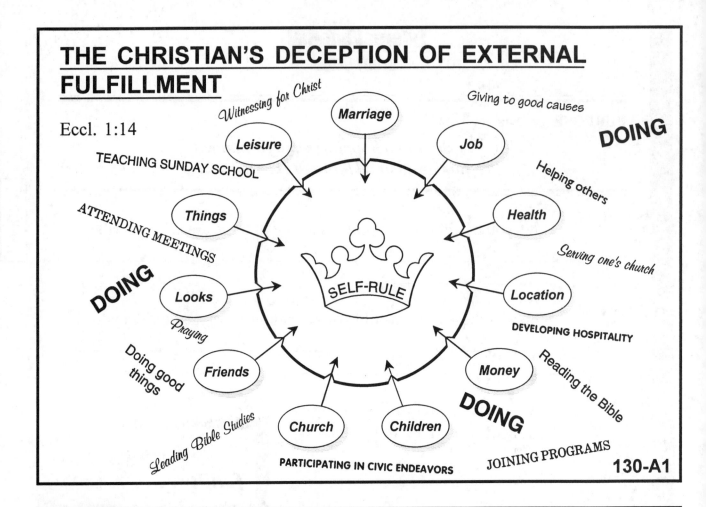

Eccl. 1:14

Witnessing for Christ

Marriage

Giving to good causes

DOING

Leisure

Job

TEACHING SUNDAY SCHOOL

Helping others

ATTENDING MEETINGS

Things

Health

DOING

Looks

SELF-RULE

Location

Serving one's church

Praying

DEVELOPING HOSPITALITY

Doing good things

Friends

Money

Reading the Bible

DOING

Leading Bible Studies

Church

Children

PARTICIPATING IN CIVIC ENDEAVORS

JOINING PROGRAMS

130-A1

VCL

VICTORIOUS CHRISTIAN LIVING Conference
Copyright © 1999 Victorious Christian Living International, Inc.

PURPOSE for Diagram **130-A1**:

To reveal the futility of a Christian trying to find fulfillment
and meaning in DOING good things.

? 1. Which of these activities are you doing now? _____
_____
_____
_____

? 2. Why? _____
_____
_____
_____

? 3. Have you been deceived into thinking that God wants you to do
things? _____

? 4. Do you believe doing good things
will gain God's favor? _____
_____

. . . our righteousnesses
are as filthy rags. Isa. 64:6
(KJV)

📖 5. Study Luke 10:38-42.

? 6. Do you see that Martha's focus was activity FOR Christ while Mary's
focus WAS Christ and knowing Him? _____
_____

? 7. Can Christian service become an idol? _____
_____

? 8. Is it possible that your Christian service for God is an attempt to find
fulfillment in external activities? _____
_____

I wasn't created to be a human doing.

EVERYTHING BUT GOD

Jeremiah 2:13

- ♦ Call a friend for advice.
- ♦ Eat food to fill the vacuum.
- ♦ Use uppers, downers, or alcohol to relieve anxiety or depression.
- ♦ Try to figure it out with your mind.
- ♦ Buy something to distract you from the pain.
- ♦ Get educated to solve problems.
- ♦ Get angry to get results.
- ♦ Work harder to overcome.
- ♦ Get overly busy to forget.
- ♦ Give money to soothe your conscience.
- ♦ Get divorced or get a new spouse.
- ♦ Spend time sleeping to escape overwhelming life situations.

Lastly, call on God!

130-B

NOTES

VCL
VICTORIOUS CHRISTIAN LIVING Conference
Copyright © 1999 Victorious Christian Living International, Inc.

PURPOSE for Diagram **130-B:**

To illustrate how believers act like nonbelievers and turn to worldly ways of coping, rather than turning to God.

? 1. Look at this diagram and note which actions apply to you.

_____

_____

? 2. Why isn't God considered first? _____

_____

_____

> *. . . come to Me, that you may have life.* John 5:40

📖 3. Study Jeremiah 2:13. What are the two sins you see? _____

_____

? 4. What pots or cisterns are you going to for life? _____

_____

_____

? 5. Are they really satisfying? _____

_____

_____

? 6. What are some of the consequences you are suffering because of your worldly choices? _____

_____

Nothing but God will work.

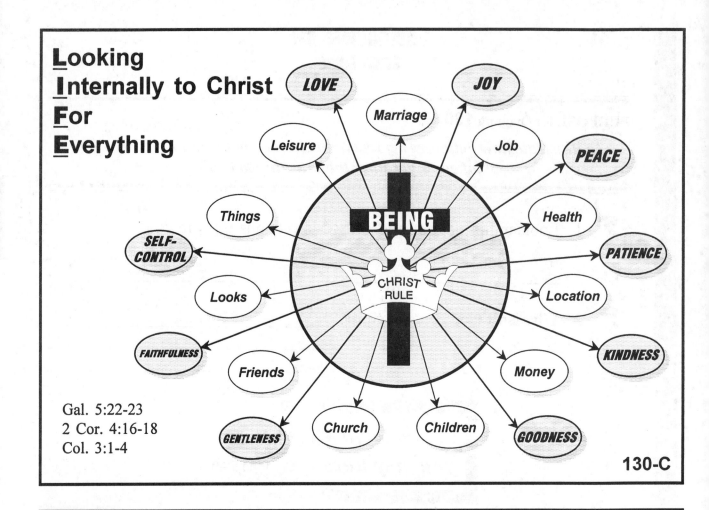

Looking
Internally to Christ
For
Everything

LOVE · JOY · PEACE · PATIENCE · KINDNESS · GOODNESS · GENTLENESS · FAITHFULNESS · SELF-CONTROL

BEING · CHRIST RULE

Marriage · Leisure · Job · Health · Things · Location · Looks · Money · Friends · Church · Children

Gal. 5:22-23
2 Cor. 4:16-18
Col. 3:1-4

130-C

VCL
VICTORIOUS CHRISTIAN LIVING Conference
Copyright © 1999 Victorious Christian Living International, Inc.

External/Internal
STUDY GUIDE

PURPOSE for Diagram **130-C**:

To illustrate that a Christian's fulfillment is based internally on being one with Christ.

1. Study Matthew 6:33.

2. Why has the direction of the arrows changed? _____
   _____
   _____

3. What is your main focus—God's kingdom or external fulfillment?
   _____
   _____
   _____

> *. . . Christ in whom are hidden all treasures . . . .*
> Col. 2:2-3

4. Study Colossians 3:1-4.
   Where is your life? _____
   _____

5. Are you allowing Christ to rule your life? How is it demonstrated?
   _____
   _____

6. Are you allowing Christ to meet your needs or are you looking to externals to meet your needs? _____
   _____

7. Will you admit to God your focus has been in the wrong direction? Will you invite Him to sit on the throne of your life and rule it now?

Jesus is life!

REVIEW

- Happiness is not found in things or people.

- Fulfillment comes from God being my focus.

- Joy comes from **L**ooking **I**nternally to Christ **F**or **E**verything.

- I must repent of all external idols such as relationships, possessions, accomplishments, job, and even Christian work.

- Real life comes from Jesus Christ.

NOTES

_____ **VCL**
VICTORIOUS CHRISTIAN LIVING Conference
Copyright © 1999 Victorious Christian Living International, Inc.

I'm really thankful to be here with you and share the EXternal deception and the INternal truth of Christ's life living within us. Please turn with me in your materials to the lesson called "External/ Internal." What I intend to do in the next few minutes is help you see a major deception of the world. A deception that I bought into for a number of years. I, also, want to help you learn how to experience the internal life of Jesus Christ and see how Christ living His life out through you functions practically today.

Many Christians are deceived into thinking that life is found in external circumstances and external things. Actually, some of us have even been deceived into thinking that service for Jesus will bring us meaning or happiness, which is not the truth. So, look with me at your explanation page. You have a short Scripture, 2 Corinthians 4:18, right in the center of the page. Let me read it to you in context. Verses 16 through 18 say: "Therefore we do not lose heart, but though our outer man is decaying, yet our inner man is being renewed day by day. For momentary, light affliction is producing for us an eternal weight of glory far beyond all comparison, while we look not at the things which are seen, but at the things which are not seen; for the things which are seen are temporal, but the things which are not seen are eternal."

Our focus should not be on the things which we can see, but our focus should be on the things we cannot see. God, His life within us empowering, should be our focus. Look with me at your explanation. Read along with me please. "How have you been pursuing happiness?" How have you been doing that in your life? "Jesus said that life does not consist in the abundance of things that a man possesses (Luke 12:15). Rather, life is to be found INternally, not EXternally. Yet we are tremendously influenced by what the world tells us is important. Most Christians easily stand against the idea that fulfillment is found in drugs or alcohol or illicit sex—and yet, more often succumb to the seductive idea that education determines success or that financial security assures happiness or that psychological understanding provides satisfactory answers to life's problems."

Let me share with you a little bit of testimony from my life. I did not come to know the Lord until I was 30 years of age. Before that time, I looked to many of these things for fulfillment and happiness in life. Actually, until the time I was 30-some years of age, my gods were sex, drugs, and speed. I liked sex a lot. I liked doing drugs and alcohol a whole bunch. And I liked going fast on anything—cars, motorcycles, boats, down a ski slope, out of an airplane free falling—whatever it took to get that rush of speed. Those were the gods in my life and I worshiped them at every available opportunity.

After I got out of the military service, I used my GI Bill and went to college and studied psychology because I knew I had a lot of problems. But, pride being what it is, I didn't really ask anybody for the answers, you know. What I wanted to do was to get out there and find the answers. My thought was pretty good, "If I find the answers then I can show those answers to somebody else someday and help that person find the answers." Well, after several years of study, expending my GI Bill, and then going into a practical internship ministering with psychological techniques to juvenile delinquents, I found out that the ways of the world, they flunk. They do not work in practical life circumstances.

Shortly thereafter through a series of circumstances, I met the Lord Jesus Christ in a personal way. A number of years later, I met the ministry of Victorious Christian Living and through the teachings and the understanding of the materials I want to share with you today, I began to see the deceptions in my life.

I actually had a contest with a guy at the steel mill where I worked 22 years. He had a T-shirt that said, "He who dies with the most toys wins." I wanted one of those T-shirts. You know what, he wouldn't tell me where he got it. Do you know why? Because he was one-up on me. He had something I didn't have. But I WANTED that T-shirt. We would compete all the time in the steel mill for toys. If somebody got a boat, somebody else would get a bigger boat, somebody else would get a faster boat, somebody else would get a shinier boat. If somebody got a tent, somebody else would get a topper for his pickup, and somebody else would get a camper. Then, someone would get a motor home. Then, somebody would get something to pull behind his motor home. All the time we were in this competition. That's all a deception. None of those things bring fulfillment and meaning to life.

Finish with me the introductory page. "Where is life? Could Jesus say to us that we are unwilling to come to Him to have life?" Could He say that to you right now? Actually, let me ask you a hard question. Why are you here? Why are you sitting here listening to me today? Why did you come? Let me explain to you why I came here. I came here because I really care about you and your walk with the Lord Jesus Christ. There's no other meaning or purpose for me to be here other than I see a lot of people deceived, floundering around, and functioning by the world's circumstances. I want to help you see the lies that the Devil and the world bombard us with

consistently, so that you can experience the truth. The truth is Jesus Christ. The only valuable experience in all that there is—a direct, personal relationship with Jesus Christ—His life. But you first need to understand how you're deceived and then I'll explain the truth to you.

THE DECEPTION OF EXTERNAL FULFILLMENT (Diagram 130-A)

Turn with me to your first diagram, 130-A, "The Deception of External Fulfillment." Isn't it true as you look at this **key diagram** in this message, that if you could put little plus signs in all of those ovals around the big center circle, that you would be happy? Isn't that true? See, none of these things around the circle in and of themselves are sinful. Let's go around the circle together and look at them.

Let's start right at the top with marriage. I am married to Juli. Juli and I are in our 27th year of marriage. I went through the 1st through 8th grades and there were 8 people in my class, 6 guys and 2 girls. As a freshman, I went to high school and the first day I discovered there were 418 freshmen and there were 4 classes in that school. I got hopelessly lost. By 6th hour, I was devastated. I sat down in study hall across the table from the most beautiful woman I had ever seen in my life.

"Juli Holmes, my name is Bill Houck."

This woman! I went home that day and I told my mom. She said, "How was your day?" I said, "I met the most beautiful woman in study hall, Juli Holmes. I think that's the girl I want to marry."

It took me 4 years of high school, dating all of her friends, before I finally got her to realize that I was alive. She started dating me and 2 years later we got married and 27 years later we are still married and having a great relationship. I wanted Juli really, really bad but, you know, within 12 hours of being married to her, I realized that somewhere along the line I got deceived, that this wasn't all that I thought it was going to be. How many of you got married and realized shortly after the wedding ceremony was over, that everything you thought was going to be there didn't necessarily happen? Marriage in and of itself won't fulfill you.

How about a job? I was talking to a businessman the other day, and he was saying, "Years ago I thought when I get to this economic level, then I'll be happy." Now he is at this rung, he said, "I finally broke the six-digit mark, I'm at this rung," and he says, "you know what, when I get to that rung, then, I think I will be happy." That happens to many of us in the job world, we think when we get to the next level then we'll be happy. That's not it. It's not getting to the next level in the job that makes us happy, significant, and fulfilled. It's not getting to that next rung that makes you significant, it's something else.

Look with me at health. A couple of years ago I got to the end of the year and I went through the annual trek of evaluating. How many of you do that? I do that periodically. I discovered at the end of that year, really, practically, if I know the Lord Jesus and I am walking with Him and I am physically healthy there isn't anything else that really matters. Everything else you can just do away with, you know, clothes, stuff, if you're healthy. But what if you're not healthy? What if you're somebody like Joni Eareckson Tada who can only turn her head a little bit back and forth like this? What if your earth suit, your body, doesn't function? Can you still be happy, significant, and contributing meaningfully to society? Absolutely, you can. Health is not the determining factor.

Neither is your location. Juli and I bought a nice little house in town and we lived there, but I got claustrophobic. When I opened the shade on my bedroom window, I was looking into the neighbor's bedroom window. Depending on which one of them was looking out at me, it was

either a good day or a bad day. We decided that what we needed to do was move out-of-town. So we went on a motorcycle ride and we saw this knoll in a subdivision and I said, "That's the place; that's where we need to build a home." She said, "Well, it's only a few miles from town, I guess that will work." So I built my own house just the way I wanted it on top of this hill. That was 20 years ago. I put a new roof on this summer. You know what, that house is never done; it's never complete; it's never finished; it's never up to date; it's always calling to me for attention. I discovered just 2 years ago, I'll never own that thing. Even when I get it all paid off, if I don't pay my taxes "my uncle" will repossess it. He's the one who really owns it. So, my deception was: "When I get that house then I'll be happy. When I get that house done I'll be happy." Juli was thinking, "When I get that house decorated then I'll be happy." Not true. See, that doesn't make you happy.

If I just made a little more money, then I'd have enough. How much is enough? Someone has asked some of the most influential rich people in the world, "When is it enough?" They said: "The next million or the next billion. That's when it's enough." Money in and of itself has never satisfied.

How about children? Juli wanted to have children. One of the endearing things about her when I met her was she said, "I want to have 12 kids." I was thinking this is a woman who likes to have sex. This is the woman I want to marry. Twelve kids! All right! But then, I told her she had to wait 5 years before she could have any babies. "Because," I said, "if you can put up with me for 5 years, you'll stick with me for the duration—I'm not going to have my kids go through a divorce." So, 5 years later we began to have children. Our first baby went right up to the day that she was meant to be born and rolling over to exit Juli's birth canal she strangled herself on her umbilical cord and she died. She died in the process of being born. That rocked my world and destroyed my wife's world.

Juli went looking for solutions to life because of that incident. That led her to a radical experience with Jesus Christ. Me, I went for better drugs and stronger alcohol to numb the pain. Juli found the truth. After a year and a half of poking and prodding at her Christianity, I finally discovered that she had something vital and I surrendered my life to the Lord Jesus Christ. Now we have 2 children, Monica and Kristopher. Monica is 21 and Kristopher is 19. Those children to this day continue to be a joy and a challenge to my life, but in and of themselves, they do not provide happiness or significance.

How about a church? We spent a year looking for the best church we could find. Do you know what the conclusion was after searching a year? There isn't a perfect church. The bottom line is if there was a perfect church and Juli and I joined it, it wouldn't be perfect anymore. See, you can't find the perfect church; that will not make you happy.

How about friends? If you just had one good friend that you could go to and bare your soul to, wouldn't that be nice? But you know what happens when you get that one friend that you can go to and bare your soul to, then you forget going to your best friend and baring your soul to Him because you go to somebody with flesh on rather than a Spirit.

How about looks? How many of us would just like to have a little more here [pointing to hair] or a little more here [pointing to shoulders] or a little less here [pointing to stomach]? Looking different: if I could just look better then I'd be happy, then I would be significant. It's a lie. It doesn't work. That's not real.

Things: if I just had more stuff. I'm staying at a guy's house who has a float-deck boat. When I first saw it, I said, "I need a boat; I want a boat." Then we talked for 25 minutes and he told me all the problems with the boat. My conclusion was I don't need a boat; I don't want a boat; I don't want one more thing in my life to fix. As soon as you get things, then you have to fix them, then you have to maintain them. Things are not the solution to life.

How about leisure? If you just had enough stuff, just had enough time to play with it, then you'd be happy, right? The worst times for me are the times when I am not involved in anything. You know why? Because I get involved in things that my heavenly Father would not have me involved with. Now the world says you need time for yourself. God says, "You need more time, more intimacy with Me. You don't need time to just lay around, you need time fellowshiping with Me, interacting with Me, and being about the making of disciples." That is the commission God has given us.

Look with me in the center of this diagram. This is really the important part—the control center. Who is in the control center? Self. Self is ruling. If you spell self backwards and put an "h" on it you have a word called "flesh." Flesh is ruling this person. Let me share with you a man who has gone the full gamut, so to speak, in this circle and that's a guy called Solomon. You see on your diagram it says Ecclesiastes, Chapter 2, verses 1 through 11. Here's what it says:

> I said to myself, "Come now, I will test you with pleasure. So enjoy yourself." And behold, it too was futility. I said of laughter, "It is madness," and of pleasure, "What does it accomplish?" I explored with my mind how to stimulate my body with wine while my mind was guiding me wisely, and how to take hold of folly, until I could see what good there is for the sons of men

VCL
VICTORIOUS CHRISTIAN LIVING Conference
Copyright © 1999 Victorious Christian Living International, Inc.

to do under heaven the few years of their lives. I enlarged my works: I built houses for myself, I planted vineyards for myself; I made gardens and parks for myself, and I planted in them all kinds of fruit trees; I made ponds of water for myself from which to irrigate a forest of growing trees. I bought male and female slaves, and I had homeborn slaves. Also I possessed flocks and herds larger than all who had preceded me in Jerusalem. Also, I collected for myself silver and gold, and the treasure of kings and provinces. I provided for myself male and female singers and the pleasures of men—many concubines. Then I became great and increased more than all who preceded me in Jerusalem. My wisdom also stood by me. And all that my eyes desired I did not refuse them. I did not withhold my heart from any pleasure, for my heart was pleased because of all my labor and this was my reward for all my labor. Thus I considered all my activities which my hands had done and the labor which I had exerted, and **behold all was vanity and striving after wind and there was no profit under the sun.**

Here's Solomon. He's got more money than anybody else. He's got more slaves. This guy had 700 concubines and 300 wives, a thousand women. He had everything you could imagine. After accumulating all that, the smartest man in the world said, "It's futility; it's not worth it." So, where is your focus? Is your focus on things?

THE CHRISTIAN'S DECEPTION OF EXTERNAL FULFILLMENT
(Diagram 130-A1)

Look with me at your next diagram, 130-A1, "The Christian's Deception of External Fulfillment." What happens to many of us is that we get saved by God's wonderful grace and then we think that we need to perform to keep that salvation. That's a lie. What happens is we often shift our focus from the Lord Jesus Christ to me and what I am doing for Jesus. That's wrong. That's a deception. Look at all these external things that have been added: "Witnessing for Christ." Is that a good thing? Sure. "Giving to good causes." Oh, yeah. "Helping Others," "Developing Hospitality," doing this, doing that, "Leading Bible Studies," doing these things, attending those meetings. Are all those things good? Oh, sure, but if you're doing those things to provide fulfillment, meaning, and significance in life, then you're functioning in a way contrary to the way God would have you live. What's actually happening here? I was counseling one day and a man next to me was really excited. He could hardly wait for me to get done. He had explained this diagram to a woman and the woman said, "I see it. I'm a human *doing*. God designed me to be a human *being*, but I'm not being, I'm doing all of this stuff." The focus becomes on the things that we do. Any of those things can become an idol in your life, even serving the Lord Jesus Christ.

EVERYTHING BUT GOD
(Diagram 130-B)

Look with me at your next diagram, 130-B, "Everything but God." What happens in many people's lives is, rather than going to God, they go to something else or someone else. I want to read to you Jeremiah, Chapter 2, verse 13, "For My people have committed two evils: They have forsaken Me, / The fountain of living waters, / To hew for themselves cisterns, / Broken cisterns, /That can hold no water." So there are two things. First, they forsake God and second, they created cisterns of their own.

God designed us to experience Him as living water. Do you remember Jesus talking to the Samaritan woman in John Chapter 4? She's talking about water out of the well and He's talking about water flowing up from inside. God wants to fill us with His living water.

But you see what happens is we go to another source. We may call to a friend for advice. We may even turn to a beautiful biblical counselor. Oftentimes, I have people come and they lay this whole scenario out before me and I'll ask them, "So, what does God have to say about that?"

"We haven't talked to God about that yet."

"When do you think you should talk to Him?"

You see, they come to somebody else rather than going to Him. You don't want to go to somebody else, you want to go to God.

You may use food to fill in the vacuum. I watched a video the other day of Patsy Clairmont. She put this list on her refrigerator door, and any time she went to get food out of that refrigerator, she had to write on the list why she was eating. She would write things like this, "I'm eating because I'm tired. I'm eating because I'm excited. I'm eating because I'm bored. I'm eating because I'm frustrated. I'm eating because I'm mad at my husband. I'm eating because the dog peed on the carpet." All these different reasons and at the end of the day she discovered very seldom did she eat because she was hungry. Why? Because we have this something inside us we want to fill, so we look for something to put in there to fill it. Maybe food is that in your life.

How about using uppers, downers, or alcohol to relieve anxiety or depression? I did that for 14 years. For fourteen years, I was on a daily basis smoking dope, drinking beer, and many other things to take the rough edges off of the world. Uppers and downers were a way of life for me.

Speed was something I did on a regular basis, flying for days. All of those things were because I didn't like life. I didn't like the way it was, and I found a pretty good chemical creation where I could alter life to where I enjoyed it. But all of that was sin. I was looking to those things to fulfill me—trying to figure out with my mind by going to study psychology. Why? So that I could understand how I worked, so I could get me to work the way I wanted.

Buy something to distract you from the pain. When the going gets tough, the tough go shopping. Right? Yeah, buy some new threads, then I'll feel good about me. Isn't that true? No, it's not true.

Get angry, that will get results. How about that? Work harder to overcome it. Pull yourself up by the old bootstraps, a little more commitment, try a little harder, that will get her done. Right? God wants you to surrender, not try harder. Get busy and you'll forget all about it. Does that work? Can you get busy enough working that for a brief moment of time you don't think about your problems? Sure, but as soon as you get unbusy do they come back? You bet they do. So, that doesn't work either.

Give money away. That will soothe it. If you have enough money, you can do that.

Get divorced or get a new spouse. Will that work? No, that doesn't work. In my counseling experience all the people who have gone through the process of divorce say they thought this would simplify their lives, that everything would be better if they could just get that other person out of there. Never, never, in the years I've been involved with counseling, has that been the truth. Every time it got worse for them and worse for the children involved. That's not the solution.

Spend time sleeping to escape overwhelming life situations. How many of you, like me, have days when the alarm goes off you just want to pull the covers up over your head and just stay in bed all day and forget all about it? Just hide out. On a regular basis, I want to do that. I do not want to get up and face the challenges of the day What I have discovered is the best thing to do is pull the covers down, look directly up to my heavenly Father, and say, "I can not survive this day without You." Before my body ever splits the sheets, "I surrender my life to You, and I want to be your body today. I am a living sacrifice unto You. I can't get out of bed; I don't want to get out of bed. So, when my body gets out of bed, it's You doing it through me." When I live life that way, the day is significantly different.

LOOKING INTERNALLY TO CHRIST FOR EVERYTHING (Diagram 130-C)

Look with me at your next diagram, 130-C. This is a **key diagram** in understanding the life of Christ functioning within you. You will notice on the upper left-hand side is the word "life" spelled out "**L**ook **I**nternally to Christ **F**or **E**verything." That is the solution. It's not just sitting cross-legged with your hands looking internally for life, it's looking internally to Christ for life.

I was sitting in my east window the other morning when the sun came up. I was actually sitting there cross-legged with my bathrobe hood up, with my Bible across my lap, and a cup of coffee next to me and I was thinking about this diagram. I was thinking: I still sit cross-legged, I still like to put my hood up, I still like to be still, but my focus is not on me and me being able to create the energy to survive this day. My focus is on plugging into, tapping into the life of the Lord Jesus Christ in such a way that my hoses are connected to His water source so it is Jesus Christ who gurgles out of me all day long. But I need time alone with Him in the morning. I need time in the evening alone with Him. I need to sneak out of the office periodically and go for a walk and spend intimate personal time alone with Him. I'm a very needy creature. I am desperately in need of the Lord Jesus Christ's life.

For how that takes place look with me at the center of this diagram. You see, this is not self-ruled anymore is it? The rulership here is Christ's rule. Christ is in control of this person's life. The control center is your spirit and soul. God is in control of the spirit and the soul of this individual. How does that take place? Well, you'll also notice that there is a cross inserted in here. Across the crossbeam it says "being." Do you realize in our human language, our English language I should say, we are called "human beings," aren't we? God, even in the language, wanted us to understand the truth of His design. We are to be "being" related to Him, "being" intimate with Him, and if you'll look at the very center of that word what is the letter on the cross? "I," correct. I am on the cross. I, Bill, have been crucified with Christ. It's no longer I, Bill, who lives in this earth suit, it's Christ who lives within me. When I am co-crucified with Christ, when I am seated in the heavenly realms with Him, when I am functioning in my true identity as a son of the most high God, my spiritual, soulistic identity is being intimately related with God. God energizing my personality. Bill is a little bit different than all the rest of you. You probably noticed that by now. God flowing through Bill looks different than you, but it's still Christ's life being empowered in me, being indwelt in me, being my very life.

Now I don't know how many of you struggle with this death issue, death to the selfish lifestyle, death to my life. See, when I came to know the Lord, I knew enough about the Word to make a clear understanding of what it was going to cost. I looked at it and I had this running dialogue with God. I said, "Okay, God, I have one life to live, right?" [God responds, "right."] "And you want me to give you my one life to live, right?" [God responds, "right."] "So, who gets to live my life if I don't?" [God responds, "I do."] "Well, what about me?" [God responds, "You'll be better off."] "I don't get to do anything?" [God responds, "right."] "But I want to do something." [God responds, "right son, it's the best for you."] I went through this ongoing dialogue, I wanted to do it. Come on, I only get one chance and you want me to give you my one chance so that you can do it through me? Yes, that is what He wants from me, that's what He wants from you. And you know what, it's the best way to live.

After living 30 some odd years in sin after my flesh, and now just the last few years, the last 11 or 12 years, walking in God's Spirit, walking after God's Spirit, this is by far the best life to experience. I cannot find the words to explain to you all the value, internally and externally, for living life this way. When Christ is in control of your life, when He is your very life, then you see shooting out of this control center all these things.

Love. When I first met Juli, I didn't really love her. I lusted after her. Now I know how to lay my life down and love her like Jesus Christ loves the church.

How about joy? Did I have fun free-falling? Oh yeah! Is there anything as joyful as walking with the Lord? Nothing. Is there anything as much of a rush as seeing the sparkle in somebody's eyes when the person begins to get a glimpse of, just a glimpse of who God is? Nothing compares with that joy. There is none.

How about peace? Peace that surpasses all understanding, being able to stand in His presence, being able to stand firm, secure in your identity in any circumstance. See, God designed us with feet that we stand on. When your feet are enclosed in the peace of knowing the Lord Jesus Christ—knowing His life that is our life—anywhere you go, no matter where you stand, you stand in peace. You can go anywhere, you can do anything, you can meet anybody because you know Christ.

In Philippians, Chapter 4, verse 13, it says, "I can do all things through Him who strengthens me." See, Bill cannot do everything. But with Christ in me, working through me, I can now do anything. I can even be patient. Whoa, I can be patient with people! I can be kind. I can be good. I can be gentle to people. I used to think gentleness was wimpy. If I went to a men's room and it said "gentlemen" on the sign, I went to find another one that said "men." I wanted a "men's" room, I didn't want a "gentlemen's" room. Do you know what I have discovered, God is the gentlest man you will ever know. Gentlemen know their heritage, they know who they are. Real men are gentle men. They know the gentleman of the universe, God himself. Being gentle is cool. Being gentle is the most manly expression. Now that's not what the world says, but that's what God says.

How about faithfulness. I was not faithful. I walked after my flesh. I did a lot of sinful things. I was not faithful to God. I was not faithful to my wife. But since coming to know the Lord Jesus Christ, it has been incredibly wonderful to be faithful to Him and faithful to my wife Juli. That faithfulness is not something I can do. That faithfulness is an expression of Him.

Self-control. Some of you watching this are sitting there thinking, old Bill is not very controlled, because I am rather animated from time to time. I am personally under the control of the Lord Jesus Christ. He controls my "self," therefore, I am self-controlled by God. God is in control of my life. He's the one who controls me.

You have several different verses at the bottom of your diagram. Let me read for you in the book of Colossians, Chapter 3, verses 1 through 4, "If then you have been raised up with Christ, keep seeking the things above, where Christ is, seated at the right hand of God. Set your mind on the things above, not on the things that are on earth. For you have died and your life is hidden with Christ in God. When Christ, who is our life, is revealed, then you also will be revealed with Him in glory."

VCL

VICTORIOUS CHRISTIAN LIVING Conference
Copyright © 1999 Victorious Christian Living International, Inc.

So, what we need to do brothers and sisters in Christ, is we need to keep seeking the things that are above, not the things that you see. Don't be looking to the next thing that you can acquire— that's not the solution to life. That's not where happiness is found. That's not where joy is. That's not where peace is. Set your mind, set your thinking on the things that are above. Keep looking heavenward. Keep looking to the Holy Spirit that lives within you for everything. Don't look at circumstances. Don't look at the people around you. Look to the Lord Jesus Christ who is your life. As you begin to walk, consistently walk in that, the One who is your life, He will begin to show up in you. So, function in this focus. Focus on Christ being your life. Surrender to Christ being your life.

REVIEW

Turn to your review with me. As you look at that, let me share with you a quote from Oswald Chambers book *My Utmost for His Highest*. On October 18 he wrote this, "The key to a missionary's devotion is that he is attached to nothing and no one except the Lord Jesus Christ Himself. It does not mean simply being detached from external things and surroundings, our Lord was amazingly in touch with ordinary things of life, but He had no inner attachment except to God. External detachment is often actually an indicator of a secret growing inner attachment to the things that keep us eternally. The duty of a faithful missionary or a faithful Christian is to concentrate on keeping his soul completely and continually open to the nature of the Lord Jesus Christ. The men and women of God that are sent out on His endeavors are ordinary human beings, ordinary human people, but people who are controlled by their devotion to Him, to Christ, which has brought them through the work of the Holy Spirit." So, focus your devotion on the work of the Holy Spirit. The work that Christ is doing in you, that's our focus, not on the things around us.

Look with me at the review points. Number 1, "Happiness is not found in things or in people." Number 2, "Fulfillment comes from God being my focus," that's fulfillment. Number 3, "Joy comes from **L**ooking **I**nternally to Christ **F**or **E**verything." What is not covered in everything? Does everything cover everything? I mean every pair of socks I wear, every T-shirt I choose, everything I eat, I should be looking internally to Christ Jesus. What are you hungry for? You guys didn't have pizza when you walked here. Want to do a pizza? How about it? You guys didn't have tacos. Do you want to do a taco? Let's do tacos. Cool!

Look internally to Christ for everything. "God, we have 10 minutes. What do you want to do in these 10 minutes?"

"All right, let's do that. Great idea. I like it." See, look internally for everything. Pray without ceasing. This is it. That's the life.

Number 4, "I must repent of all external idols such as relationships, possessions, accomplishments, job, and even Christian work." There is a process: I must turn from the idols of my life. Is there a man or woman in your life that is more important than God? If there is, that's an idol. Are there children in your life that are more important than God, more important than your wife or your husband? Is there? Then they have become an idol. Is there some thing in your life that you think about more than God? Is there? If there is something—whatever it is, boat, car, motorcycle, job, money, you know, what ever it is that you value—you think about more than God, that has become an idol in your life and you must repent. You must turn from that and turn back to God. God is number one. He is a very jealous God. He will not tolerate us having other idols as more important than Himself, not even Christian work.

I had someone say to me in counseling the other day, "Oh, it would be so easy to be a Christian if

EXT/INT

I had your job." And I said, "Do you want to know the truth? The truth is the hardest place to be a Christian is in my job." He says, "Huh?" I said, "The reality of living in the position that God has given me, is it's more difficult to be real, doing what I do, than any other job. It would be much easier to become a Pharisee and just fake it, as if I've made it. But the reality is, I haven't made it. I need Jesus."

Many people put on the air: I know it all, I'm so high and lifted up. That's pride. That's not the life of Christ. We never fully comprehend the reality of God until we get there. Always be growing. Always be reaching for more of it.

Number 5, "Real life comes from Jesus Christ." Jesus is the way; He is the truth; He is the life. You don't find the truth, you find Him. You don't find a way to live, you find Him. That's life. He is it. Look nowhere else. Look to no one else, to nothing else, but Him. Have you been looking elsewhere? Let's spend a few minutes and go before the throne, and I'll give you a chance to turn from that right now and experience Christ as your life.

Let's pray. "Father, thank You for revealing to us this very day the deception that we get distracted by stuff and people. Things, Father, we confess that we momentarily, hourly, daily, get distracted by those things. Father, we admit to You that they've become idols in our life. Right now we lay them before You. We humbly receive from You Your love, Your washing, Your forgiveness. Thank You, God, thank You for forgiving us. Thank You, Lord Jesus, for providing a way for us to be redeemed. Holy Spirit of God, thank You for Your anointing, thank You for Your presence, thank You for Your fellowship right now. Minister personally to each one of us, oh Holy Spirit, in a practical way that leads us to a greater dependency and a greater demonstration of Your life in this world today. Be honored, be glorified because of our turning to You, because of our humbleness, magnify Yourself. Thank You, Lord Jesus, in Your precious and perfect name we pray. Amen."

VCL
VICTORIOUS CHRISTIAN LIVING Conference
Copyright © 1999 Victorious Christian Living International, Inc.

GODSHIP ——————————————————————

REJECTION ——————————————————————

EXTERNAL/INTERNAL ——————————————————

PROBLEMS, PROBLEMS, WHY PROBLEMS? ➤

MY FLESH—GOD'S ENEMY ——————————————

REPENTANCE ——————————————————————

WHAT'S NEW ABOUT YOU? ——————————————

ACCEPTING YOUR RIGHTEOUSNESS ————————

EXTENDING FORGIVENESS ——————————————

SEEKING FORGIVENESS ——————————————

REST, ABIDE, WALK ——————————————————

LOVE ——————————————————————————

GODSHIP

REJECT

EXT/INT

PROBLEMS

FLESH

REPENT

WHAT'S NEW

ACCEPT RIGHT

EXTEND FORGIVE

SEEK FORGIVE

REST

LOVE

PROBLEMS, PROBLEMS, WHY PROBLEMS?

> . . . God causes <u>all</u>
> <u>things</u> to work together
> for good . . . .
>
> Romans 8:28

Scripture says that God causes all things to work together for good to those who love Him and are called according to His purpose (Romans 8:28). Is this true in your experience as well as in your theological belief? If so, do you become aware of the process only after the good has been worked out? Do you know God's heart and walk with Him, so that you can rejoice in the completion of God's good purpose while actually *in the pressures* of the moment?

Seek to understand the experiences of your life from God's perspective. Victorious Christian living is rooted in victorious Christian thinking—especially in regard to the problems of life. There are three kinds of problems in life: **(1) problems God allows for His glory, (2) problems God allows because He loves us and wants to bring us to maturity, (3) problems that are the result of our own wrong choices.**

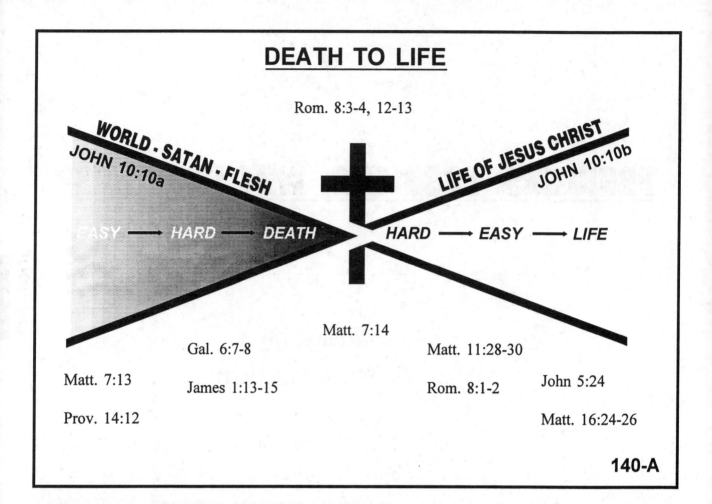

DEATH TO LIFE

Rom. 8:3-4, 12-13

WORLD · SATAN · FLESH
JOHN 10:10a

LIFE OF JESUS CHRIST
JOHN 10:10b

EASY → HARD → DEATH   HARD → EASY → LIFE

Matt. 7:14

Gal. 6:7-8

Matt. 11:28-30

Matt. 7:13

James 1:13-15

Rom. 8:1-2

John 5:24

Prov. 14:12

Matt. 16:24-26

140-A

NOTES

VCL
VICTORIOUS CHRISTIAN LIVING Conference
Copyright © 1999 Victorious Christian Living International, Inc.

PURPOSE for Diagram **140-A**:

To show how the world's ways start out easy, but lead to death and to show how God's ways start out hard, but lead to life.

1. Study Luke 15:11-32. What appealed to the son that started out easy? _____ How did it get hard and lead to death? _____ _____ What hard thing did the son have to do that led to life? _____

2. What problem have you had that started appealing or easy and ended in misery or death? _____
_____

3. What is the most pressing problem you face today? Describe.
_____
_____

4. Where are you on this diagram?
_____
_____

> **Enter by the narrow gate.**
> Matt. 7:13a

5. Study John 10:10. In which part are you living? _____
_____
_____

6. Do you want to stay where you are? _____
_____

7. What would entering the narrow gate look like for you? _____
_____
_____

Give it up!
My way isn't working anyway.

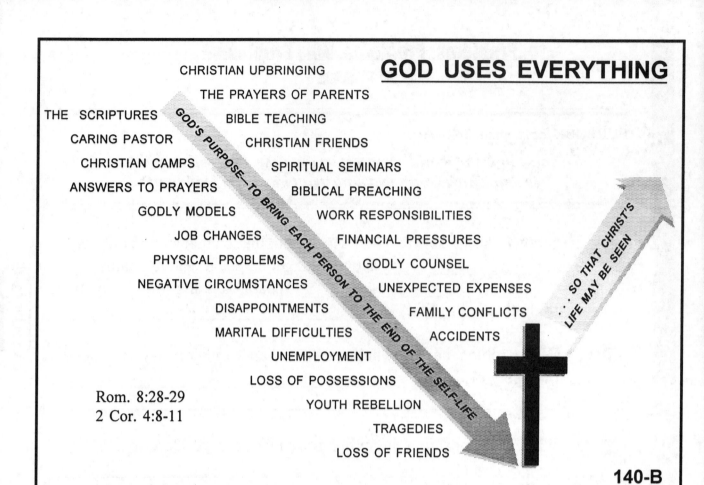

CHRISTIAN UPBRINGING

THE PRAYERS OF PARENTS

GOD USES EVERYTHING

THE SCRIPTURES

BIBLE TEACHING

CARING PASTOR

CHRISTIAN FRIENDS

CHRISTIAN CAMPS

SPIRITUAL SEMINARS

ANSWERS TO PRAYERS

BIBLICAL PREACHING

GODLY MODELS

WORK RESPONSIBILITIES

JOB CHANGES

FINANCIAL PRESSURES

PHYSICAL PROBLEMS

GODLY COUNSEL

NEGATIVE CIRCUMSTANCES

UNEXPECTED EXPENSES

DISAPPOINTMENTS

FAMILY CONFLICTS

MARITAL DIFFICULTIES

ACCIDENTS

UNEMPLOYMENT

LOSS OF POSSESSIONS

Rom. 8:28-29
2 Cor. 4:8-11

YOUTH REBELLION

TRAGEDIES

LOSS OF FRIENDS

GOD'S PURPOSE—TO BRING EACH PERSON TO THE END OF THE SELF-LIFE

. . . SO THAT CHRIST'S LIFE MAY BE SEEN

140-B

NOTES

VCL
VICTORIOUS CHRISTIAN LIVING Conference
Copyright © 1999 Victorious Christian Living International, Inc.

PURPOSE for Diagram **140-B**:

*To show that God uses all that happens to us
to bring about His eternal purposes.*

1. Study Romans 8:28-29.

2. What does God say is the good that He predestined for us? _____
   _____
   How have you defined what would be good for you? _____
   _____
   Whose good is guaranteed? _____

3. How do you see God conforming you to the image of His Son by the
   problems you are now facing? _____
   _____
   _____

4. Study 2 Corinthians 4:8-11. How is this problem being used to bring
   you to death? How can Christ's life be seen in you as you walk
   through your problem? _____
   _____
   _____
   _____
   _____
   _____
   _____

   > *. . . death . . . that the life
   > of Jesus be manifested . . .*
   > 2 Cor. 4:11

5. What area of your self-life (godship) does God want to bring to death?
   _____
   _____
   _____

*God uses everything to conform me to
Christ's image.*

PROBLEMS

WELL-MEANING DETOURS

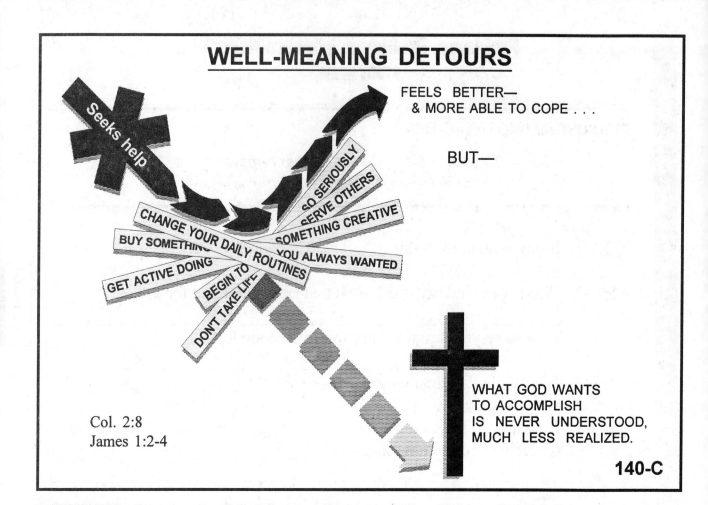

FEELS BETTER—
& MORE ABLE TO COPE . . .

BUT—

Seeks help

DO SERIOUSLY
SERVE OTHERS
SOMETHING CREATIVE
CHANGE YOUR DAILY ROUTINES
BUY SOMETHING
YOU ALWAYS WANTED
GET ACTIVE DOING
BEGIN TO
DON'T TAKE LIFE

Col. 2:8
James 1:2-4

WHAT GOD WANTS
TO ACCOMPLISH
IS NEVER UNDERSTOOD,
MUCH LESS REALIZED.

140-C

NOTES

VCL
VICTORIOUS CHRISTIAN LIVING Conference
Copyright © 1999 Victorious Christian Living International, Inc.

PURPOSE for Diagram **140-C**:

*To warn of the danger of being sidetracked before
God's purposes can be accomplished.*

1. Study James 1:2-4. How are we told to consider trials?_____
   What do trials produce in us? _____

2. What are you doing to get out of your trials? _____
   _____
   _____
   _____

3. If you get out of your trials, how will you become mature? _____
   _____
   _____
   _____

> *. . . philosophy
> and empty
> deception . . . .*
> Col. 2:8

Let God finish what He started.

DEAD TO THE SELF-LIFE
AND ALIVE TO CHRIST'S LIFE

1 Thess. 5:18
Eph. 5:20

SEE GOD in what is happening.

LET GOD BE GOD in what is happening.

THANK GOD in what is happening.

God's purpose: bring each one to the end of the self-life

TRUST GOD in what is happening.

OBEY GOD in what is happening.

140-D

VICTORIOUS CHRISTIAN LIVING Conference
Copyright © 1999 Victorious Christian Living International, Inc.

PURPOSE for Diagram **140-D**:

To move a person to godly action concerning a problem.

1. Study Philippians 3:8.

2. What would it take to bring you to the point where you could say with Paul, "I Count all things to be lost in view of the surpassing value of knowing Christ Jesus my Lord, for whom I have suffered the loss of all things, and count them but rubbish in order that I may gain Christ."? _____

_____
_____
_____
_____

. . . to become conformed to the image of His Son . . . .
Rom. 8:29

3. Study Jeremiah 29:11-12.

4. Why can you trust God? _____

_____
_____
_____

5. Study Ephesians 5:20 & 1 Thessalonians 5:18. Can you thank God in what's happening? _____

_____

6. Are you ready to be obedient to God in what is happening? _____

_____

LIFE comes out of death!

REVIEW

- Problems in life cannot be avoided.

- God uses *everything* in our lives to accomplish His purposes.

- Often problems cause us to come to a point of weakness either physically, spiritually, financially, or relationally so we will give up doing things our way.

- God wants us to trust Him because of His sovereignty, love, and power.

- We can even thank God for the problems He permits, because they cause us to come to Him and totally depend on Him.

NOTES

VCL

PROBLEMS, PROBLEMS, WHY PROBLEMS?

Lesson Transcript by David Ritzenthaler

About 14 years ago, I was on my motorcycle heading south on Pima from my home. As I came toward an intersection, I noticed a pickup truck pulling out to turn left. It's a very serious thing to drive defensively riding a motorcycle, so I observed the truck ahead and took note of it. As it got a little closer, the pickup truck pulled out again and stopped. I said to myself, "Watch out. There's an indecisive driver up there." Just a few feet before I got into the intersection, the young man driving the pickup truck jammed the pedal to the floor and pulled left in front of me. I was doing about 50 miles per hour. I slid sideways on my motorcycle, hit the side of that pickup truck, drove the door in about a foot, and the pickup box grabbed my motorcycle, took it backwards about 150 feet. I flew about 25 feet into the intersection sitting on my bottom in the middle of July in Arizona, when the temperature was about 118 degrees. I sat on that pavement and I decided the first thing I wanted to do was get off the pavement. As I looked down to get off the pavement, I noticed that this wrist [right] was busted over here and this one [left] was busted over here. My thought as I looked at my wrists was, "Man, these would make a good monster movie." You wonder why these things happen. What in the world is this all about?

About 3 years ago, I was awakened one morning by a telephone call from my youngest daughter. It was obvious as I listened to the tone of her voice that she was in distress, because she called and asked that we would immediately come— there had been an accident. So we got dressed, got over to her home about 4 o'clock in the morning to find her sitting in the backseat of a police car. The street was filled with the ambulance and other emergency vehicles and we wondered what was happening here. As I went to comfort my daughter, the policeman told me not to touch her hands. Then she proceeded to tell us that her husband laid a little pistol behind his head on a shelf, and it accidentally fired and hit him.

Then just about a year ago in the process of writing a book, I had gone with some friends and my wife, Suzanne, to California to get away from the busyness of the schedule here. Suzanne and I walked about 5 miles one day and came back and had dinner. After we finished dinner, I sat down and began to read. My wife was watching television with our very good friends. I asked her a question, but she didn't respond and, all of a sudden, I realized there must be something wrong. I looked around and went over and got down in front of her and realized that she was having a stroke. She was paralyzed on the left side. She couldn't speak and was drooling from the left side of her mouth. You want to ask yourself why is this happening. What's this all about?

I don't know if any of you have problems in your life, but I want you to know they're the most wonderful things that can happen. As I share those stories with you, you could say, "Man, you must be crazy to say that about all those things happening."

Turn with me to the first page of "Problems, Problems, Why Problems?" I want you to look at the purpose of problems. Hopefully, by the time we finish this lesson, you truly will say problems are one of the most wonderful things that can happen to you. In many years of counseling, I have found that as people began to understand what the purposes were when God designed problems—though no problems changed, nothing got fixed, no circumstance got better—their lives became better. Many times just from understanding the reasons for problems, life became exciting in the midst of those problems. I want to show you why.

In the box at the top, Romans 8:28 says, ". . . God causes **all things** to work together for good . . . ." You've maybe said at times, "Why me?" or "Why did this happen?" or "What's the good here?" Well, hopefully, in the next few minutes I will show you the purposes of the problems in those three stories I just told. At the end of the introductory page, you will notice there are three kinds of problems. The first one is problems that God allows only for His glory. I'm sure you're familiar with the story of the man blind from birth that Jesus and others came around. The disciples were concerned whether he had sinned or whether his parents sinned and what that was all about. In John 9:3, "Jesus answered, 'It was neither that this man sinned, nor his parents; but it was in order that the works of God might be displayed in him.'" So one of the reasons God allows problems is to bring glory to Himself. That is one of the reasons.

Many people want to promote the idea that the only things that happen to Christians are good things. Let's take one of the people that God used to write the majority of the New Testament and in a major way to prepare the gospel and to share the gospel with the rest of the world. That was Paul. Let me read to you what he says in 2 Corinthians 11:24-26: "Five times I received from the Jews thirty-nine lashes. Three times I was beaten with rods, once I was stoned, three times I was shipwrecked, a night and a day I have spent in the deep. I have been on frequent journeys, in dangers from rivers, dangers from robbers, dangers from my countrymen, dangers from the Gentiles, dangers in the city, dangers in the wilderness, dangers on the sea, dangers among false brethren." Here's Paul—obviously a

servant of God, greatly used of God—writing about all kinds of problems he had. Well, if problems are not something you want in your Christian life and if problems are not something that God wants in your life, why did God allow all these problems to happen to one of His most significant servants, Paul? After Paul had sought why he had a personal problem, he writes in 2 Corinthians 12:9-10: "And He has said to me, 'My grace is sufficient for you, for power is perfected in weakness.' Most gladly, therefore, I will rather boast about my weaknesses, that the power of Christ may dwell in me. Therefore I am well content with weaknesses, with insults, with distresses, with persecutions, with difficulties, for Christ's sake; for when I am weak, then I am strong." God has a purpose for problems and the first one is for the purposes of His glory.

Now we're not going to cover that in this lesson, but I wanted you to understand that is one of the purposes. Most Christians never get the privilege of being used of God with problems in their lives for His glory because the other two issues of why problems have not been dealt with yet. They haven't grown to a place of maturity that they could receive problems in their lives totally for the purpose of bringing glory to God's name.

Let's look at the second reason that problems happen: God allows problems because He loves us and He wants to mature us. Most of us never get to that place of maturity where we understand the purposes of problems and we're not afraid of them anymore. We actually go through problems with joy in our lives, and we actually recognize that they all happen for good. When we get to that maturity, then God can even use problems for the purposes of glory to His name.

The third kind of problem, is the kind that comes from our own wrong choices. I will tell you that after 30-plus years of counseling, the majority of the problems that people have in their lives when they come in for counseling are due to the fact that they have made wrong choices and are reaping problems in their lives. Now God understood all that. He knew that people would make wrong choices, but God made a system which we are going to look at in depth. He set up a system so that when people made the wrong choices, it would cause problems to come into their lives that would produce maturity, so that they wouldn't choose problems anymore. They wouldn't choose wrong choices and, therefore, have more problems. So God uses even wrong choices to produce a sanctifying process of maturity in the life of a believer. But I do want you to know that many, in fact probably most, of the problems in our lives we do not have to have. If you'd like to have a more problem free life, then it's a matter of learning to choose choices according to God's ways because many problems happen due to our wrong choices. I hope we'll see that in our next few minutes together.

DEATH TO LIFE (Diagram 140-A)

Turn to your first diagram, 140-A, "Death to Life." The first type of problems that I want to deal with are ones that come from our wrong choices. Due to the fact that those are the majority of the kinds of problems we have, I want us to see how God set this system up and how we end up reaping problems and how those very problems are the vehicles that finally mature us and sanctify us. You're probably very familiar with the section of Scripture in Matthew where he talks about the narrow gate and the wide gate. On your diagram on the left side, you'll notice a wide gate that comes down in this triangle to nothing. It dead ends; it's called death. There it says easy, hard, and death. Look at Matthew 7:13-14 it says, "Enter by the narrow gate; for the gate is wide, and the way is broad that leads to destruction, and many are those who enter by it. For the gate is small, and the way is narrow that leads to life, and few are those who find it." So on the left-hand side is a great big, wide gate. The Bible says many go in that gate and it's easy to get in that gate. It's easy to choose the ways of the world, the influ-

ence is great. Just look around you, it's obvious—television, radio, newspapers, advertising. Most things that are promoted to you are promoted with the idea of getting you in a worldly gate that satisfies all the lusts of your flesh, all the lusts of your eyes, and all the pride of life. That's why it's easy to get there. Sin is easy. In fact, sin is joyful, wonderful, pleasurable—for a moment. That's why it's easy to get in this gate.

You'll notice in the middle of the diagram there's a cross. And notice just to the right of the cross is another triangle that has a wide gate on the right side, but it has a little narrow gate where the triangle from the left side fits in. Notice that at the little narrow gate, the word "death" fits right in there if you slide that triangle in. The reason is that the many problems that come as the result of wrong choices—the wide gate that is easy to get in, brings a person to a living-death experience. It's a death experience at that cross because it's through the cross that you get through the narrow gate. It's how you get in the gate that is narrow that produces a life that is wide. You'll notice on the top of the diagram on the left it says "World-Satan-Flesh." In John 10:10a, most people don't know the first half of this verse, they only know the John 10:10b on the right-hand side of the triangle where Jesus says, "I came that they might have life, and might have it abundantly." Do you know what the first part of that verse is? Most people never hear, never quote, "The thief comes only to steal, and kill, and destroy." He comes to steal the Christian's joy, for example, because the joy of the Lord is our strength. In the presence of the Lord is the fullness of joy. One of the things Satan would like to do is to deceive you that there are other places than in His presence to get life and joy. So he steals the Christian's joy. He also destroys your relationships because if he can destroy your relationships he can also take away your joy. In fact, ultimately, he can kill the potential ministry that you could have in your life because your life is a miserable mess, and there is no life or overflow

VICTORIOUS CHRISTIAN LIVING Conference
Copyright © 1999 Victorious Christian Living International, Inc.

of joy to pass to the next person for the healing of the person's life. So the left side there, Satan's work, is to deceive you into the ways of the world as the best way to get fulfillment for your life.

The ways of the life of Christ are not things that most of us want anything to do with because they require death to the self-life to get through the narrow gate. They require us to die to our ways. They require us to face the issue of godship and of fulfilling life through our own means and methods. In order to get through that gate, it's a hard decision. See, the Bible says the way of the transgressor is hard. It ends up a hard, miserable, living-death experience. It's hard to get into the Christian life. It is hard to make a decision that's righteous and holy because it's contrary to the stream of the flow of the world's society that we live in—so it's a hard decision. But notice, it says it becomes easy and it becomes life. That's why Jesus says, "Come to Me all you who labor," there's the hard part, ". . . and I will give you rest" (Matthew 11:28). I will make your life light and easy it says in the last verse of that chapter. See, the Lord's way produces life and it produces a life that is light and easy. So why is it we choose these things [that end up hard]? Well, I don't think most of us purposely choose because we want to choose the end result of misery. Is that true? I don't think so.

Let me just give you an illustration of that. I mentioned to you about the accident on the motorcycle. You see, one of the things that the Lord had been saying to me for some time was that He wanted me to take time during the day, not my private devotional time in the morning with Him, but during the day as I was directing the ministry of VCLI. He wanted me to stop during the day. Now realize that when you're involved in counseling, you have many staff members, you have board members, you have friends and many of them are in need of help in counseling, you have all your administrative

activities, you have the responsibility of raising support, and you have the responsibility to manage everything—you've got lots of things going. So it's real easy for a guy like me that can get involved in doing a lot of things to say, "Well, Lord, I tried, but I was really busy yesterday, I had some really important things that had to be taken care of and I just never got to it." In fact, I did that for 2 years because I really felt that I was fairly important and many of the things that I was doing were fairly important.

So, the Lord said, "Oh, okay. So you don't want to choose to do what My Spirit keeps convicting you that you should do. Well, I tell you what, let me help you out."

Slap, up side the pickup truck. Busted my right hip and busted both my wrists. I was in the emergency room for 6 hours. When I woke up after surgery the next day, I was hanging from the ceiling in a sling because of a broken hip. I had a steel cast-thing on this arm over here [left]. This one [right] was cast from my fingers all the way up to my elbow. I realized as I was looking up, the first moment that I became conscious after the anesthetic, that I was totally helpless. I had to be fed and everything else that was involved with being helpless. As I lay there looking up, I realized this was rather significant that I'm looking up. In fact, the first words that I heard from the Spirit of God were: "Well, David, do you have time to pray now?" I realized the Lord is incredible. He took my wrong choice, my failure to submit to His Spirit, and He slapped me up side a pickup truck. I tell you, He was very gracious because He gave me no internal injuries, just broken bones and just totally incapacitated me, so that I couldn't walk, I had to be fed and everything else. He had me hanging face up in a sling in a bed, not able to do anything but pray. He does have kind of a sense of humor, too, doesn't He. God causes all things to happen together for good.

Do you think I have any consciousness or awareness or sensitivity about praying during the day

VCL
VICTORIOUS CHRISTIAN LIVING Conference
Copyright © 1999 Victorious Christian Living International, Inc.

now? You see, the Lord can get something through to us much better than anybody else can. God causes all things to happen together for good because He loves us. Because we love Him and we're called according to His purposes, He wants us to act according to His purposes. He wants us to do whatever He has called us to. He has amazing resources to do anything necessary to sanctify and mature and grow us and to cause us to reap the consequences of our choices. See what Galatians 6:7-8, listed on your diagram, says, "Do not be deceived, God is not mocked; for whatever a man sows, this he will also reap. For the one who sows to his own flesh" (Doing his/her own program, doing his/her own thing) "shall from the flesh reap corruption," (misery, pain) "but the one who sows to the Spirit shall from the Spirit reap eternal life." God has a process because He set up a law of life that's called "sow and reap," cause and effect.

Many of the problems we have in our life, we have because we've chosen, and, therefore, caused or sowed things that make us reap certain things. The reaping is a living-death experience when we have been sowing to the flesh. By the way, where does that fit in the relationship of the cross to the narrow gate? Just to the left of it. It's what sets us up to be willing to go through the gate. It's what sets us up to face the cross because of the living death that we're experiencing. It's what helps us stop and listen and do whatever He has us do.

So as I lay there realizing what He had said and what He had asked, I began to make some commitments. In fact, I found that the real pain wasn't the accident, the surgery, or the physical recuperating. I remember even a month later as I was learning to walk, it took me 20 minutes to get out of the bed and into a wheelchair, 20 minutes to be able to go to the bathroom. I still couldn't use my hands because of the way they were cast and the way they were put together. But the real pain was realizing that I didn't

consider God important enough to do what He asked me to do.

The real challenge was to find out that I had to actually schedule in my life the time to have that appointment or it didn't happen. So even weeks later as I finally began to schedule appointments, I found that I made appointments with other people. That was because I had appointments. I didn't have an appointment to meet with God and I didn't make it. I found that I had to actually begin to, and I do this to this day, schedule prayer into my day. God has wonderful ways of causing all things to happen together for good.

Now God doesn't always limit it there, He can do all three of these problems at the same time in our life. For example, during the time that I was in surgery—the doctor informed me a few days later—they had taken bets on me which I thought was kind of funny and I laughed and asked him what that was about. He said: "We were convinced when you came in that you were probably on drugs. You were having too good a time for the kind of condition you were in. So we took bets, and I want you to know I lost 5 bucks."

"You lost 5 bucks?"

"Yeah. I bet you were on drugs. But after we did all the blood tests and everything, we found out that you were not on any kind of drugs whatsoever. What is puzzling us now is, it's a few days later and you're still having a good time and we don't understand it. We'd like to know what makes you tick."

As the Spirit spoke to me at that moment, the Spirit said, "Don't tell him." Now I decided after my last experience of the accident that I was going to be obedient to the Spirit of God the next time He spoke to me. I was very attentive to what He was saying. Do you understand what I mean here? I didn't want to get slapped up the side of another pickup truck. So I

VICTORIOUS CHRISTIAN LIVING Conference
Copyright © 1999 Victorious Christian Living International, Inc.

decided not to tell him a thing and so my response was, "Well I do as little as possible." He laughed and I laughed and that was the end of the discussion. He didn't ask me anything else.

About 2 weeks later, he took me down to take some more x-rays; and as he was taking these x-rays, he began to talk to me. He said, "You know if I ever have problems in my marriage, I'm going to call you." Now why would he say that to me?

A month after I was released from the hospital he called me one day and he said, "I'm coming out to visit you." I thought, "This is great. I didn't realize doctors still made house calls." So, when he arrived, I went to the door. I still couldn't do much except get in my little chair and push the buttons because my arms were cast and I couldn't walk. I'd push a little button and I'd go around the house in that little cart. I went out to the door and said, "Come on in." As the doctor walked in the door he said, "I'm not here to see you." I thought well what did you come out for.

"I thought you were coming to do a doctor's visit?"

"No, I'm here for you to see me."

"Oh, okay. So what do you want me to see you about?"

"Well, I want to tell you this, can I sit down and talk to you?"

"Sure. Go ahead and sit over there."

He sat down in a chair and for the next few minutes he began to tell me that he was in the midst of a second divorce. He had been divorced before, and he was in the process of being divorced again. He just thought maybe I could help him. He didn't know why, but he thought I could.

"Well you know it's an interesting thing, but I can help you. I'd like to tell you what the solution is."

I began to explain to him the problem of godship in his life. I began to explain to him the reasons problems happen. Just like we're having a discussion here right now. And as I began to explain to him the purposes of problems and that they are designed to bring us to the end of our self-life and to bring us to the place where we recognize we have a need that is bigger than we are that we don't know how to answer. Then I told him the answer. I told him the answer is in the person of the Lord Jesus Christ. As he knelt on the floor there at the table in my office, he prayed and asked the Lord Jesus to come into his life. As he got up from the table, the first thing he said to me, "Now I know what's different about you." You see, the Lord decided to display His glory in the midst of my disobedience. Now the Lord wanted to display His glory. He decided to use me to introduce him to the most wonderful thing that ever happened to him. In fact, so wonderful, a few days later he called and said, "Is there any way that I can bring my wife to see you?" I said: "Well, I'm really not going anywhere. She might as well come. At least I enjoy visitors." So she came and I had an opportunity to talk with her. I had the opportunity to introduce her to this great life in Christ Jesus.

But it didn't end there. You see for the next 10 years as we dialogued together, we got to know each other. Months later after being introduced to Christ, she quit her job and she went to work for him. For the next 10 years, they worked together every day in his practice. Not only were they married, now they worked together every day. You see, God allowed all those problems to cause the works of a brand new life, not only individually for them each knowing Christ, but in their marriage with each other as well. He just retired a couple of years ago and they are now enjoying the latter years of their

VCL

VICTORIOUS CHRISTIAN LIVING Conference

lives together as husband and wife, in love with each other. God uses and causes all things to work together for good.

GOD USES EVERYTHING
(Diagram 140-B)
In your next Diagram, 140-B, you'll notice that it says at the top "God Uses Everything." As you look down through the list, you'll notice many wonderful, positive things like Christian upbringing, praying parents, Bible teaching, Christian friends, Scriptures, caring pastors, camps, answers to prayer, godly models, etc. You see many wonderful things that God uses to do the work of sanctification in our lives. But I'm convinced in 30-plus years of counseling, the most significant things God uses to sanctify are not the good things. It's all the things that we would call bad things, that to God are good things.

You see again this issue of godship. What I call good, you call bad. Now God calls problems joy. In fact, we're going to see that He says to thank Him **for** them and thank Him **in** them. God sees problems as one of the most wonderful vehicles to sanctify and produce a work. In James 1:2-4 it says, "Consider it all joy, my brethren, when you encounter various trials, knowing that the testing of your faith produces endurance. And let endurance have its perfect result, that you may be perfect and complete, lacking in nothing." How many of you as believers would like to experience a maturity and a completeness in your life that everything that happened to you in your life you actually could get excited about? The worst things you could think of could happen and you could be at peace, because you know all things happen together for good.

I shared with you that our youngest daughter called and we arrived and all the emergency vehicles were there. Finally, after talking with Michele, Suzanne then took over, and I went in to see about Stuart. Just as I went in to see

about Stuart—her husband of 3 years; she was 26, almost 27, and he was 30 years of age—the paramedics were bringing him out of the house. As I looked at him, his head was bandaged, but he was breathing and he wasn't on any equipment, so I said to Michele, "It looks like he will be fine." We followed the vehicles to the hospital, and as we got to the hospital the police came. They did what they call a dusting of Michele's hands, because you see they didn't really know what had happened and they were investigating the case. I realized at that point, the reason they didn't want me to touch Michele's hands was because she was a suspect. But they dusted her hands and an hour later they came back and reported to us that she was fine, she wasn't a suspect.

Of course, we were relieved to know that they realized that. We knew, but we were just glad that they now knew. About an hour after that all happened, the doctor came out and he began to explain the details of what had happened and in the process trying to explain, he said, "You know I really don't know how to even explain it to you." He said, "Let me just show you the x-rays." As he started to pull the x-rays out, Michele said she didn't want to look so I went with the doctor by myself. I looked at the x-rays and I saw that the bullet that had hit the back of his head had shattered many pieces of skull into his brain. The doctor said, "There is no way we can do surgery without killing him through that, and if we don't do surgery we can tell you he is going to die anyway." So, one hour later, we realized that this 3 years of marriage to Stuart was going to end.

Now, here's Stuart, not only was he significant in our daughter's life because he was her husband, but Stuart had become involved with our organization. He had gone through the VCL Conference and he was excited about the messages of our ministry. He'd come to work full time on our staff. He was by that time head of the training in our center in Phoenix. In fact, because of who he was, a very unusual young man at 30 years of age, he had also built all the computers in our operations and programmed all those computers and networked them all together with each other. Besides that, he was on the national speaking team. He was speaking in these VCL Conferences as part of the speaking team. And besides that, he was one of my motorcycle riding buddies. He was a friend, not just a son-in-law.

Besides all of that, he with a couple of other guys had started a church and he was pastoring a church at 30 years of age besides working full time for me. I didn't pay him a nickel because you see besides all of that he earned a living outside of that building computers for corporations. Somewhat of an unusual 30-year-old wouldn't you say? And yet, Stuart was gone—no longer part of our family. But I thought you said all things happen together for good. Well, let me tell you about that so you can begin to see that the second thing I said about problems happen for glorifying God. I said that problems happen because we make wrong choices, but I also said that problems happen for the purpose of sanctifying us.

When Stuart was alive, he had wanted Michele many times to travel with him and speak. Our daughter Michele was at that time fairly timid and, in fact, if I would just mention that she was in the audience when I was speaking, she would be embarrassed. Stuart, however, desired very much for her to actually speak with him. He also desired very much along with that, that she could know the thrill he had of knowing who he was in Christ. You see, Stuart came from a background where he had 5 stepmothers and 4 stepfathers. His second stepfather hit him with a two-by-four and broke his jaw. He had been whipped so badly that when he lay down to go to bed, the sheet stuck to his back. As his mother pulled the sheet off, the skin ripped off his back. Stuart had come from a terrible situation in his background, but when he discovered

who he was in Christ, his past was no longer a problem. In fact, that's why he started pastoring a church. He wanted people to know the incredible life in Christ. And he, in fact, was challenging our daughter, Michele, to go through the training at VCL that he was the head of because he wanted her to discover more of the incredibleness of this life in Christ. Well, now all this had happened.

Michele had the benefit of many believers around her encouraging her, helping her understand how you walk through this kind of thing and that was a great benefit and great blessing. A few months later she was asked to speak because of the healing and the work that had taken place in her life. She was asked by a woman whose husband had died that year. When she came through our center, she watched Michele and saw what was happening in her life, and she wanted her to come and share at her church. This woman had started a group in her church for people who had lost someone in their family.

So, I was asked to speak and Michele was asked to come and share her testimony. When we arrived at the church there were some 15 people who had all lost their spouses that year. They were all approximately my age except for one young couple who had lost an 11-year-old boy in a car accident. Michele at 27 years of age began to speak. That evening I never did have a chance to speak and I was very grateful for that. They didn't want to hear from me, they wanted to hear more from her. In fact, one woman in the midst of her conversation actually stopped the entire presentation she was making. She said, "Stop. Stop. Stop. Stop." and said to Michele, "How can someone at 27 years of age have such an incredible understanding of life?"

As Michele began to speak, the first thing she said was, "You know, I couldn't wait to get here to speak to you." As her father that was puzzling to me, knowing who she had been all of the years of her life, I looked over to see if this was actually Michele. I looked and saw it was

Michele. You know how you do that. I looked again, because I thought she couldn't be saying she couldn't wait to get up here and speak. This is not Michele. Well you know, she not only has spoken many times without me now, she has been conducting a grief group for people who go through these kinds of things. The same woman who at 27 was insecure, wasn't sure, today is confident, capable, and allowing God to use her in a mighty way to touch other people's lives. See all things happen together for the purpose of sanctifying and maturing us and growing us.

God has incredible ways. And you know what is exciting is that Stuart now is enjoying observing the benefits of his life being the vehicle through which God produced that work he wanted for his wife. He became the vehicle for that to happen. God uses all things, causes all things, to work together for good. So you see in this diagram Romans 8:28. There's another verse there, 2 Corinthians 4:8-11, here is what it says, "We are afflicted in every way, but not crushed; perplexed, but not despairing; persecuted, but not forsaken; struck down, but not destroyed; always carrying about in the body the dying of Jesus, that the life of Jesus also may be manifested in our body. For we who live are constantly being delivered over to death for Jesus' sake, that the life of Jesus also may be manifested in our mortal flesh."

You see those things that we would say are problems that we wouldn't want in our life, the Lord says to us through His servant James as he wrote to us these words and I want to paraphrase these now to you backwards (James 1:2-4). Would you like to be mature, complete, lacking in nothing? Then, "Let patience have its completing work in you. Stay in that situation, walk through the process, endure through it because the testing of your faith produces that patience." That means then, "Let the testing of your faith happen." And it says, "that all kinds of trials and tribulations and temptations are the things that cause your faith to be tested. There-

fore, get all excited when they come into your life. Don't count them as intruders but count them as friends." Do you now see the picture of those verses? When things come into our lives, if we understand that God is going to use them to mature and sanctify us, we can get excited because we will start looking for the result. In fact, even when we make wrong choices and they produce a living death in our experience we will start getting excited because we realize that the process that is bringing us death is the same process that is going to produce the life of Christ in us. So all of the problems—our wrong choices, God by His choice causing afflictions—are for the purpose of maturing us and bringing us to the end of the self-life, so that Christ's life may be seen!

I would like to read to you one more. This is kind of a special one. It's about David. In Psalm 119, that longest chapter in the Psalms, but I want to read you just three verses because David, too, was realizing the significance of problems. Listen to what he says starting in verse 65 (NKJV). He says, "You have dealt well with your servant, / O Lord, according to Your word." Before, this is verse 67, "Before I was afflicted I went astray, / But now I keep Your word." And then in verse 75 (NASB), "I know, O Lord, that Thy judgments are righteous, / And in faithfulness Thou has afflicted me." Who afflicted David? The Lord God of heaven. Why? So that he wouldn't go astray. That he would walk according to the statutes. God knows that one of the best ways to bring us into the sanctifying process of the maturity of the completing in Christ is through problems. Don't run from problems. Stay right in them. Endure in them. Let God teach you until you come to the place where you begin to say thank you in all the problems. It's at that place that you begin to be completed.

WELL-MEANING DETOURS
(Diagram 140-C)
You see in Diagram 140-C, many well meaning

people want to turn you away from your problems. They want to distract you from your problems. They want you to do superficial things to not face the problem or the need that is bringing you to the cross. So they will suggest to you, "change your daily routine," "go shopping," there are many ideas that people have that are ways of the flesh to keep you from dealing with what has to happen. Those are simply philosophies of the world.

In Colossians 2:8, it says, "See to it that no one takes you captive through philosophy and empty deception, according to the tradition of men, according to elementary principles of the world, rather than according to Christ." Many of the self-help philosophies that are being taught today are ideas encouraging you to live independent of Christ, sufficient in yourself. God wants us to realize that in and of ourselves, we can do nothing. But in Him and through Him we can do anything. We are not limited by the death of a spouse. God is capable of doing supernatural things.

DEAD TO THE SELF-LIFE AND ALIVE TO CHRIST'S LIFE
(Diagram 140-D)
Look at Diagram 140-D, "Dead to the Self-Life, Alive to Christ's Life." What the Lord wants us to see in 1 Thessalonians 5:18 is that we should consider "all things" good. In 1 Thessalonians 5:18 it says, "*In* everything,"—in the circumstance, in the problem, all things are things for which we should give thanks. "*In* everything give thanks; for this is God's will for you in Christ Jesus."

Look at Ephesians 5:20. It says, "Always giving thanks *for*," notice the first one was "in everything," in every circumstance give thanks. This one is "Always giving thanks *for* all things in the name of our Lord Christ Jesus to God, even the Father." Always give thanks to the Father *for* all things in the name of the Lord Jesus. You see the Lord wants us not only *in* the circumstances

to be thankful, but He wants us *for* the thing to be thankful. So that we can begin to recognize that all these things are happening together for our good. As we begin to be thankful, we will begin to see the good thing that God wants to do. When we are unthankful, when we are resisting what God's doing, it is hard to ever see the good that God is doing.

When my wife had a stroke, I spent the next four days in intensive care. During that time I had no idea whether I would talk to her again. I had no idea whether I would be able to enjoy the some thirty-five years we had had of marriage. I didn't know what would happen, and the doctors didn't know what would happen. She was in intensive care with tubes in her and with a lack of response at times. In fact the fourth day, the head nurse and I tried to wake her up in the morning. We couldn't get her to respond. And due to that fact, when the doctor came in and saw that we were unable to get a response from her, that she couldn't wake up, he decided to order another cat scan.

It was at 8 o'clock we tried to wake her up, at 10 o'clock they took her in for the cat scan. At this time they wanted me to sign off on a permission form because they wanted to put dye into her brain to really find out what all had been damaged and what had been hurt. So I signed off so they could do that and they proceeded to fill her brain with dye and then took the cat scan. Forty-five minutes later the doctor came to get me. I had walked out of intensive care to the reception area because some friends had come to visit. I was standing there talking to them and the doctor said, "Can I talk to you. I need to tell you what we observed." And I said, "Sure, you can tell me right here." He said, "It is a pretty grave situation, do you mind if I tell you right here?" And I said, "This is fine, my friends can hear too." Well, he began to explain the gravity of the situation to me. And in the process of explaining the gravity, he wanted to prepare me for the worst of worst because he basically said, "From the dye in the x-rays it is a pretty serious situation because both sides of the brain have been affected."

The one thing the doctor didn't know is that night about 1:00 a.m. the Lord had been showing me what it was He wanted to teach me through this situation. All things happen together for good, and I was asking Him for what that was (Romans 8:28). He was wanting to point out to me that it had to do with a need for me to learn to be more sensitive to Suzanne. I was learning that lesson by reviewing the day. He helped me review the day and I realized that she had been walking behind me. Now my wife was in much better physical condition than I was so this was a very unusual thing. But I had not been aware, I didn't have any conscious realization that she had been walking behind me. As we walked, I started to limp because my right hip is screwed together, so she had asked me a number of times if I wanted to stop and rest. I said, "No," because it is nothing you can really do anything about. I just limp because of it.

When we got to our destination where we were going to turn around, we sat on the bank and we started to look over the San Diego Bay. She asked me things about what I was thinking and I was sharing those things with her. And as we walked back, she was asking me other questions. Here I was now at 1:00 a.m., realizing I hadn't asked her any questions that day. In fact, I not only had not asked her any questions and wasn't aware of anything that she was thinking, I wasn't even aware of the fact that she had been walking behind me. I had been sitting about three feet from her as we were eating dinner and she was telling her friend she had been having a pain in her left side all day, and I never heard that. I wasn't aware of anything, until I was sitting in intensive care and the Lord was reviewing this information for me.

The Lord has very dramatic ways to speak to hardheaded people like me. Unfortunately, as I was sitting there, I was realizing that Suzanne was having to suffer the consequences of my hardheaded, insensitive, unawareness of what was happening. So as I became aware of this, I said to the Lord, "Lord, You know I believe I have learned, I see now what You are talking about. It would just be wonderful if she could enjoy her grandchildren, if she didn't have to suffer the consequences of my insensitivity. If there would be any way that you could change the consequences of what is happening here it would be wonderful. But I do want you to understand, Lord, if I have to take care of her the rest of my life, have no communication, but just give myself in sensitiveness to her the rest of my life, I am willing to do that because I believe you have now finally got my attention."

The Spirit said, "Go in and pray for her." I was sitting in the next cubicle in intensive care during the night. They let me sleep in another bed right there. So I got up out of my chair and I walked into her room. I prayed for her and I asked the Lord if He would choose to heal her. About 3 o'clock that morning, I went back into the room and I noticed something totally different. She was so still, which was unusual, that I thought she wasn't breathing, and I thought her heart wasn't beating. I looked up at the monitors. I could see that the heartbeat was there and I went over and listened to her and she was breathing. She was so calm, I thought she had died. Well, 8 o'clock that next morning was when the nurses were trying to wake her up and we couldn't wake her up. And I know they didn't understand this, but I was thinking maybe the Lord just had her in such a deep sleep He was just healing her, and we were disrupting that. So, I said that to the nurses, and I think they thought I was a little crazy. They didn't know what I was talking about.

When the doctor was standing and telling me the gravity of the situation, what the doctor didn't know was that one-half hour earlier when they brought her out of the cat scan, and took her back into the intensive care room, she sat up, got out of the bed, sat down on her chair and started talking to the nurses. So, I said that to the doctor, "Well, I understand the gravity which you are saying but I want you to know she is sitting up talking to the nurses." He thought I was joking. He thought I was trying to make light of this terrible, grave situation. So he said, "No, no, I am serious about this and I think you should go into the x-ray room with me and let me show you the x-rays." So we went into the x-ray room and I wanted to see those anyway. He showed me the gravity of the situation but I was still standing in there aware of the fact that just one half hour ago she was sitting up talking to the nurses. So I said to the doctor, "I appreciate what you are saying, but I think now it is your turn, you need to come with me now." And I said, "I don't know anything about this kind of thing, maybe she has relapsed, but she was actually sitting up talking to the nurses." His comment was if that were the case that would be nothing short of miraculous. So we walked into her room, and there she was sitting and talking to the nurses. I walked around the back of the bed and he stood in the front. We stood there for two minutes looking at each other. He finally walked away. I wanted to know what he was thinking, so I walked after him and he was over at the nurses station writing in the thing. And I said, "Well, doctor how do you explain this?" He said, "I don't." I said, "Well, should this situation relapse and she goes back into a coma or whatever. What's going to happen?" He said, "Don't ask me. I don't know. All I can tell you right now is what you see is what you get." I said, "Good, that's what I am planning on."

You see, all things happen together for good. Because of that circumstance, Suzanne and I have the best relationship I believe we have ever had in our marriage. Because God knows how to use all things to do what he wants to do.

You see in Diagram 140-D a number of things that you and I want to do. We want to "See

God" in everything that is happening; we want to "Let God Be God"; we want to "Thank" Him in these things"; we want to "Trust" and to "Obey" Him. God's purpose is to bring us to the end of our self-life, to this cross down at the bottom so we can have His supernatural life.

REVIEW

Look at what it says: There are three kinds of problems. "Problems in life cannot be avoided." Everybody is going to have them. You're going to have them because you made wrong choices. You are going to have them because God wants to sanctify you. You're going to have them because God wants to glorify Himself.

Number two, "God uses **everything** in our lives to accomplish His purposes." So, there is no problem that is wasted. It's only wasted if we don't learn the good from it. It's only wasted if we aren't thankful in the midst of it. But all problems happen together for our good.

Number three, "Often problems cause us to come to a point of weakness either physically, spiritually, financially, or relationally so we will give up doing things our way." God has a process of bringing us to the cross and the end of our self-life, so He can begin to give us His supernatural life and we can enjoy His life instead of our own.

Four, "God wants us to trust Him because of His sovereignty, love, and power."

Number five, "We can even thank God for the problems He permits, because they cause us to come to Him and totally depend on Him."

Problems are exciting and I hope from this day forward you will get all excited when all kinds of trials and tribulations come into your life because they test your faith. And the testing of your faith causes you to become capable of enduring. When you let endurance have its completing work in you, you will become mature, complete, lacking in nothing. You will be able to walk through everything in life when Christ becomes your life.

VCL
VICTORIOUS CHRISTIAN LIVING Conference
Copyright © 1999 Victorious Christian Living International, Inc.

GODSHIP —————————————————————————

REJECTION —————————————————————————

EXTERNAL/INTERNAL —————————————————————

PROBLEMS, PROBLEMS, WHY PROBLEMS? ——————————

MY FLESH—GOD'S ENEMY ➡

REPENTANCE ————————————————————————

WHAT'S NEW ABOUT YOU? ——————————————————

ACCEPTING YOUR RIGHTEOUSNESS ——————————————

EXTENDING FORGIVENESS ————————————————————

SEEKING FORGIVENESS ———————————————————————

REST, ABIDE, WALK ————————————————————

LOVE ——————————————————————————————

GODSHIP

REJECT

EXT/INT

PROBLEM

FLESH

REPENT

WHAT'S NEW

ACCEPT RIGHT

EXTEND FORGIVE

SEEK FORGIVE

REST

LOVE

MY FLESH—GOD'S ENEMY

> *Because the mind set on the flesh is hostile toward God; for it does not subject itself to the law of God, for it is not even able to do so . . . .* Romans 8:7

This lesson deals with the condition within each of us whereby we desire to operate in our own strength, reason, and selfish desires. This condition is called the flesh or the self-life. The flesh may be described as "my claim to my right to myself" (Oswald Chambers). Paul says in Romans 8:6 that "The mind set on the flesh is death." This is a crucial lesson to uncover a basic reason Christians are not living in victory. They are choosing to walk after the flesh. There is good news—victory is possible because **I am not my flesh**.

Consider this quote to help clarify the "flesh."

"We have all learned to rely on our own strategies for getting our needs met. The Bible calls this mechanism for servicing our own needs the *flesh*. Every person has developed his flesh-life in order to get what he wants out of life as much of the time as possible. Don't think of flesh as skin, but as personal *techniques* for meeting your own perceived needs, apart from Christ. . . ." From *Grace Walk* by Steve McVey, page 28.

MAKING LIFE OR DEATH DECISIONS

Deut. 30:19-20

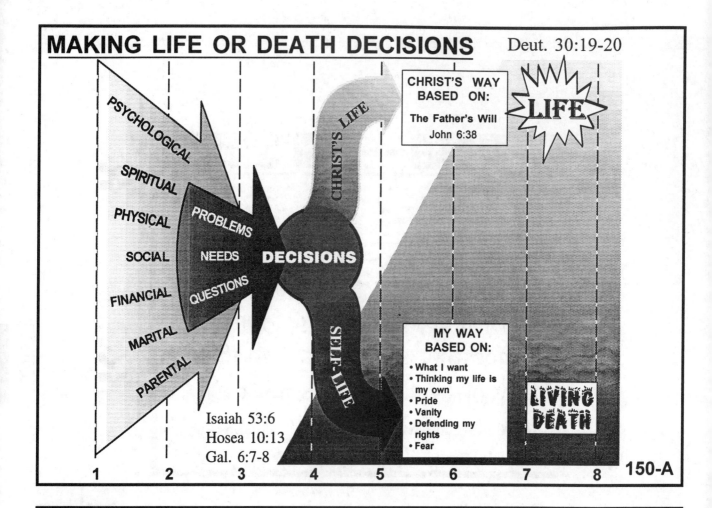

CHRIST'S WAY BASED ON:
The Father's Will
John 6:38

LIFE

PSYCHOLOGICAL
SPIRITUAL
PHYSICAL
SOCIAL
FINANCIAL
MARITAL
PARENTAL

PROBLEMS
NEEDS
QUESTIONS

DECISIONS

CHRIST'S LIFE

SELF-LIFE

MY WAY BASED ON:
• What I want
• Thinking my life is my own
• Pride
• Vanity
• Defending my rights
• Fear

LIVING DEATH

Isaiah 53:6
Hosea 10:13
Gal. 6:7-8

1   2   3   4   5   6   7   8   150-A

VCL
VICTORIOUS CHRISTIAN LIVING Conference
Copyright © 1999 Victorious Christian Living International, Inc.

PURPOSE for Diagram **150-A:**

To show that all decisions will reap life or death
depending upon whether they are made my way or Christ's way.

? 1. Study Deuteronomy 30:19-20.

? 2. What is God's desire for you? Is He interested in every decision you make? Why? _____

_____

_____

3. List a decision you need to make in one of the seven areas of life.

_____

_____

> ## Choose life!
> Deut. 30:19

? 4. How have you typically made decisions in the past? Which of the six ways of deciding "my way" have you used? _____

_____

_____

_____

? 5. How have you experienced a living death? _____

_____

📖 6. Study John 6:38.

? 7. How can you know what God's will is regarding your decision?

_____

_____

📖 8. Study John 5:30. Is doing your own will hindering you from considering God's will? Explain. _____

_____

My life is not my own.

SELF-LIFE

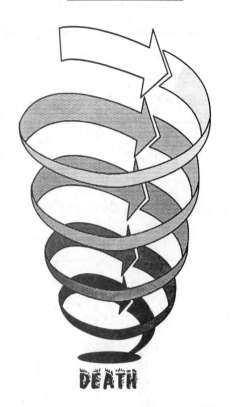

DEATH

Matthew 16:25a

SELF-LIFE	*James 3:16*
SELF-COMMENDATION	*2 Cor. 10:17-18*
SELF-OCCUPATION	*Phil. 2:4*
SELF-PLEASING	*Rom. 15:1-3*
SELF-CONDEMNATION	*Rom. 8:1*
SELF-DEFENSIVENESS	*Gen. 3:11-13*
SELF-PITY	*Jonah 4:8*
SELF-DESTRUCTION	*Phil. 3:19*

150-B

NOTES

VCL
VICTORIOUS CHRISTIAN LIVING Conference
Copyright © 1999 Victorious Christian Living International, Inc.

PURPOSE for Diagram **150-B:**

> *To reveal the cause and the process of death brought about through the self-life.*

---

1. Study Matthew 16:25.

2. Have you been seeking your own way? _____
   _____
   Have your decisions reflected that mindset? _____
   _____

3. Study James 3:16. How might your selfish ambition lead to every evil thing? _____
   _____

4. Which of these steps in the spiral can you identify with now? _____
   _____

5. If you are living your life for yourself, you are headed down further.

6. Study John 12:25.

7. Are you ready to admit an infatuation with yourself? _____

> *For the mind set on the flesh is death . . . .*
> Rom. 8:6

Self-life leads to death.

FLESH

TEST YOUR MOTIVES

1.

Is my decision for the **FLESH**?

- Am I doing it for my self-interest? *Phil. 2:3-4*
- Is it against God's word? *Ps. 119:11*
- Is it contrary to those in authority? *Rom. 13:1; Heb. 13:17*
- Am I feeling frustrated, angry, or fearful? *Gal. 5:16-21*
- Is there a lack of contentment? *1 Tim. 6:6*

If so, the result is DEATH, LOSS, and CORRUPTION!

2.

Is my decision for the **SPIRIT**?

- Am I doing it in recognition that my life is not my own? *2 Cor. 5:15*
- Am I acknowledging God's sovereign control in everything
  and trusting Him to work things out? *Rom. 8:28*

If so, the result is **LIFE & PEACE!**

150-C

NOTES

VCL
VICTORIOUS CHRISTIAN LIVING Conference
Copyright © 1999 Victorious Christian Living International, Inc.

PURPOSE for Diagram **150-C:**

To provide a means to determine if motives
are from the Spirit or the flesh.

1. Do you have any doubts that your decisions are motivated by the Spirit? _____

2. Study Galatians 5:16-21.

3. Are your decisions or actions found in this list? _____

4. What principles in God's Word speak to you about the decision you are facing? _____

5. Is it contrary to those in authority over you? This would include for example: your pastor, parents, husband, or boss. Have you checked? _____

6. Are you feeling angry, frustrated, fearful, or discontented? What do these feelings show you? _____

> ## This is the way, walk in it. Isa. 30:21

7. Are you unwilling to ask for help and guidance from anyone? (See Diagram 100-A.)   Yes   No

8. If you're acknowledging that your life belongs to God would it affect your decision? _____

9. If you could really trust God would it affect your decision? _____

Motive is the key.

CHRIST'S LIFE

EVER-EXPANDING

John 15:16	MINISTRY to OTHERS
Matt. 28:19-20	OUTREACH
Gal. 5:1	SPIRITUAL FREEDOM
1 John 4:11-12	MATURE LOVE
Psalm 62:5	EXPECTATION From GOD
Psalm 50:23	WORSHIP & PRAISE
Matt. 16:24	DAILY CROSS-BEARING
Luke 9:23	DENY SELF

150-D

NOTES

VCL
VICTORIOUS CHRISTIAN LIVING Conference
Copyright © 1999 Victorious Christian Living International, Inc.

PURPOSE for Diagram **150-D:**

To show how Christ's life can be expressed in a person.

1. Study Acts 16:22-31.

2. How does this diagram illustrate this passage? _____
_____
_____
_____
_____

> *. . . whoever loses his life for My sake shall find it.* Matt. 16:25

3. Study Luke 9:23.

4. What would denying yourself look like? _____
_____
_____
_____

5. How would it affect your decision-making process? _____
_____
_____

6. Are you ready to confess decisions you have made based on your own desires and commit to follow His will and not your own? _____
_____

7. Can you begin to praise God that your life is turning around? _____
_____
_____

8. Study John 15:16. Have you considered how you can minister to others? Who? How? _____
_____

Blessed to be a blessing.

REVIEW

- The flesh or self-life is a condition that exists within every person, believers and nonbelievers alike.

- A believer has been born of the Spirit and does not have to carry out the deeds of the flesh.

- However, when a believer chooses his or her own way over God's way that person is walking after the flesh and it will produce death.

- By checking my motives, I can determine if I am walking after the flesh or walking after the Spirit.

NOTES

VCL

VICTORIOUS CHRISTIAN LIVING Conference
Copyright © 1999 Victorious Christian Living International, Inc.

MY FLESH—GOD'S ENEMY

Lesson Transcript by Mark Ford

I'd like to ask you to turn in your manuals to the section on MY FLESH—GOD'S ENEMY. On many occasions I deal with young men who are struggling in their marriages. Often they say things like: "Mark, I really love my wife. The thought of losing her terrifies me. Can you help me somehow? Can you share something with me that will give strength and stamina to my marriage? I have trouble controlling my thoughts and my words. It isn't helping my marriage at all."

As we go through the Scriptures together we always agree as to what is true and should be done, and yet frequently when they return the next week they come back totally defeated. They say things like: "I don't know what happened. When I got home and my wife started in on me, it was like something came over me and dragged me into my anger. I wound up seeing my anger accelerate and the next thing I knew, I was doing all of the things we agreed I shouldn't do. I feel totally helpless."

It brings us to a very important question. "Why do some situations render us helpless, without strength to do what we know is righteous?" We are going to answer that question. Sometimes it seems that situations somehow gain power and seize precedence over all that's happening. What can we do for people who genuinely desire to walk with the Lord, but find no power to do it?

A major point is the will. I may have an idea of what life should be and find that God has a different idea. God takes His children through hard times to purify them and teach them to become comfortable with having to trust only in the Lord. Certainly the Lord did that with His people in Israel. In hard times God's people may say: "This is not what I signed up for God. I am not interested." They look for ways to arrange some kind of a compromise with God. Sometimes Christians will pursue their own desires, walk away from God and the church for a while, hoping that God doesn't punish them too severely. Christians argue: "I like that kind of music. I don't think that God wants me to listen to it, but I want to listen to it."

Others struggle with the kind of friends they choose. "I don't think that God wants me to spend time with these people, but they make me laugh. I enjoy being with them."

The Word says that we are not to be unequally yoked with unbelievers; yet, we see it in marriage and business. Many Christians struggle between their will and what they know God wants. It really does bring havoc.

Sometimes Christians play this deadly game: "This is what I want. I know God doesn't want me to do it, but what will He do to me if I do it? I really don't want to abandon God, so I will do it and confess it later." Where does this kind of thinking originate? It comes from unbelief. It comes from the flesh which demands its desires and to be in control to fulfill them. Our flesh knows God isn't going to deliver what it wants. Flesh knows that God won't help in its plans, and so, it must rely on self to make them happen.

In this lesson we will study four things:
- We will identify for you what the flesh is.
- We will teach you how the flesh works and what it does to you.

- We will show you how to identify your flesh.
- We will show you how to escape the power of the flesh and walk in peace and righteousness.

Let's look at our title page and answer the question, "What is the flesh?" Look at Romans 8:7 in the box. "Because the mind set on the flesh is hostile toward God; for it does not subject itself to the law of God, for it is not even able to do so." That answers part of our question. The flesh is hostile to God. If you are subjecting your decision making process to the control of the flesh, you will not be successful. You will not experience life and peace. The flesh does not even have that capacity. That's important.

The text under the box says, "This lesson deals with the condition within each of us whereby we desire to operate in our own strength, reason, and selfish desires. This condition is called the flesh or the self-life. The flesh may be described as 'my claim to my right to myself' (Oswald Chambers). Paul says in Romans 8:6 that 'The mind set on the flesh is death.' This is a crucial lesson to uncover a basic reason Christians are not living in victory. They are choosing to walk after the flesh. There is good news—victory is possible because **I am not my flesh**."

We have a quote here from the book *Grace Walk,* written by Steve McVey, which I believe is very helpful. Here is what he said: "We have all learned to rely on our own strategies for getting our needs met. The Bible calls this mechanism for servicing our own needs the *flesh*. Every person has developed his flesh-life in order to get what he wants out of life as much of the time as possible. Don't think of flesh as skin, but as personal *techniques* for meeting your own perceived needs, apart from Christ."

Here is another way of looking at it. The flesh is *another will*. Let's consider the origin. Turn in your Bibles to Isaiah 14:13-15. Notice the five

"I wills" of Satan. "But you said in your heart I will ascend to heaven, I will raise my throne above the stars of God, and I will sit on the mount of the assembly in the recesses of the North. I will ascend above the heights of the clouds. I will make myself like the Most High." Notice God's comment. "Nevertheless you will be thrust down to Sheol to the recesses of the pit."

Maybe as you hear the comments of Satan you may be thinking, "Well I don't want to ascend above the throne of God, I don't want anything like that." I don't either, but we don't have to take it to that extreme to buy into independence from God. Have you ever heard yourself telling God, "I don't want to do that"? Or maybe saying, "God, I can't" or how about, "Lord, I know you want me to do this, but not right now." Or "I'm just not into that kind of thing. Can't you find someone else?" If we say things like that to God, it may not sound so blatant as "I will be like the most High," but any time we don't do what God wants, when He wants it done, we are basically saying: "God, I am the god of my own life. I make my own decisions." There is no difference.

Since the fall in the garden of Eden, man has lived with the flesh, perverted by sin—believer and unbeliever alike. For the unbeliever, the flesh is his life. It is everything to him. It is his decision maker, it is in absolute control of every single thing he does. That's the power of the flesh. The believer on the other hand has an option. He does not have to sin. According to Romans 6:6-10 he can yield his life to God. He doesn't have to yield his body as an instrument of unrighteousness unto sin. He can yield himself to God. The believer has flesh, but he also has an option. For the believer the flesh remains God's enemy and ours, but it becomes a very good reason to pursue the Lord. The fruit of following the flesh is always death. There are no exceptions.

VCL

VICTORIOUS CHRISTIAN LIVING Conference
Copyright © 1999 Victorious Christian Living International, Inc.

MAKING LIFE OR DEATH DECISIONS (Diagram 150-A)

Let's consider how the flesh works. Turn to Diagram 150-A. Let's look at Deuteronomy 30:19-20: "I call heaven and earth to witness against you today, that I have set before you life and death, the blessing and the curse. So choose life in order that you may live, you and your descendants, by loving the LORD your God, by obeying His voice, and by holding fast to Him; for this is your life and the length of your days, that you may live in the land which the LORD swore to your fathers, to Abraham, Isaac, and Jacob, to give them." Notice what He said. Life comes by loving the Lord, by obeying His voice, and by holding fast to Him. Hosea 10:13 says, "You have plowed wickedness, you have reaped injustice, / You have eaten the fruit of lies. / Because you have trusted in your way, in your numerous warriors." What is the value of numerous warriors? They are resources. If we trust in our own resources, we are not trusting in God. We can take God's resources and abuse them for our own purposes. That is what this lesson is all about.

Let's look at the diagram. You can see in the large arrow off to the left that there are basically seven areas of life: psychological, spiritual, physical, social, financial, marital, and parental. Notice that each of those areas can bring problems, needs, and questions that force us to make decisions. Somebody once said that every sin issue is really a trust issue. Because I have concerns that God will not do what I want, I determine what I want and trust in my own way and resources to make it happen if I can. "My will" is the element in the decision making circle that tips the scale down to the self-life.

The option is to allow the Christ-life, or God's will, to tip the scale and lift us to submission to God. That is based on John 6:38, "For I have come down from heaven, not to do My own will, but the will of Him who sent Me." Here is the question. Do I want what God wants or what my flesh wants?

Now let's look at what happens. Suppose we choose to do what Hosea describes, trusting in our own way. Look in the "my way" box and see how it works. My way is based on "what I want." That's what Satan did, wasn't it? That's also what Eve did in the garden. She knew what God wanted. It was God's tree. God gave his instructions regarding the tree. But she said: "I know what you want God. I have a better idea. It would be better for me to know the difference between good and evil, and then I would be just like You." She chose to pursue her own agenda. Notice the basis, "what I want."

The second one is "thinking my life is my own." 1 Corinthians 6:19-20 tells us clearly that we are not our own. We are bought with a price. Our responsibility is to glorify God who is in heaven. But if I take the body God gave me to pursue my own desires, I am telling God that I belong to myself and I can do what I want.

Pride and vanity often drive us in "our way." Have you ever heard someone say, "I can't possibly go out in public looking like this." I used to have a 1979 Toyota Celica and I've actually had people decline to ride in it. It defiled their image.

I may choose my way based on defending my rights. This is a problem for many people. "I have rights and I'm going to defend them. Your right stops where my right begins."

What about fear? Many function out of fear. I may know what I'm going to do is not God's way, but I'm afraid this is my only chance to achieve my goal or stay in control.

What we need to see from this diagram is that if we pursue the self-life, it inevitably culminates in living death. Galatians 6:7-9 tells us that God is not mocked. If we sow to the flesh, we are from the flesh going to reap corruption. We will reap death.

Let's consider the other option we have as Christians. In the decision making process we may choose the Christ-life. Notice what the Christ-life is based on. It is based on the Father's will. Notice what John 6:38 says. "For I have come down from heaven, not to do My own will, but the will of Him who sent Me." That was life for Jesus and if you are living the Christ-life, that is your life as well.

Let's consider the life of a golfer. He worked all week long and he is looking for his reward. He wakes up at 6:00 Saturday morning, grabs his clubs and is on his way out when his wife hears that noise and says, "Where are you going?" He says, "I'm going golfing." She says to him: "You can't do that. My mother is coming in a few days. You've got to paint the living room and the bedroom." The agenda begins to roll. The first words that come out of his mouth are: "Your mother is coming? You didn't say anything to me about that." The fire begins to build and the words begin to fly. The next thing you know, the two are yelling at one another. What happened? The wants of two people came into conflict. This describes many lives.

How can we identify the cause? We find a concise list of the works of the flesh in Galatians 5:19-21. Here they are: immorality, impurity, sensuality, idolatry, sorcery, enmities, strife, jealousy, outbursts of anger, disputes, dissensions, factions, envying, drunkenness, and carousing. You know for certain that if you are experiencing an outburst of anger, the Bible says you are walking after the flesh. When you have walked after the flesh what do you need to do? You need to recognize that you have made the self-life choice. It's going to be based on one of these things—what you want—perhaps pride or defending your rights. You may be certain that it is going to culminate in death.

Let's use our diagram to track through the conflict with our golfer and his wife. It begins with the social world in our seven areas of life. He wants to go golfing with his buddies. His problem was that his wife said, "You need to stay home and paint." He must make a decision. What decision might he make if he decides in favor of the Christ-life? He begins with John 6:38. Jesus didn't come to do His own will. He exists to do the will of God who sent Him. So, too, it is with our golfer. Perhaps he needs to prefer his wife and stay home and paint. There's nothing wrong with golf. In 1 Corinthians 9:27, Paul talks about something our flesh doesn't like to hear about. Buffeting our body keeps us from becoming enslaved to our flesh.

There are other verses to consider. Ephesians 5:25 says, "Husbands, love your wives, just as Christ also loved the church and gave Himself up for her." In the Greek that word "gave himself up" could also be translated "he abandoned himself" for her. What would be wrong with him abandoning himself and his desire to go golfing for his wife? What would he be doing if he stands and argues with his wife? He is basically saying, "The only thing that is important here right now is what I want. Paint it yourself."

We could consider other of the seven areas from our diagram. Finances come up often. People who are struggling financially will sometimes go into business with unbelievers because they have money. They might think: "I have the business, I need the money. I know that God's Word says that I am not to be unequally yoked with unbelievers, but God doesn't understand. My business is going to fail if I don't get some money. He's got the money. I'll just do this quickly, turn my profit and pay him off. Then I will get back on track with God again." It ends in death.

Consider parenting. I was standing in the checkout line at the grocery store where I saw a battle between a mother and her child. The child grabbed a candy bar from the rack. Mother did not want her baby to have the candy. When the two realized they had come to an impasse, the child played the trump card. He let out a screech that felt like a steel bar going right through my

VCL
VICTORIOUS CHRISTIAN LIVING Conference
Copyright © 1999 Victorious Christian Living International, Inc.

ears. You know what happened? Mom grabbed the candy bar and gave it to Junior and paid for it. Was that God's will? It was MY will. The pain was excruciating. I would have bought the kid the candy bar if she didn't. It wasn't my child. I didn't have to worry about the child. Mother gave the child the candy because the mother didn't want to deal with the scream. She didn't want the embarrassment. The Bible tells us that we are to train our children. What kind of training was she giving? For the moment it was more convenient for the sake of her vanity or pride to give him the candy. For 35 cents she saved her pride. That is self-life. In ten or fifteen years payday is coming. Mom and Dad are going to have to deal with the legacy of teaching their child that if he makes people uncomfortable enough, he can have anything he wants, anytime he wants it. It's easy for a while, but living death is coming.

There is another element not quite so obvious. In Jeremiah 17:9 the Bible says, "The heart is more deceitful than all else / And is desperately sick; /Who can understand it?" The truth is, you cannot trust your heart or your emotions. That is why we need God to tell us what to do. If we take our lives into our own hands and do things our own way, we're going to run into lots of trouble.

I served as a missionary in Papua New Guinea for three and a half years and was totally convinced that what I was doing was absolutely righteous. If you would have looked at my life you would have thought I was doing what God wanted. I want you to understand how what I was doing was not at all what God wanted, and I'm going to show you how you can tell in your own life.

I wanted to become a dedicated missionary. When I went to the mission field in Papua New Guinea, I already had a plan. I suppose I was more concerned about what I was willing to do than I was about how God wanted me to do it. That was the way I went to the mission field. I got involved in learning language, doing all of the good things that a missionary should do.

SELF-LIFE (Diagram 150-B)

Let's look at Diagram 150-B. Notice the life that ends in death begins with the self-life. I want to illustrate this diagram with my life. Let's read James 3:16. "For where jealousy and selfish ambition exist, there is disorder and every evil thing." Where jealousy (which is what I want) and selfish ambition (which is the essence of the drive of what I want) exist there is disorder and every evil thing.

My life began with the self-life. I wanted to gain personal value through becoming a good, accomplished missionary. Did you notice what I said there? "I will have personal value." Does that sound anything like what we looked at in the words of Satan, "I will be like the Most High"? It doesn't matter if I say: "God, I don't want your throne. I don't want my throne to be above the stars of heaven. I just want to do what I want to do." There is no difference. That's why the Lord deals with that same issue in Luke 12:18. That's where the man says: "Here is what I will do. I will tear down my barns and build new. And then I will sit back and say to myself, 'Soul, you have laid up much for yourself.'" What did God say? "Bad choice. Your soul is going to be required of you tonight and then who is going to get all of your stuff?" Don't you think it makes a lot more sense to let the God who knows everything be the One who directs your life?

Notice how my life failure progressed. I arrived on the mission field and jumped right into the middle of language study. The first thing that I began to hear from my tribal friends was just what I was searching for, "Mark, you sound Kuman." That was the tribe I lived with. Notice as we move from self-life down to self-commendation. "Mark, you are a great missionary. You sound Kuman. Mark, you are Enduga." Wow! I'm Enduga. That was the clan in my tribe that

FLESH

adopted me. I belonged to them. I fit in. I began to get very excited about how that felt.

You will notice the next slip down the cycle is self-occupation. The more I gave myself to that whole process, the more occupied I became with it. When you become enamored with what you are doing, that is self-occupation. That is exactly what I was, self-occupied. As I became more involved with the tribal people there were things like weddings, funerals, all kinds of events that began to clamor for my attention. The more involved I became, the more acceptance I gained. That is what I was pursuing.

Notice the next step down, self-pleasing. I wanted to please myself. I loved my work so much. For the first time in my life I was having more fun than I thought I would ever have and I pursued it. You could say I sold my soul to pleasing myself, and I actually believed I was giving myself to the Lord. The reality was I had no clue that I was literally being eaten alive by my own lust for self-approval.

As my wife began to see me going down this spiral, my wife began to say: "I'm not going to march in your parade any more. Mark, you are a runaway locomotive and I'm going to get out of your way." My wife started talking about going home. It shocked me. It frightened me.

"You are NOT going home."

My wife should have been able to receive some support from me. What she got was: "Come with me, Sue. If you will come with me, I'll get you value just like I am getting. Come on, Sue. Learn the Kuman language. Come to the funeral with me. Come to the wedding party with me."

I got so involved in taking care of Mark, my wife decided that she needed to get involved in taking care of Sue. She began to decline attending funerals. I told her she couldn't stay home. If she stayed home the message she would be communicating to them would be that she didn't want anything to do with them. They weren't important. I couldn't let her do that. She had to go.

From there it became nasty. She defied me and wouldn't go. She told me that I was the missionary, she wasn't. If I wanted, I could go, but she would not. I told her: "No, you ARE going. Let's get this clear." She began to tell me what a lousy husband I was: "You care more about the tribal people than you do about me." I told her, "Well, you are a lousy missionary." She reminded me that she really never wanted to be a missionary and that I was abandoning my family. I told her to leave if she wanted. I was committed to the work of God and I would stay and do it. I walked away with my fingers in my suspenders. I won the argument. I still had my spiritual integrity and she had just admitted to being a spiritual dwarf. So now that we had established that, she was God's problem and that's where I left it.

"God, if you want me to stay out here and do this awesome work, you are going to have to do something about my wife."

I became self-defensive, and it wasn't long before I moved into self-pity: "God, why in the world did you saddle me with this woman? Her sole mission is to destroy my work." I was so self-righteous about it. You will notice on the bottom that the end is self-destruction. That is exactly what happened. My wife and I had such an impasse with the whole thing that it really did bring destruction.

OVERCOMING THE FLESH
(Diagram 150-C)

Let's consider how to identify the flesh. We use this diagram to give relief and direction. This diagram will help you identify your motives. How can you discern your flesh?

Look at box number one. Is my decision for the flesh? Am I doing this for my self-interest? Is it

VICTORIOUS CHRISTIAN LIVING Conference
Copyright © 1999 Victorious Christian Living International, Inc.

against God's word? Is it contrary to those in authority? Am I feeling frustrated, angry, or fearful? Or is there a lack of contentment?

Let's apply the principles. You know we can nail the golfer's flesh right off the bat. Is he doing it for his self-interest? Of course. Things like that are easy. Is it against God's word? Well, if you are talking about something like adultery, lying, or stealing, of course it is.

What about things that are more subtle. There are many people in ministry, and I would have included myself, who are totally convinced that what they are doing is righteous, yet they are destroying their families. Wouldn't it be nice if God gave us a way to look at what we are doing and know, "THAT'S FLESH"? He has.

Look at box number 2. Is my decision for the Spirit? Am I doing it in recognition that my life is not my own? Am I acknowledging God's sovereign control in everything and trusting Him to work things out? Notice that it says, "If so, the result is life and peace."

Let's use the diagram and track my life through it and see how it works. What about my going to the mission field? Was I doing it for my own self-interest? The honest answer is "yes," but I couldn't see it. Was it against the Word of God? Absolutely NOT. "Go ye into all the world and preach the Gospel." I thought that if I didn't go I would have been disobedient. Is it contrary to those in authority? No. Boy, I'm flying through this list. Look at the next one. Am I feeling frustrated, angry, or fearful? That one had me cold. By checking on our emotions and motivations, we can find the reality of what is going on inside our hearts.

We could move on. I could check it out: "Is my decision for the Spirit? Am I doing it in recognition that my life is not my own?" No, I was doing it my own way. That was pretty obvious. "Am I acknowledging God's sovereign control in

everything and trusting Him to work things out?" Absolutely not. I was trusting in my own re-sources. The way to determine fleshly motives is actually very simple. The Lord gives peace doesn't He? The Bible says to let the peace of God rule in our hearts.

Let's say in the scenario of my life that our struggle was all my wife's spiritual problem. That was not the case, but let's suppose it was. If I am trusting in God's sovereignty even if my wife is trying to destroy the ministry, it is God's problem. I don't have to worry about it do I? I can just sit down and say, "Okay God, you take care of this." I can continue to patiently love and accept her and show her the love of Christ. I didn't do that. I was very hard on my wife. I was very hard on my kids because I was protect-ing my agenda. God had to allow tragedy to come into my life to bring me to my knees. For the first time in my life I had not one solution. I came to VCL a broken man.

CHRIST'S LIFE (Diagram 150-D)

Look at Diagram 150-D. Luke 9:23 says this, "And he was saying to them all, 'If any one wishes to come after me, let him deny himself and take up his cross daily and follow me.'" I had to come to this. My first step was: "Mark, you have done a poor job of evaluating your needs, what your goals ought to be, and how you ought to accomplish them. Look at your family. Look at your wife. Look at your ministry. Everything has absolutely gone to seed. I quit. Lord, I take whatever is left of my life and I put it at the cross. I have been running my own life my own way, doing my own thing. I have literally experi-enced living death. So Lord, if you can do anything with this life that is left, You can have it. It is Yours."

As I began to deny myself and daily bear the cross the Lord had given me, I began to live. I was in pain from my choices, but I realized I was reaping what I had sown. I chose to obediently reap them in order to honor what God says in

Galatians 6:7. The pain was the natural consequence of my bad choices. As I quit fighting them and began to walk with the Lord through them, God began to fill me with praise and worship.

One more thing about this diagram. These "spiral out" steps are not *goals* for us to try to meet. This is the natural result of what happens when we are living the Christ life. That's important to remember. As I continued and all of this became a flow of peace and joy in my life, I had expectations from God. I began to watch the Lord heal my relationship with my wife. I began to see the Lord heal my children. I am a man who brought serious destruction to his family actually believing I was serving the Lord. When I came to the Lord and said: "I give up. You are the King, You are the Head. I am your servant and I belong to You. You tell me what to do and I'll do it. I have ruined my life." God moved me so rapidly through this cycle, it was so wonderful to see. I had expectations from God, that He was in charge and He would heal.

As we grow in expectations from God, we move into mature love and spiritual freedom. As God weans us away from the selfishness that drives us, we begin to lead lives that are poured out for the sake of others, just like the Lord Jesus. That is my testimony and here is the deeper blessing. Two of my kids are training for ministry now, learning how to disciple others. Because they saw transformation and reconciliation active in their father, they began to put their lives in the Lord's hands as well.

REVIEW

Let's consider the review. The flesh or self-life is a condition that exists within every person, believers and non-believers alike. Point two: A believer has been born of the Spirit and does not have to carry out the deeds of the flesh. When we choose to obey the Lord, we walk in liberty. Point three: However, when a believer chooses his or her own way over God's way, that person is walking after the flesh and it will produce death. Point four: By checking my motives, I can determine if I am walking after the flesh or walking after the Spirit. Consider this: Your life is not your own. You belong to the Lord. Maybe you have made a real mess out of your life as I did. May I just encourage you? There is One who has the answer. There is One who has the solution. There is One that has more power than you can ever imagine, and all you have to do is give it up.

Let's pray: "Father, thank you that you love us enough to chase us anywhere in the world, even to the fields of New Guinea to make your point, to show us that only you are God. Only you can direct life. And this thing of the flesh and trusting in it is absolute death. Lord, I thank you for what you did in my life. I praise you for it. Lord, I pray for those who are struggling right now who are hearing this message. I pray in Jesus name that you would lay your hand on their shoulder, that you would fill their hearts with hope as they walk in faith, knowing that as they direct their lives to You, they can live the victorious life in Christ. Thank you, Lord, for what you are going to do, in Jesus name. Amen."

VCL

VICTORIOUS CHRISTIAN LIVING Conference
Copyright © 1999 Victorious Christian Living International, Inc.

GODSHIP ————————————————————————————

REJECTION ——————————————————————————

EXTERNAL/INTERNAL ————————————————————

PROBLEMS, PROBLEMS, WHY PROBLEMS? ————————

MY FLESH—GOD'S ENEMY ——————————————————

REPENTANCE ⟶

WHAT'S NEW ABOUT YOU? ——————————————————

ACCEPTING YOUR RIGHTEOUSNESS ——————————

EXTENDING FORGIVENESS ————————————————

SEEKING FORGIVENESS ——————————————————

REST, ABIDE, WALK ————————————————————

LOVE ——————————————————————————————

GODSHIP

REJECT

EXT/INT PROBLEMS

FLESH

REPENT

WHAT'S NEW

ACCEPT RIGHT

EXTEND FORGIVE

SEEK FORGIVE

REST

LOVE

REPENTANCE

> ## Or do you think lightly of the riches of His kindness and forbearance and patience, not knowing that the kindness of God leads you to repentance?
> Romans 2:4

We came to Christ by repentance. Do we need to repent after salvation? Yes! Have you looked for life and fulfillment in things, people, or your performance instead of looking to God for fulfillment? Have you been going your own way ignoring God's right to be God in your life? Maybe you have been rejecting yourself or God. If any of these things are true, REPENTANCE is needed. Pride works against taking such action. And yet, we see throughout Scripture that true repentance is the gateway to wholeness and joy and peace with God. God is "against the proud" (1 Peter 5:5), but always ready to meet the repentant soul with forgiveness, cleansing, and restoration.

Spirit—Eph. 2:1
Mind—Eph. 4:17-18
Will—Titus 3:3
Emotions—Eph. 4:19
Body—Gal. 5:19-21

NATURAL MAN: UNREGENERATED

IN THE FLESH & WALKING **AFTER** THE FLESH

1 Corinthians 2:14

160-A

NOTES

VCL
VICTORIOUS CHRISTIAN LIVING Conference
Copyright © 1999 Victorious Christian Living International, Inc.

Repentance
STUDY GUIDE

PURPOSE for Diagram **160-A:**

*To illustrate the utter hopelessness of the person
who is not born again spiritually.*

1. Study Ephesians 2:1-3.

2. Where is God in this diagram? _____
   _____

3. How did you become a Christian? _____
   _____
   _____

4. Have you had any doubts you were really a Christian? _____

5. Study Ephesians 4:17-19.

6. How would you describe your heart
   in regard to the things of God?

   _____
   _____

> **You were dead in your trespasses and sins.**
> Eph. 2:1

7. Is it hard to choose the right things to do? _____
   _____

8. How do you feel after you sin? _____
   _____

9. Study Matthew 7:21-23.

10. If you are unclear about your relationship to God, go over the verses
    on the page titled "How to Commit Your Life to Christ" before "Godship."

Jesus didn't come to make bad people good, but dead people alive!

REPENT

SPIRITUAL MAN: FUNCTIONING SPIRITUALLY:

REGENERATED; **IN** THE SPIRIT & WALKING **AFTER** THE SPIRIT

Rom. 6:12-13; Rom. 13:14; Col. 3:9-10

160-A1

NOTES

Repentance
STUDY GUIDE

PURPOSE for Diagram **160-A1**:

An illustration of a person who has accepted Jesus Christ and is walking after the Spirit.

1. Study Romans 8:11.
2. Where is God now? ____________________
3. Study Romans 6:6, 14.
4. Is your old self really dead? ____________________
5. What happened to sin's power? ____________________
6. In what ways are you currently being tempted? ____________________
7. Does this diagram accurately describe your walk with God today? ____________________
8. If not, check the next diagram and see if it does.

. . . our old self was crucified . . . .
Rom. 6:6

REPENT

The indwelling Spirit makes me spiritual—not my behavior!

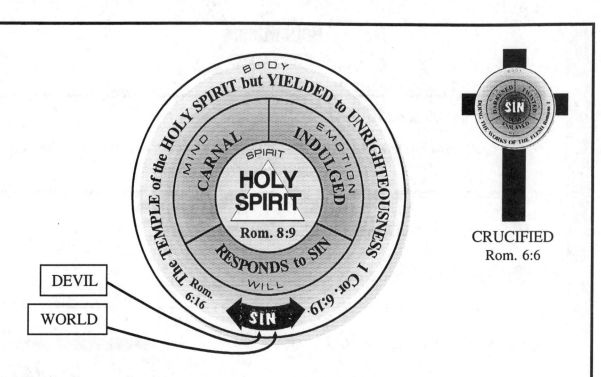

CRUCIFIED
Rom. 6:6

DEVIL

WORLD

SPIRITUAL MAN: | FUNCTIONING CARNALLY: |

REGENERATED; **IN** THE SPIRIT BUT WALKING **AFTER** THE FLESH

Rom. 7:22-24; 1 Cor. 3:3; 1 Cor. 6:15

160-A2

NOTES

VCL
VICTORIOUS CHRISTIAN LIVING Conference
Copyright © 1999 Victorious Christian Living International, Inc.

PURPOSE for Diagram **160-A2**:

> *To show how a spiritual man or woman can make sinful choices and function as a natural man or woman.*

---

1. Study James 1:13-15.

2. How do you handle temptations? _____
   _____

3. How does this diagram depict your life? _____
   _____

4. Are you led into temptation by your thoughts? _____

5. Are you led into temptation by your emotions? _____

> **You are not in the flesh but in the Spirit . . . .**
> Rom. 8:9

6. Study 1 John 2:15.

7. How are your thoughts and emotions being influenced by the Devil and the world? _____
   _____

8. Are you ready to consider the process of repentance?   Yes   No

9. If so, then go to the next diagram.

Christians can be carnal by behavior, but never carnal by nature.

REPENT

REPENTANCE

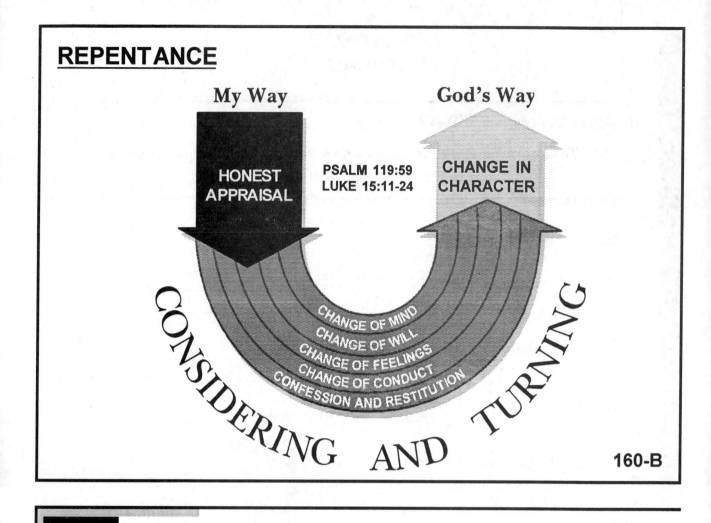

My Way   God's Way

HONEST APPRAISAL

PSALM 119:59
LUKE 15:11-24

CHANGE IN CHARACTER

CONSIDERING AND TURNING

CHANGE OF MIND
CHANGE OF WILL
CHANGE OF FEELINGS
CHANGE OF CONDUCT
CONFESSION AND RESTITUTION

160-B

VCL
VICTORIOUS CHRISTIAN LIVING Conference
Copyright © 1999 Victorious Christian Living International, Inc.

PURPOSE for Diagram **160-B:**

This is a key diagram. To illustrate repentance as a U-turn.

---

1. Study Psalm 119:59.

2. What two steps do you see? _____
   _____
   _____

3. How have you been living
   according to your own way?

> *I considered my ways, and turned my feet to Thy testimonies.* Ps. 119:59

   _____
   _____
   _____

4. Study Luke 15:11-24 and describe the repentance process in the story
   of the Prodigal Son. _____
   _____
   _____
   _____

5. Study the "Considering" section of Diagram 160-C.

6. What sin have you been committing, how long, how often, who else is
   involved, and do you want to repent now? _____
   _____
   _____
   _____
   _____

7. Are you ready to follow his example and repent? _____
   _____

   If so, walk through the steps found under the word "Turning" on
   Diagram 160-D.

It's never too soon to repent!

CONSIDERING

Considering your way begins with HONEST APPRAISAL.

> HONEST APPRAISAL leads to as clear a statement as is possible for you to make, as to *WHAT IS*: that is, what the TRUTH is about your own purposes, motives, methods, and patterns—without the varnish of self-protection, without enhancing or guarding your reputation, and without using devious means to maintain personal objectives.

One difficulty encountered immediately is that of overcoming procrastination. Honest appraisal must be undertaken in obedience to God without waiting for the feelings. Honesty requires *facing the truth*. Often a person may need help in this process.

The following factors are suggested:

1. Pray specifically for God to reveal your "own way" or your self-life.

2. Wait upon God; listening to Him. You may want to record what God reveals.

3. Allow yourself no excuses, rationalizations, or alibis. Do not allow blaming others to stop the process.

The purpose of HONEST APPRAISAL is to bring about in you an attitude of cooperation with the Holy Spirit in which CHANGE OF MIND, CHANGE OF THE WILL, and CHANGE OF FEELING may follow.

TURNING

- ◆ Quit doing what you were doing.

- ◆ Choose to appropriate the life of Christ to empower right decisions.

- ◆ Admit your sin to the Lord and thank Him for forgiveness.

- ◆ Admit your wrong to those you offended and seek their forgiveness.

- ◆ Make restitution when necessary.

- ◆ Walk in the freedom of who you are in Christ.

Note: Forgiveness is covered in detail in the VCL Conference "Extending Forgiveness" and "Seeking Forgiveness" lessons.

160-C

VCL
VICTORIOUS CHRISTIAN LIVING Conference
Copyright © 1999 Victorious Christian Living International, Inc.

There is no study guide for 160-C

MY OPINION ABOUT SIN

	I'M TRULY REPENTANT	I'M UNREPENTANT
AS TO THE NATURE OF SIN	I see my sin as disgusting and detestable. I am contrite and ashamed that I ever desired such a thing or actually ever did it. I see my own sin as hateful and deserving of hell.	Inwardly I harbor the secret opinion that my sin is desirable and "worth it." I see that it will ruin me, that God will punish me—but I still love it. I may see that it will adversely affect my character; but if it could end in happiness, I would never abandon it.
AS TO SIN'S RELATION TO GOD	I view my sin with God's righteous evaluation. I do not question the severity of the judgment—but heartily agree with it.	I don't see why God threatens my sin with such great judgment & punishment. When deeply convicted I may see it quite as God does, but only in fleeting glimpses.
AS TO THE TENDENCIES OF SIN	I see my sin's destructive tendencies and accept in my own mind the rightness of God's dealings with it. I acknowledge that total abandonment of it is necessary.	I initially cannot grasp that sin's tendencies should lead to eternal death. I may see sin as ruinous to myself and others, in body and soul for time and eternity, and the very opposite of all that is good & lovely—and still rationalize my continuance of it.
AS TO WHAT SIN DESERVES	I have no doubt whatsoever about the justice of God's condemnation of my sin. I see this as a fact of God's character and, therefore, a valid and necessary action on God's part.	I admit in theory that sin deserves eternal death, but do not really believe it. (If I believed it, my unrepentant attitude would be impossible.) My real opinion is different than I think it is. I am self-deceived. **160-D**

MY FEELINGS ABOUT SIN

	I'M TRULY REPENTANT	I'M UNREPENTANT
TOWARD SIN'S NATURE & RELATION TO GOD	I see my sin as distinct from its consequences and really hate and detest it in my heart—not for what it brings, but for what it is, an insult to my holy God. Deep and profound sorrow crushes me when I'm repentant.	My feelings of regret are centered on my sin's consequences to me. I feel sorry my sin was discovered. But all this is pure selfishness. I really care nothing for what my sin does to God; its nature is unknown to me.
TOWARD SIN'S TENDENCIES	I have a fervent desire to stop what I have been doing. My heart is set on fire to deliver myself and others from the direction, destruction, and ramifications of my sin.	I rationalize my refusal to deal ruthlessly with sin by telling myself that for *my* action I have special safeguards. Sin will never trap me (I think) because I am too shrewd. I view my own actions as excusable, because I "will never go as far as others have gone." I feel myself able to walk dangerously close to the edge of the cliff but never fall to my doom. The challenge to do so excites my passions and boosts my ego.
TOWARD WHAT SIN DESERVES	I feel right about what God says my sin deserves. Far from arguing with God's sentence, I am overwhelmed with wonder that God can forgive me.	I fully agree intellectually that God's condemnation is deserved, but my heart continues to argue that my own case is different. My sin should be excluded (and this is supported by my long list of mental reasonings). The rightness of God's judgment produces no *feelings* of agreement. **160-D1**

Repentance
STUDY GUIDE

PURPOSE for Diagram **160-D & D1:**

*To distinguish the differences between
the truly repentant person and the unrepentant person.*

1. Study Psalm 139:23-24.

2. Study these diagrams.

3. Your opinion about sin is important. What sin in your life have you considered "worth it" to continue rather than stop and repent of it?_____
_____
   What do you think the Lord wants you to do? _____

4. Do you sometimes question the severity of God's judgment? If so, write an example here: _____

5. Study Deuteronomy 32:3. How do you believe God wants you to view His judgment of sin?_____
_____

> *Search me, O God, and know my heart . . . .*
> Ps. 139:23

6. Write an example of a time you rationalized sin.
_____
_____
_____

7. What opinion(s) about sin do you believe you could be deceived in?_____
_____

8. Your feelings about sin are important also. Are your feelings of regret centered on the consequences of your sin, or the insult sin is to God? _____
_____

9. Is your desire to stop sinning a fervent desire, or do you refuse to deal with sin ruthlessly? _____

10. What is God convicting you of right now? _____
    What will you do about God's conviction? _____
    When will you do that? _____

It's time to repent—Now!

REVIEW

- Repentance is God's way of bringing us into His family.

- As God's child I can choose to walk after the flesh and sin.

- Every time I turn to sin I need to turn back to God's way by repentance.

- God uses people and circumstances to get my attention, so I will repent and stop doing things my way.

- After repentance I can start making right choices.

NOTES

VCL
VICTORIOUS CHRISTIAN LIVING Conference
Copyright © 1999 Victorious Christian Living International, Inc.

VICTORIOUS CHRISTIAN LIVING CONFERENCE

REPENTANCE

Lesson Transcript by Ted Sellers

Let's talk about the subject of repentance. Repentance isn't something that you hear about very much today, but it's an important subject in the Bible. In fact, the New Testament uses the word "repentance" over 30 times. Repentance means a change of mind and a change of life. You could sum up repentance in one word and that word would be—"turn" or "to turn." And the way I think of it, it's like a spiritual U-turn. Probably all of you have had your hands on a steering wheel [holds up **steering wheel**] recently, even today as you came to this meeting. What is the purpose of a steering wheel? It is used to turn the car. Every time a person turns toward sin, he/she needs to turn away from sin with a spiritual U-turn. Hence, the use of a steering wheel as a visual aid.

I remember an experience I had when I drove a truck for a living. I delivered the Wall Street Journal. I needed to make a delivery to a location across the street on the left. I saw an intersection and I thought the best thing to do was to make a U-turn. The only problem was a big sign, "NO U-TURN." I knew that sign was not for me. It was posted for people who were tourists and not people who were actually working for a living. I was working, earning money, earning a living and I had something to do. So I stopped, made the U-turn quickly, and pulled into the place of business. Then I looked in my rearview mirror and saw something that made my stomach turn over. It was two little red flashing lights going bing-bing, bing-bing, bing-bing and I knew I was busted. I opened the window and the policeman gave me a ticket. He said, "You're not supposed to make a U-turn there."

Making U-turns when a sign says not to is a bad thing. It's breaking the law. However, when we make a spiritual U-turn that's a good thing. It's good because we're turning back to the Lord. Don't ever ignore sin in your life. Look at the verse on page one, Romans 2:4. Do you see any emotional words as God thinks about us? What does He feel? Listen to this. "Or do you think lightly of the riches of His kindness and forbearance and patience?" Wow! How does God treat us when we sin? With kindness, forbearance, and patience. Notice the word "kindness" is repeated again, ". . . the kindness of God leads you to repentance."

We become children of God through repentance. As I began to study for this message, I wondered, "Does repentance really have a place in the life of Christians?" I believe it does. Everytime we as Christians turn toward sin, we need to turn back toward God. How do we do it? By repentance. Here are a couple of quotes from people who talk about repentance. David Wilkerson says, "The longer I walk with Jesus the more I am convinced, repentance is not just for sinners but also for believers. It is not simply a one time thing but something God's people are called to do until Jesus returns." Oswald Chambers writes this, "The new life will manifest itself in conscious repentance and unconscious holiness. Never the other way around. The bedrock of Christianity is repentance. If you ever cease to know the virtue of repentance, you are in darkness." These men are both saying that repentance is for the child of God.

It reminds me of a pastor who was repainting the church. He got a bunch of men to help him. As the Saturday wore on, different men had to

REPENT

leave and after a while, he was the only one left. He was at the very tip of the steeple. He was almost finished. As he was painting, he noticed his paint was running out. There was no one to help him. So, instead of climbing all the way down to get more paint, he thought, "I know what I'll do, I'll add some paint thinner to the paint and stir it up to stretch it." It worked! The paint went a little farther. Soon he was running out of paint again. He was almost finished with the steeple. He got the paint thinner can again and started pouring the thinner into the paint can. As he did, he heard a voice thunder out of heaven which said, "Repaint, Repaint and thin no more." Now that didn't happen. But it does make a point. Many times in our life we try to pour thinner into things. We are trying to do things our way, we're trying to cut corners and make things go the way we want them to go. When we do that, when we try to thin it out, we need to repaint. Repentance is an important subject.

NATURAL MAN (Diagram 160-A)

Turn to page 2 in your lesson. Look at your first diagram. This is a picture of a person who needs to repent. This is a natural man, an unregenerated man, a person who is not a Christian. Every one of us entered the world a natural man or woman. That is how we were all born. What's the position? In the flesh. What's the function? After the flesh. This natural man is dead spiritually, his mind is darkened, he cannot understand the things of the Spirit of God. First Corinthians 2:14 says, "They are foolishness to him." The *New International Version* translates "natural man" this way, "The man without the Spirit." This person is without the Spirit. This person is dead spiritually. His mind is darkened. He thinks the things of God are foolishness. Have you ever talked to someone who's not a Christian about spiritual things? What do you get? Often just a blank stare. The person doesn't get it. The person doesn't understand it. It's foolishness to the non-Christian. You talk about praying about some-

thing and the non-Christian says, "Why do you want to pray about it, just do it." The person doesn't understand the things of the Spirit of God. They're foolishness to a non-Christian.

This person's emotions are twisted. I believe non-Christians are either callused to their emotions or controlled by them. In being callused they have learned to deny what they feel and do what they want. In being controlled, if they feel something, they just do it. They have no sense of challenging their feelings. Their feelings control them. Our feelings should be our servants or our slaves, but they often become our slave drivers and we have no freedom with twisted emotions.

This person's will is enslaved. The person can't even make godly decisions. If you work with a natural man or woman or you know someone like this in your family, don't even expect the person to be nice. In the flesh, the person may sometimes be nice when that's what it takes to get the result he or she desires, but natural men or women aren't capable of living that way consistently. You think, "Well, they ought to act this way." No. They're spiritually dead. Where is God? God is outside their life. See the triangle? God's outside the life. This is a body-soul existence.

As you look at the three rings, the outside ring is the body. The inner ring is the soul, which includes the mind, the will, and the emotions, and the center ring is the spirit. The spirit is dead and sin is in the center. So this person is living a body-soul existence, as if there were no spirit. It's the principle of animal life. The Spanish Bible, translates l Corinthians 2:14 as, "the animal man," not the natural man. That's very accurate. It's a person living like an animal because an animal doesn't have a spirit. Sin is at the heart. These people believe the lie that you can have meaning and purpose in life apart from a relationship with the giver of life. They're trying to find life and they seek it through things, people, relationships, and experiences. However, right in the middle is sin and there's a vacuum. One man has said, "Within every person there's a god-shaped vacuum and only God can fill a god-shaped vacuum." People are trying to fill that vacuum with other things or people. There's still a vacuum.

Notice the word flesh. This person is in the flesh walking after the flesh. Write the word "flesh" under the notes. Now spell it backwards. What do you get? H-s-e-l-f. Do you see the word "self"? It has the letter "h" in front of it. Now what does the "h" stand for? It's either him or her—himself or herself without God. A person living without God. Himself or herself, that's the flesh. As Oswald Chambers says about the flesh: "It's my right to my claim to myself." I want to do what I want to do when I want to do it and I don't want you to stop me. I'm living selfishly. I'm self-centered. I'm self-serving. People walking after the flesh are very much concerned about "self." If you talk to them very long they'll talk about themselves because that's their life.

What did Jesus say? He said, "I came not to call the righteous, but sinners to repentance" (Matthew 9:13; Mark 2:17; Luke 5:32 KJV). Notice He said the same thing in Matthew, Mark, and Luke. This is the picture of a sinner. This is a picture of a person who is not a Christian. Jesus didn't come to make bad people good; He came to make dead people alive. That's a big difference. He wants to give us life, not just teach us how to be good. The only way we can be good is by having Him living in us. So you may need to consider repenting and turning from sin and actually receiving Christ. Letting Him fill the god-shaped vacuum that's in your life. If you do, that's the initial act of repentance. Something very wonderful will happen.

SPIRITUAL MAN—FUNCTIONING SPIRITUALLY (Diagram 160-A1)

As you turn to your next diagram, you'll see the picture of the spiritual man who is functioning spiritually. How do I get from being a natural man to becoming a spiritual man? John R. W. Stott, a British theologian says: "Our biography is written in two volumes. Volume one is the story of the old man, the old self, of me before my conversion, that's the natural man. Volume two is the story of the new man, the new self, of me after I was made a new creation in Christ. Volume one of my biography ended with the judicial death of the old self. I was a sinner. I deserved to die. I did die. I received my desserts in my substitute with whom I have become one. Volume two of my biography opened with my resurrection. My old life having finished, a new life to God, has begun." I'm living in volume two, not in volume one. In volume two I'm a spiritual man or woman functioning spiritually. What's the position? In the Spirit. What's the function? After the Spirit. This is the way I believe every child of God can live. It's the normal Christian life. The indwelling Spirit is what makes me spiritual, not my behavior. And that's where we get confused. We think it's our performance or our behavior. We're going to try harder or do better. It's the Holy Spirit that makes me spiritual. In the center of this spiritual person is the Holy Spirit. This person has been born again, born anew and the Spirit lives there. The triangle that used to be outside, which was symbolic of God is now on the inside, right in the center of that person. That person is indwelt by the Holy Spirit.

Take note of the cross on the right side of the diagram. What's on that cross? The natural man. Everything that we just saw on that first diagram was put on the cross. Crucified with Christ. Romans 6:6 says, "Knowing this," this is something that we need to know, "that our old self was crucified with Him, that our body of sin might be done away with, that we should no longer be slaves to sin." And that's what we said was true of the natural man, a slave to sin, but our old self was crucified with Him. That's an amazing thing. I used to remember singing that song, "Were You There When They Crucified

My Lord?" As I sang it I thought of us all standing around holding hands, humming. Then I thought one day, I was there. I wasn't just standing around humming, I was there because I was in Christ. I was participating in what happened on the Cross. Praise God. That's what it says, "I have been crucified with Christ" (Galatians 2:20). That's why that whole natural man, natural woman is on the cross. That life is gone. I have a new life now, a spiritual life and it is even better than the Garden of Eden. Think about that, in the Garden of Eden the Lord came and met with Adam and Eve. He walked with them and talked with them—remember that song? Well, the problem is He can leave the garden and there I am all by myself again. I don't even care if He holds my hand. I don't want Him to hold my hand, I want Him to come in and live inside of me, having an indwelling relationship, an intimate relationship, much better than Adam and Eve ever had.

Notice what is happening in the soul. The mind is being renewed. How? By spending time in God's word and seeing what God has to say about things instead of what I think or what I feel. What about my emotions? They're being brought under control. Emotions aren't bad, but they do not need to be the bastion of truth in my life. My will is choosing the truth and my body has become a weapon of righteousness. It's not yielded to sin. How does all this happen? What actually happens inside of a person? It's very much like what happens when a caterpillar becomes a butterfly. I brought this [holds up paper butterfly], my little boy made this in Sunday School. You know what that is don't you? Yes, it's a butterfly.

Several years ago I had the privilege of going to Calaway Gardens in Georgia, and I visited the Butterfly House. It was a huge building with hundreds and hundreds of butterflies. You could just hold out your hands and they would land all over your arms. I just stood amazed. They also had a movie about butterflies. It was made by the Moody Institute of Science from a biblical perspective. Several times it said, "The Creator did it this way; the Creator did it that way." It wasn't based on evolution. What was explained that I'd never known before was how the caterpillar becomes a butterfly. It said: "The little caterpillar goes around and just gorges itself, eats everything in sight. Then it's ready to go into the chrysalis stage and hooks a little hook on a branch and hangs for several days and then comes out as a butterfly." What happens when it's in there in that chrysalis? I thought the caterpillar grew wings and came out. NO, that's not what happens. During that time, the caterpillar inside that little chrysalis liquefies, turns completely to liquid, and something brand new that has never existed before emerges—a butterfly. Something brand new.

When you and I receive Christ and He comes into us, He changes us and makes us brand new—something that has never existed before. It's interesting to note what the job of the butterfly is in this last or fourth stage of the development. It is two things, to disburse and multiply. After we know who we are in Christ, we want to disburse. We want to tell other people about that and then multiply and even have other people come into the kingdom.

However, have you ever seen a butterfly crawling along the ground like a caterpillar? I never have. If you did, what would you know about that butterfly? Something's wrong with that butterfly, right? It's sick; it's got a broken wing; it's confused; it's got an identity crisis. It doesn't know who it is and doesn't know where its house is. It is back with the old gang in the dirt. As a Christian I can make a bad choice like that. I can start living like I used to live when I was a natural person and going and doing the things that I did before I became a child of God. That would be very foolish. That would be dumb, but you could do it. That's what the next diagram illustrates. This is what happens if you choose to go crawl around in the dirt. You become a spiritual man or woman functioning carnally. You are not functioning spiritually anymore.

SPIRITUAL MAN—FUNCTIONING CARNALLY (Diagram 160-A2)

I want you to look at Diagrams 160-A1 and 160-A2. Observe the words "Devil" and "world." Now check the lines between them and the word "sin." In Diagram 160-A1, you'll see that the little arrowheads on sin are broken off—the power of sin has been broken. On the "Spiritual Man: Functioning Carnally," 160-A2, they're welded back on and also the lines are darker between the Devil, the world, and the individual. This person has looked at the world, listened to the flesh, and has turned his or her eyes away from the Lord. Watchman Nee, says, "All temptation is designed to get us to take our eyes off the Lord." That's a good definition of temptation, just getting your eyes off the Lord. Look at that thing, that possession, that person, just don't look at the Lord. When I do look to other things I give power or energy to the world and it becomes stronger. Then what happens? My will can respond to sin. My mind becomes carnal and my emotions are indulged. Then I am called carnal. What does carnal mean? It means walking after the flesh. The exciting thing is, my position in the spirit has not changed. My true identity has not changed. I'm making a bad choice, possibly making a stupid choice, but my identity has not changed.

What I've done is I've started to function carnally. It's like chili con carne. What does that mean? I mean chili with flesh or meat. It's the flesh part that is dominating and I'm functioning like an animal. Once again I'm trying to be an animal man. I'm not an animal man—a body-soul existence. No. I have a spirit that's alive, but I'm not functioning according to the Spirit. I'm functioning just the way I did when I was a natural person. There is no connection with the Spirit. I like what John McArthur said, "Christians can be carnal in their behavior, but they're never carnal by nature." Never carnal by nature. That is a miserable person, a spiritual man or woman functioning carnally. You know why this person is miserable? Because the person is living contrary to his or her real identity.

You know people that are not Christians—natural men or women. Do they have any trouble sinning? Do they have any trouble going out and doing things wrong? No! They enjoy it. They even want to tell you what they did. You may not want to hear it, but they don't care. A carnal Christian who is walking after the flesh does not want to tell you about his or her sinful choices. It's not enjoyable, it's not pleasant. But it's exciting to know carnal Christians don't have to stay that way. First Peter 2:11 says, ". . . Abstain from fleshly lusts which wage war against the soul." Because I don't have to live like that, I can abstain from fleshly lust.

Do you have a beeper? I think a person who has a beeper is a very, very important person. Because even here, in the middle of this meeting, there are people who need you, and they want to be able to contact you. It is because you have vital information that they need. I probably never will have a beeper because I'm not that important. Important people have beepers. Being tempted is like having a beeper. Before you became a Christian, your beeper went off and you picked it up and said "Oh, okay I'll do that." Whatever the sin was you did it. When the beeper of temptation went off, you responded by yielding to sin. But after you become a Christian, the little arrowhead of sin, the power of sin is broken. Do you think the beeper will still go off? Do you think you'll still be tempted? Yes! Have you ever seen people look at their beeper when it beeps and ignore it? Sometimes I wonder why they have the beeper, when they never call the people, they just ignore it. That's the way you can live as a child of God. When your beeper of temptation goes off you can say: "Oh yeah, I remember. I used to call that number a lot. You know what? I don't think I'll call it. I don't need to. I don't have to. I know who I am."

When Satan tempted Jesus, he said: "Here, aren't you hungry? Come on, forty days and forty nights without food, let's eat something. Think about yourself. Notice these rocks. All you need to do is speak the word and make loaves of bread out of them." Jesus could have easily said: "You know what Satan? You've got a point there. If my real identity were just flesh, I might consider it. After all I am hungry and I don't just want some bread, I want it hot, out of the oven, with butter and strawberry jam on it. That's what I think I want." But He didn't say that because in effect He said: "That's not my identity. I don't need that in order to live. I'm going to live by every word that proceeds out of the mouth of God. I'm going to look to my Father for my sustenance, not bread because I know who I am." He didn't call up the number of temptation to meet His bodily needs in that manner.

I don't have to call those numbers either. I can ignore them. The interesting thing is, in a moment, in a flash I can move from functioning spiritually to functioning carnally by responding to sin. I'd like to think about this for a minute. Are we all tempted? Yes, we are, even Jesus was tempted. Is there any sin to being tempted? I've had people in counseling who think they have sinned just because they were tempted. Also, they think they have sinned just because they've thought about something sinful. One man said, "I did think about it, so I might as well do it if thinking about it is a sin." No, no, no, no. no. The the old saying is, "You can't keep the birds from flying over your head, but you can keep them from building a nest in your hair." Temptation is like the birds flying over your head. What can we do to keep them from building a nest in our hair? Remember the steering wheel? [Holds up **steering wheel.**] Once I sin I need to make a spiritual U-turn and repent.

Let's keep with the driving theme. [Holds up green **GO** sign.] When I am tempted I can see it as a **green light**, step on the gas, and say: "I'm going in. It's probably wrong. I'll probably regret it, but I think it's what I want to do." And so we go for it. We may have people encouraging us and saying: "You deserve this. You know, God wants you to be happy. That's what He really wants. He's a loving God, He wants you to be happy and this will make you happy, so, go for it. It's okay." Especially non-Christian people will tell you to make sinful choices. Or you can say: "No, I don't want to do that. I don't want to go for it. I want to **stop**." [Holds up red **STOP** sign.] This is like responding to the **red light** at an intersection. And as I think about this, I think about a person stepping on the brake and pushing hard with all his or her might. By their own strength people try to not sin. Trying to stop sinning is like what happens when I step on the brake with all of my might. Have you ever pushed on the brake and all of a sudden your foot goes to the floor? Why? No brake fluid. The master cylinder is broken. That's a picture of someone trying to overcome temptation by his or her own strength. This is trying not to sin by exerting the power of the flesh. Can you see how senseless that is? Me, by the power of my own flesh, trying not to sin. That doesn't make sense, but that's the way a lot of people live. Often we are encouraged to live like that. Haven't you heard people say: "You need to try harder. You can do it. Do your best and God will do the rest." Think about that one. You do your best. No, my best is trusting in Him. Not me trying hard not to do that. Have you ever tried hard to not think about something? How does that work? Are you tempted with food? OK. I don't want any of you to think about a chocolate sundae with a little brownie under it, with hot fudge dripping over it, with a little cherry on top, with nuts and whipped cream. Don't think about that, okay. Stop. Stop. Stop thinking about it. You were thinking about it. Now stop it. Are you thinking: "Okay, I'm going for it. [Holds up green **GO** sign.] As soon

VCL
VICTORIOUS CHRISTIAN LIVING Conference
Copyright © 1999 Victorious Christian Living International, Inc.

as this meeting is over, I'm out of here. I'm going to the Dairy Queen."

Now, so what can I do? What can I do? [Holds up **ONE WAY** sign.] Go to the Lord. There's only **one way**. Jesus said, "I am the way, and the truth, and the life" (John 14:6). There's only **one way** and He's it. I go to Him. I turn to Him. I yield to Him. Because whatever it is, this thing is moving me away from Him. I want to turn toward Him and see that He's the only one that can deliver me. Jesus doesn't give you victory. **He is your victory.** It's not saying, "Give me this, or help me with this." It is saying, "It's you Lord, Yourself in me, live through me by Your power, for Your glory, You're the one that makes the difference." Second Peter 2:9 says, "The Lord knows how to rescue the godly from temptation." That's an excellent, excellent verse. So if I find myself functioning carnally, what do I need to do? What do I do if I see temptation as a **green light** and sin? I need to repent. That's the title of this lesson.

REPENTANCE (Diagram 160-B)

Look at page 5 and note the U-turn diagram. I begin the repentance process with an honest appraisal. I have to consider my way. Isaiah 53:6 says, "All of us like sheep have gone astray / Each of us has turned to his own way . . . ." And we think that's a good way, but it's not.

Turn to Luke 15. Consider the story of the prodigal son. This is an interesting story the Lord made up to teach us about repentance. It also demonstrates the Father's love when we have gone astray. You'll see here that there's a change of mind, will, feelings, conduct, confession, and restitution. Now these may occur in any order, that's why they're all congruent. It's interesting that in this particular story, they do line up in that order. Look at Luke 15:17 and you'll see a change of mind. The prodigal son, "Came to his senses." He came to his senses, he woke up and said, "How many of my father's hired men have more than enough bread and I'm dying here with hunger!" He came to his senses. He had a change of mind. In the next verse you see a change of will. "I will get up." There it is. "I will get up and go to my father." That's a change of will. Verse 19 shows a change of feelings. He says, "I'm no longer worthy to be called your son." He feels unworthy. Verse 20 records a change of conduct. "And he got up." He just didn't think about it or pray about it, he did it. He got up and came to his father. Luke 15:21 records his words of confession and restitution. He says to his father, "Father, I have sinned against heaven and in your sight; I am no longer worthy to be called your son." I like what happened at the end of this chapter when the older brother was all upset. The father says, "We had to be merry and rejoice, for this brother of yours was dead and has begun to live, and was lost and has been found." He's begun to live. As a person becomes a child of God he begins to live. If I walk, and continue walking away from the Lord, it's as if I'm a dead person. I don't have life. I know where life is, but I'm not drawing on it. I'm not experiencing God's life. As I repent, I can experience His life again.

This past year our church sent a team of ten people to India. They went to Calcutta, probably one of the most destitute places on the planet. They had an excellent time representing our church in India. Before they left the church had all kinds of events regarding the India Team. As these events took place, I started remembering that last year my wife and I went to Russia. Now, we were not sent out from our church, we went with another organization. The church did do some things for us, they helped provide finances and gave us time to speak to the church, but the India Team was everywhere. They had a 24-hour prayer vigil, they had bulletins printed telling where they were every day of their trip. My son learned about India in Sunday School. I remember opening the itinerary bulletin and praying for the India Team. On the second day I thought, "I don't want to pray for these people."

I couldn't figure out why. Why don't I want to pray for the India Team? These people are sacrificing, they're going in some pretty distressed areas of the world, and I'm not going to pray for them. Why? It hit me. I was jealous. I was jealous because so much attention was paid to this team, and we did not get so much attention when we went to Russia. I had to repent. I got down on my knees and I said, "Lord, I see what I'm doing," That was an honest appraisal. Then came a change of mind. "I'm jealous because so much attention was paid to these people, and that's wrong. I'm sinning and I would appreciate it if you would cleanse me. I thank you Jesus, that You already died for that. I apply what you've done for me. I thank you." Then I could pray for the India team and I haven't had any twinges of jealousy since. That was honest appraisal. Sometimes the honest appraisal has to happen by getting away from other people or the situation that's going on.

My wife said I could share this incident that happened last Valentine's Day. She had several things planned that we were going to do for Valentine's Day. We were going to spend it together as a family and have a wonderful time. We were going out to dinner and going to a movie. When I got home from work, I had to do some things. Then I thought I better check our coupon for the restaurant where we were going and found out it had expired. Oh no! I called the restaurant, because a lot of places don't care if the coupon has expired. I said, "I have a coupon that's expired, what do you think?" They said: "Nope, won't honor it. It's expired." That changed things. We had to consider a different restaurant. All along I can see time is ticking away. I checked the time of the movie and found out to my dismay that the movie had already started. Susan got upset. She said, "I don't know why I get my hopes up. Why do I get excited about a night like this, and it just goes to pot?" My little boy and I were listening. Finally I said, "Honey, why don't you just take a few minutes and go in the bedroom and just talk to the Lord?" My son said, "Busted! Busted! Mom got busted." Because she was caught with a bad attitude. Sometimes Elliott is, but this time it was Mom. She went in the bedroom, and came out in about 10 minutes. She said, "Hey family, I'm sorry. I didn't need to get all upset like that and lose my cool, let's go out and have a nice time together." That was taking time away to get with the Lord, have an honest appraisal and then repent. The sin only involved two people and she admitted what she had done. Confession only needs to be made as wide as the area of sin.

Two weeks ago in my home fellowship group, we were studying a book and as we met for the evening, I said: "Okay we're going to discuss Chapter 11. How many of you have actually read Chapter 11?" There were 16 people in the group. Only two people had even read the chapter. I got disgusted and said: "This is really sad. I spent time preparing and evidently you really don't want to study this chapter because you didn't even read it. If you don't want to discuss it, then we'll do something else." And they said, "No, no we want to discuss it." So we did. At the end of our meeting I closed in prayer. As I was praying the Lord seemed to say: "You need to seek this whole group's forgiveness. You need to repent." As I finished praying I said: "The Lord spoke to me and I need to please ask you to forgive me, I was kind of harsh and rough at the beginning of the meeting because a lot of you hadn't read the assignment. So would you please forgive me?" One of the men, my son-in-law, said, "Sure Dad. I was a little surprised because you know we're studying the book *Grace Walk* and you were a little rough on us, kind of like Law walk or legalism." So they all forgave me. What did I do? I had to take a hold of the spiritual U-turn wheel and turn around from the way I had acted at the beginning of the meeting. Because my action had been to the whole group, I needed to ask forgiveness from the whole group.

VCL
VICTORIOUS CHRISTIAN LIVING Conference
Copyright © 1999 Victorious Christian Living International, Inc.

CONSIDERING/TURNING
(Diagram 160-C)

Let's look at page 6A. This "Considering and Turning" shows you how to go through repentance. First step: Honest appraisal. What are the facts? What's the truth? Check out your own purposes and motives. Sometimes we don't do that. We need to overcome procrastination. I like what Psalms 119:59 says in *The Living Bible*. It says, "I thought about the wrong direction I was heading and I turned around and came running back to you." That's someone who's not involved with procrastination. Then pray specifically for God to reveal your own way or your self-life. Wait upon the Lord. Write down if the Lord shows you anything. Don't permit any excuses or alibis. Also deal with it right away. Now consider turning. Remember anytime you turn toward sin you need to turn back toward the Lord by repentance. This is the cure for godship. Consider how godship can help in this process. Every time you feel upset, see what area of godship you might be exercising. Were you walking after the flesh? Were you becoming self-centered, self-focused, selfish? What do you do? Choose to appropriate the life of Christ to empower right decisions. Admit your sin. Thank Him for forgiveness. Admit you're wrong if there were other people involved. Make restitution and then walk in the freedom of who you are in Christ. There are two lessons in the Victorious Christian Living Conference that show how to extend and seek forgiveness.

What happens after you repent? You need to start making right choices. I like what Charles Hodge says in his book on 1 and 2 Corinthians about repentance. He says: "Sorrow in itself is not repentance, neither is remorse, nor self-condemnation, nor self-loathing, nor external reformation. These are its attendants or consequences, but repentance itself is a turning from sin to holiness. It's a real change of heart. It is a change of views, feelings, and purposes resulting in a change of life." Isn't that similar to what we've been sharing? He said: "Further consider Peter and Judas. Both of these men had denied the Lord. One repented, Peter, and was restored to faith. One was bitter and did not repent and committed suicide."

MY OPINION ABOUT SIN/ MY FEELINGS ABOUT SIN
(Diagrams 160-D & D1)

These two charts "My Opinions About Sin" and "My Feelings About Sin," will clarify whether you are truly repentant. If you have any questions about whether or not there is something that you need to repent for, read through these lists, see if they apply to what you're going through.

REVIEW

Turn to your repentance review sheet. It says: "Repentance is God's way of bringing us into His family" and "As God's child I can choose to walk after the flesh and sin," but "Every time I turn to sin, I need to turn back to God's way by repentance. God uses people and circumstances to get my attention, so I will repent and stop doing things my way. After repentance, then I can start making right choices." It's never too soon to repent. When I am aware that I am walking away from the Lord, even one or two steps—I don't have to get all the way into the far country like the prodigal son, just down the road a piece—it's time that I come back. Or, if you already are in that far distant land and you think, "What good is it?" It's always the right time to repent and come back to the Father because He's waiting. He's looking, He's anticipating your return and He wants to welcome you with arms of love.

However, do you see yourself as a natural man or woman? Then your repentance is unto salvation. You could pray and open the door to your life and ask Jesus to come into your life as your Savior and Lord. He wants to take up residency in you.

Has the Holy Spirit been convicting you of any sin in your life? Maybe from some of the other lessons you've heard in this VCL Conference. Now is the time to repent. Also, is there a dullness or a dryness, a coldness or a weakness in your Christian life? It could be, you need to repent. You need to come back to where you were and discard the clog in your life so that God's life and God's love can flow freely again. Could be that you were setting standards, trying to control, involved with greed, or self-centered. It's time to come back through repentance.

Remember the pastor we talked about at the beginning of the message. Is it time to repaint and stop thinning? Is it time to repent and stop doing things your way, being self-focused, self-centered, selfish? Praise God that we can repent and come back to Him and He will receive us.

Let's pray. "Lord, we do praise your name. That you've opened up this opportunity, that we can repent. We thank you that you've provided the way through your cleansing, by the blood of Jesus. We pray in Jesus name, Amen."

VCL
VICTORIOUS CHRISTIAN LIVING Conference
Copyright © 1999 Victorious Christian Living International, Inc.

GODSHIP ————————————————————

REJECTION ————————————————————

EXTERNAL/INTERNAL ————————————————————

PROBLEMS, PROBLEMS, WHY PROBLEMS? ————————

MY FLESH—GOD'S ENEMY ————————————————

REPENTANCE ————————————————————

WHAT'S NEW ABOUT YOU? ➤

ACCEPTING YOUR RIGHTEOUSNESS ——————————

EXTENDING FORGIVENESS ————————————————

SEEKING FORGIVENESS ——————————————————

REST, ABIDE, WALK ————————————————————

LOVE ————————————————————————

GODSHIP

REJECT

EXT/INT

PROBLEMS

FLESH

REPENT

WHAT'S NEW

ACCEPT RIGHT

EXTEND FORGIVE

SEEK FORGIVE

REST

LOVE

WHAT'S NEW ABOUT YOU?

> ℐf any man is in
> Christ he is a <u>new</u>
> <u>creature</u> . . . .
>
> 2 Corinthians 5:17

God created you a God-conscious being. He gave you the ability to think in terms of your own personal identity as related to Him. You have a built-in need to view life in terms of meaning and purpose. Meaning and purpose in life flow from identity. Personal significance is a driving objective. The constant search for meaning has always motivated man (Psalm 8:3-4). This need is met only when a person experiences Christ as his/her very life and identity (Philippians 1:21; Colossians 3:3).

God's purpose is that through an intimate, obedient, dependent, love relationship with Him, you will receive and demonstrate the very life of Christ. His life, love, purity, patience, faithfulness, and power are meant to become yours and then be manifested through you.

Adam and Eve lost the security of life through unbelief and disobedience. Following their rebellion, they tried to "make life work" with only human resources. Life's meaning and purpose thus had to be sought *within* the person, now that man had become god of his own life (Genesis 3:5). Identity, significance, and purpose must now be achieved by personal appearance, accomplishments, social status, possessions, or the earned acceptance of others.

Sin is the deception that man can find meaning and purpose in life apart from a personal love relationship of obedience to the Creator of life.

If you are a Christian living without a true picture of "who you are in Christ" you may be functioning in a manner that is lacking (if not contrary to) true freedom. This is an identity crisis!

In this lesson dare to take God's Word at face value, neither blindly affirming its truth without honest examination, nor rationalizing your failures and calling them acceptable. The greatness and victory of Christ's atonement is yours in reality.

MAN—A TRIUNITY

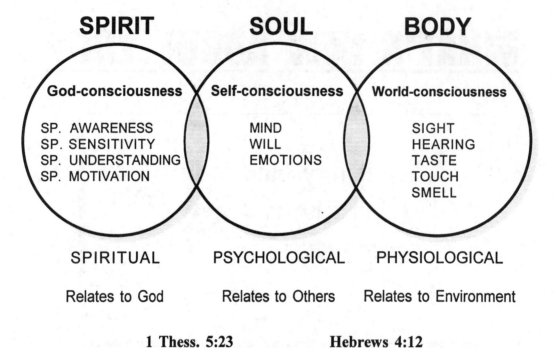

SPIRIT   SOUL   BODY

God-consciousness   **Self-consciousness**   **World-consciousness**

SP. AWARENESS	MIND	SIGHT
SP. SENSITIVITY	WILL	HEARING
SP. UNDERSTANDING	EMOTIONS	TASTE
SP. MOTIVATION		TOUCH
		SMELL

SPIRITUAL   PSYCHOLOGICAL   PHYSIOLOGICAL

Relates to God   Relates to Others   Relates to Environment

1 Thess. 5:23   **Hebrews 4:12**

170-A

VCL

VICTORIOUS CHRISTIAN LIVING Conference
Copyright © 1999 Victorious Christian Living International, Inc.

PURPOSE for Diagram **170-A:**

To explain the nature of man as a spiritual, psychological, physical being, and to introduce the significance of this in self-understanding.

? 1. Do you think of yourself as a body? Examples: I am fat, I am in great shape, I am beautiful, etc. If so, explain _____

_____

? 2. Do you spend a lot of time, money, or energy to improve your body or appearance? This could include clothes, exercise, diets, surgery etc. If so, explain _____

_____

? 3. Do you think of your intellect as who you are? Examples: I am smart, I am decisive, I am a deep thinker or maybe even I am slow and not very smart. If so, explain: _____

_____

? 4. Do you spend large amounts of time trying to figure things out or think situations or circumstances through? If so, explain _____

_____

_____

_____

> *. . . may your spirit and soul and body be preserved complete.*
> 1 Thess. 5:23

WHAT'S NEW

? 5. Do you define yourself by what you are feeling? Examples: I feel happy so I have joy or I feel guilty so I must be guilty. If so, explain _____

_____

? 6. Do your emotions or how you are feeling determine whether or not you are having a good day? If so, explain _____

_____

? 7. If you could believe your true identity was spiritual, how would that change your daily routine? _____

_____

I am a Spirit . . .
I have a soul . . .
I live in a body . . .

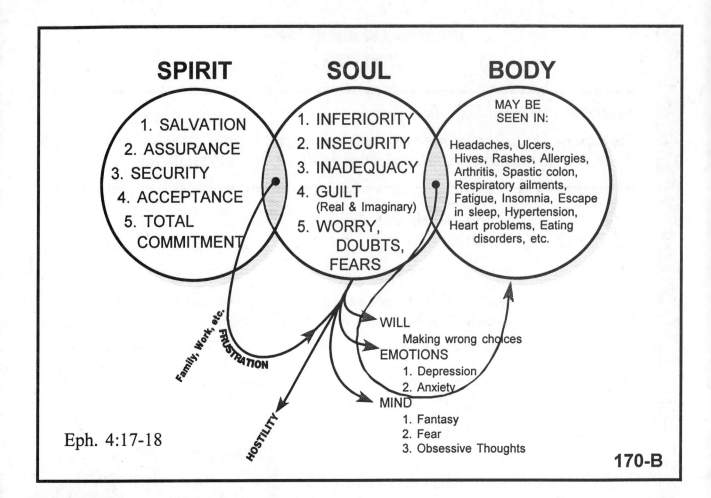

SPIRIT

1. SALVATION
2. ASSURANCE
3. SECURITY
4. ACCEPTANCE
5. TOTAL COMMITMENT

SOUL

1. INFERIORITY
2. INSECURITY
3. INADEQUACY
4. GUILT (Real & Imaginary)
5. WORRY, DOUBTS, FEARS

BODY

MAY BE SEEN IN:

Headaches, Ulcers, Hives, Rashes, Allergies, Arthritis, Spastic colon, Respiratory ailments, Fatigue, Insomnia, Escape in sleep, Hypertension, Heart problems, Eating disorders, etc.

Family, Work, etc. FRUSTRATION

HOSTILITY

WILL
   Making wrong choices
EMOTIONS
   1. Depression
   2. Anxiety
MIND
   1. Fantasy
   2. Fear
   3. Obsessive Thoughts

Eph. 4:17-18

170-B

VCL

VICTORIOUS CHRISTIAN LIVING Conference
Copyright © 1999 Victorious Christian Living International, Inc.

PURPOSE for Diagram **170-B:**

To show that the difference between what is true in the Spirit and what is felt to be true in the soul creates inner problems which express themselves in disturbing ways.

? Do you ever experience any of the following feelings?
(an extra sheet of paper may be necessary)

> *Walk no longer . . . in the futility of their (your) mind.*
> Eph. 4:17

1. Inferiority _____ Describe_____

2. Insecurity _____ Describe_____

3. Inadequacy _____ Describe_____

4. Guilt _____ Describe_____

5. Worry, doubt, fear _____ Describe_____

6. Depression _____ Describe_____

7. Anxiety _____ Describe_____

8. Obsessive thoughts or behavior _____ Describe_____

9. Why do you think you experience these feelings? _____

10. Study Proverbs 3:5-8.

? 11. How would your life experience change if you lived according to what God says about you, instead of how you feel or what you, others, or the world think?

_____

My feelings may not be true.

WHAT'S NEW

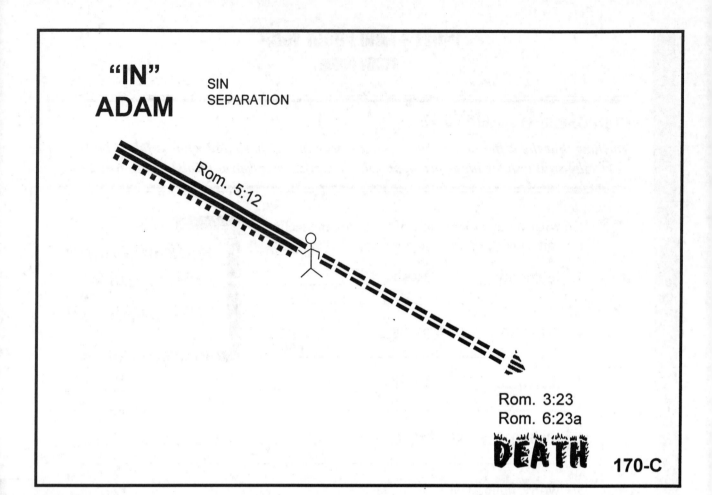

VCL
VICTORIOUS CHRISTIAN LIVING Conference
Copyright © 1999 Victorious Christian Living International, Inc.

PURPOSE for Diagram **170-C:**

*To give an understanding of how all persons became sinners
through their descent from Adam.*

1. Study Romans 5:12.

2. What did you learn about you? _____
_____

3. What does it mean to be "IN" Adam? _____
_____

4. Study Romans 3:23, 6:23.

> ### *All have sinned . . .*   Rom. 3:23

5. What did you learn about sin? _____
_____
_____

6. Are you a sinner? _____
_____

7. What will happen to you when you die? _____
_____
_____

Born once—die twice!
Born twice—die once!

IT'S YOUR CHOICE

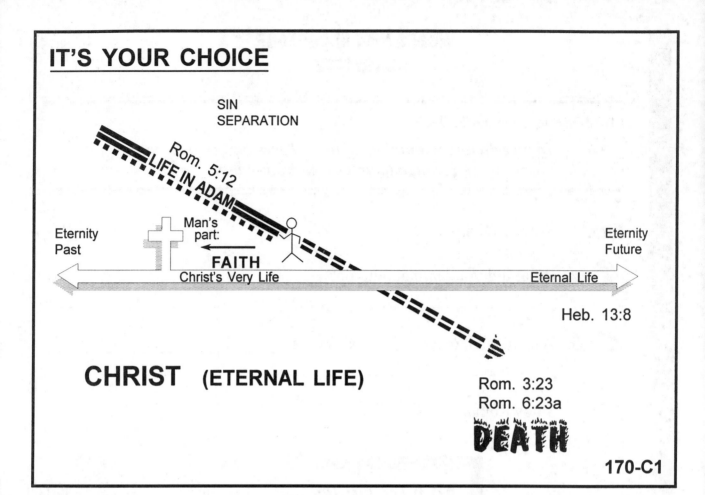

SIN
SEPARATION

Rom. 5:12
LIFE IN ADAM

Man's part:
← FAITH

Eternity
Past

Eternity
Future

Christ's Very Life

Eternal Life

Heb. 13:8

CHRIST (ETERNAL LIFE)

Rom. 3:23
Rom. 6:23a

DEATH

170-C1

VCL

VICTORIOUS CHRISTIAN LIVING Conference
Copyright © 1999 Victorious Christian Living International, Inc.

PURPOSE for Diagram **170-C1:**

To show the sinner the choice of eternal life in Christ as an alternative to death.

> *. . . while we were yet sinners, Christ died for us.*   Rom. 5:8

1. Study Romans 5:12, 17-19.

2. What did you receive because of Adam's sin? _____
_____

3. What did you receive because of Christ's obedience? _____
_____

4. Study Romans 10:9-10.

5. Do you have to end up in spiritual death? _____
   Why not? _____
_____

If you are not sure you are truly "In Christ," then now would be a wonderful time to open your life up to Him and receive Him as your Savior and Lord. He is knocking and waiting (Revelation 3:20).

I wouldn't choose death, would I?

LIFE IN CHRIST

SIN
SEPARATION

Rom. 5:12
LIFE IN ADAM

God's part: TRANSFERRED

1 Cor. 1:30
Col. 1:13
Jn. 5:24

Gal. 2:20

Man's part:

Eternity
Past

Rom. 6:6 **FAITH**

Christ's Very Life

Eternal Life

Eternity
Future

Eph. 1:4

2 Cor. 5:17
Heb. 13:8

"IN" CHRIST (ETERNAL LIFE)

170-C2

NOTES

VCL
VICTORIOUS CHRISTIAN LIVING Conference
Copyright © 1999 Victorious Christian Living International, Inc.

PURPOSE for Diagram **170-C2:**

To show the believer in Christ is actually removed from being "in Adam" and placed "into Christ."

 1. Study 1 Corinthians 1:30.

2. Whose work was it to move you from the old path to the new path?

_____

 3. Study Romans 6:6.

4. What happened to your old self that was in Adam?

> . . . *your life is hidden with Christ in God.* Col. 3:3

_____

 5. Study Colossians 1:13.

6. How did you get into Christ? _____

_____

 7. Study Galatians 2:20. Whose life do you have now? _____

_____

What's new about me—everything!

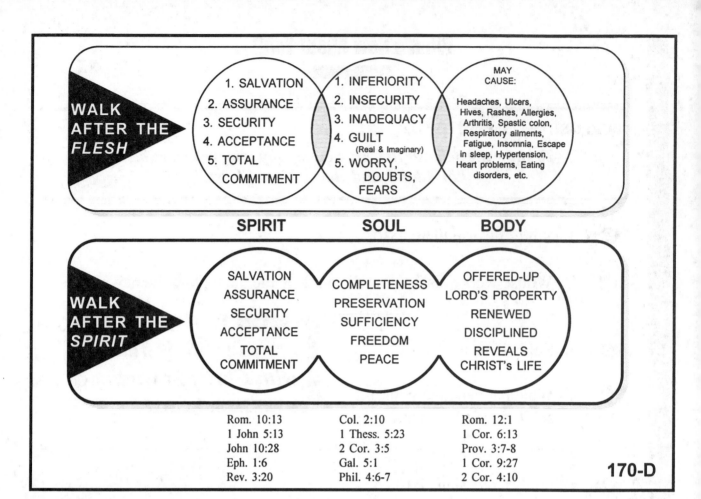

SPIRIT	**SOUL**	**BODY**

Rom. 10:13	Col. 2:10	Rom. 12:1
1 John 5:13	1 Thess. 5:23	1 Cor. 6:13
John 10:28	2 Cor. 3:5	Prov. 3:7-8
Eph. 1:6	Gal. 5:1	1 Cor. 9:27
Rev. 3:20	Phil. 4:6-7	2 Cor. 4:10

170-D

NOTES

VCL
VICTORIOUS CHRISTIAN LIVING Conference

PURPOSE for Diagram **170-D:**

*To show the difference between walking after the flesh
and living in the true identity of Christ.*

 1. Study Romans 8:5-6.

2. Do you see that feelings of inferiority, etc. are focusing on self, and
feelings of completeness, etc., come from focusing on the Lord?

_____

 3. Study John 8:32.

4. How do you change from walking after
the flesh to walking after the spirit? Where
is your focus now? _____

_____

> *You shall know the
> truth and the truth
> shall set you free.*
> John 8:32

5. What is more true—God's word or your feelings?

_____

6. Are you ready to choose to believe what God's word says about you?

_____

God said it—that settles it!

REVIEW

- I am given the life of Christ.

- I am no longer dead, but alive "in Christ."

- I am no longer a slave to sin. It is a choice now.

- I am a new creation—God's child!

- I am to be transformed by the renewing of my mind.

- I am to appropriate His *very* life.

NOTES

WHAT'S NEW ABOUT YOU?

Lesson Transcript by Bill Houck

I'm very thankful to be here with you in this time that the Lord has provided for us to look at the "What's New About You?" If you haven't already, please turn to your lesson "What's New About You?" I will be sharing with you on our identity, who we are. Some of the most critical questions that any of us can ask are: "Who am I? Why am I here? What is the meaning and purpose of life?" Those are some of the most fundamental and most important questions we can ask. I intend to answer those in the next few minutes.

In thinking about identity, I was looking at a book the other day called *Illustrations Unlimited*. Within that book I found a neat story about a man who went out into the woods and he was looking for a bird of interest. He happened to find a young eagle. He took that eagle home to his farm and put him in the chicken yard with his chickens. The eagle learned to eat chicken food. Five years later, a naturalist happened to stop by the farm and saw this eagle eating with the chickens and said to the owner, "That's an eagle you have living there." The owner said, "Oh, no, I've trained him to become a chicken." Even though this eagle had a 15-foot wingspan, the farmer still was confident that he had trained that eagle to be a chicken. Well, the naturalist said: "No, no, he's an eagle. Will you allow me to free him?" And the farmer said, "You're free to try, but he's a chicken." So the naturalist picked the eagle up. He looked the eagle in the eye and he said: "Eagle, thou art an eagle. Soar into the heavens." The eagle looked away from the guy and he looked down at the chickens and he hopped down into the chicken yard. And the farmer said: "See, I told you.

He's a chicken." The naturalist said: "No, no, he's an eagle. I'll come back tomorrow and we'll try it again." So the naturalist came back the next day and he took the eagle up onto the roof of the farmer's house. He held the eagle up. He looked the eagle in the eye and said: "Eagle, thou art an eagle. Soar up into the heavens." And he turned him around and the eagle looked down at the chickens and went right down to the chicken yard and started eating. The farmer said: "See, I told you. He's a chicken. I trained him to be a chicken." The naturalist said: "No. Let me try one more time tomorrow morning." The farmer said, "Okay." The naturalist came early in the morning and took the eagle out into the wilderness. He took the eagle up onto a high rocky knoll, looked him in the eyes, and said: "Eagle, thou art an eagle. Soar like an eagle." The naturalist turned the eagle around and he looked around a little bit. The eagle was trembling by this time, scared. Then the naturalist turned the eagle's head and pointed his head directly into the sun. The eagle seemed to puff up and he soared away, never to return again. He always was an eagle, but he had lived with chickens so long he began to think he was a chicken.

Now, we have been created in the image of God; but men have made us think we're chickens, so we believe we are even though we are eagles. What God would have us do is to stretch forth our wings and fly in our true identity. If I was going to summarize this whole lesson for you in a nutshell, it is that when someone becomes a Christian a massive change takes place in the person's life. That person becomes completely new when he or she becomes a Christian. There are several promises that I'd like to make you as we move into this lesson. I'll show you man's past identity in Adam. I will also show you your identity in Christ. The next thing I'd like to do is to show you how God made you.

So, if you'll turn with me to your introductory page, "What's New About You?", you'll see a Scripture verse, 2 Corinthians 5:17, "If any man is in Christ, he is a new creature . . . ."

"God created you a God-conscious being. He gave you the ability to think in terms of your own personal identity as related to Him. You have a built-in need to view life in terms of meaning and purpose. Meaning and purpose in life flow from identity. Personal significance is a driving objective. The constant search for meaning has always motivated man. This need is met only when a person experiences Jesus Christ as his or her very life and identity." So God created you with something inside of you that wanted to have meaning, purpose, value, and identity that can only be established in relationship to Jesus Christ.

Now there are many things in life that some of us find as identities. I'll just share with you a few of them from my past to illustrate. Years ago, I used to own a Harley-Davidson motorcycle and one of my identities was that I was a Harley rider. Have any of you who ever noticed, there are motorcycle riders and then there are Harley riders? Those who have a Harley-Davidson are set apart from all the rest. I don't exactly understand why that is—a great marketing tool on Harley-Davidson's part. Anyway, that was one of my identities. Another vehicle that I had that I would choose for an identity was an old beat-up Chevrolet pickup truck called "Bessie." When I drove Bessie, I was a totally different individual than when I rode on the Harley-Davidson. If I chose to enter the garage and drive the 1965 Corvette coupe that was stashed in there with a high performance small block engine in it, I was a totally different individual altogether. I also had a family buggy and if I was going to be the family man, I would

take the big Ford LTD and put the family in it. I was a different person when I drove that car than when I drove the Corvette, than when I drove Bessie, than when I rode the Harley-Davidson. Then if I really was in a cruel mood I had a Vega with a Chevrolet 350 high performance engine. If I just wanted to get out and rip and tear something up and do wheel stands, I'd pull the Vega out of the garage. It was the one that took all the abuse in those days. But whichever vehicle I drove was my identity.

Now there are other things that people find identity in. How many of you have met someone and when you said, "Hi. Who are you?" They say, "I am pastor so and so of such and such church and we have so many in our congregation." That's an identity statement. How many of you have met anyone who when you meet say: "I am an electrician. I'm a carpenter. Hi, I'm a Bible counselor. Hi, I'm a chef. Hi, I'm a mother, I'm a father, I'm a sister, I'm a brother, I'm a nothing." People have all sorts of different things that they find identity and meaning and purpose in. All of those are not their true identity. The only real identity that we can have, the truest one, is our spiritual identity which is either related to Adam, Adam of Eden, or Jesus Christ, God of the universe. Those are the only two identities you have. Primarily you are a spiritual creature and I'll share more of that with you.

If you'll look with me at the next paragraph on the introductory page, I'd like to explain to you why I am here and why you are here. It's very simple. "God's purpose is that through an intimate, obedient, dependent, love relationship with Him, you will receive and demonstrate the very life of God. His life, love, purity, patience, faithfulness, and power are meant to be yours and then to be manifested through you." That's why I am here, to have an intimate, loving relationship with God. It is very personal and we'll talk more about that.

Now then, look with me at the next paragraph. "Adam and Eve lost the security of life through unbelief and disobedience. Following their rebellion, they tried to 'make life work' with only human resources. Life's meaning and purpose thus had to be sought *within* the person, now that man had become god of his own life. Identity, significance, and purpose must now be achieved by personal appearance, accomplishments, social status, possessions, or the earned acceptance of others." This is the paragraph that begins to share with us a deception of the world. In the world, what you do is often who you are. That is not the truth. What you do is not who you are. Secondly, what you do is not the most important thing about you. Thirdly, who you are is more important than what you do. Who you are, who you are related to is more important than what you do.

The last part of this page on your explanation has a definition for sin in bold. Some people define sin as adultery, stealing, or murder. This is truly what *sin* is: Sin is the deception that man can find meaning and purpose in life apart from a personal love relationship of obedience to the Creator of life." Sin is a deception that you can find meaning or purpose or value in anything apart from God. See, every time that I sin, I'm deceived into thinking that is going to fulfill, that is going to meet, that is going to give me what I need. It's a deception.

The last part says on that page, "If you are a Christian living without a true picture of 'who you are in Christ' you may be functioning in a manner that is lacking (if not contrary to) true freedom. This is an identity crisis! In this lesson dare to take God's Word at face value, neither blindly affirming its truth without honest examination, nor rationalizing your failures and calling them acceptable. The greatness and the victory of Christ's atonement is yours in reality."

MAN—A TRIUNITY (Diagram 170-A)

Look with me at Diagram 170-A, "Man—A Triunity." In these first two diagrams, what I want to do is help you understand how God has created you. Let's look up 1 Thessalonians 5:23 from the bottom of this diagram. I'll read 1 Thessalonians 5:23-24: "Now may the God of peace Himself sanctify you entirely; and may your spirit and soul and body be preserved complete, without blame at the coming of our Lord Jesus Christ. Faithful is He who calls you, and he also will bring it to pass." So as God looks at you, He says you are a spirit, soul, and body. Now think with me for a minute. Is that the way the world defines you? Does the world say you're a spirit, a soul, and a body or do they flip it around and say your body is the most important part? If we look at it that way, then all of our focus goes on our body—so we have to exercise it, we have to puff it up, we have to build it up, we have to take care of it, we have to primp it, we have to . . . —if our body is not healthy our identity all changes. Our soul, as it is explained on your diagram is mind, will, and emotions. If we are primarily soul-oriented in our thinking, then intellect is most important. Or emotions, if we happen to be bent that way, then sensitivity becomes our identity. But, see, God designed us differently than what the world says. We are spirit creatures, that's who we are. We have souls and we live in bodies. That's truly who we are. The spiritual aspect of you is the most important part, so let's look at that one first.

The spirit as you see on your diagram is the part of us that is God-conscious—spiritually aware, spiritually sensitive, has spiritual understanding, and spiritual motivation. That's the spiritual part of us that relates to God. By far, that is the most important. This individual on this diagram is not a believer, is not a Christian, and has not been born again.

You'll notice that they do have a soul, though. That is our self-conscious part. Within the soul are our mind, our will, and our emotions. That's the psychological part of us that relates to others. Our mind is thinking, our will is choosing, and our emotions are our feelings. Now if you're explaining this to a child, you'd use a thinker, a chooser, and a feeler because children have these components within their soul. I want to prioritize these for you. By far what you choose to be the truth is the most important thing. What you think is second and how you feel is third if you could prioritize them. So you want to be choosing the truth, you want to be thinking on the truth, and when you do that, your emotions will follow. Now some people like me tend to be emotionally oriented and I feel things long before I can figure out what I am thinking about them. Even in that circumstance, I need to be choosing what is the truth because if I continue to choose the truth, my thoughts and emotions will come in line.

The third part of me is the body which is world-conscious and you see there sight, hearing, taste, touch, and smell. This is the physiological part that relates to my environment.

Hebrews 4:12 also talks about us having a spirit, soul, and body. That's just another reference to this triunity of man.

SPIRIT/SOUL/BODY (Diagram 170-B)

If you'll look with me at Diagram 170-B, you'll see a similar creature, but there are some significant changes. Within the spirit of this individual, the person is born again and is complete. This is a believer, this is a Christian who has been saved by God's grace. God gives the person assurance, He gives the person security, He gives the person acceptance, and He is totally committed to the person—100 percent. This person is in the kingdom of God. He is in Christ Jesus.

Now, what this diagram also explains to you is the deception that many Christians live in. They do not, in their souls, believe to be true what God has done for them in their spirits. Consequently, within their souls, they think they are inferior, they believe they are insecure, they think they are inadequate, they feel guilty, they worry about things, they doubt things, and they

are afraid of things. What happens when you have a discrepancy between what's true about you in your spirit and what you believe in your soul, is that you have a frustration gap. You see that comes out of there. So when you are living with family, or working in the world, frustrations come out and you don't know why. Well, it's because of what you believe, what you think, or what you choose in your soul. You'll, also, see that the will is making wrong choices. The emotions—you may be depressed or anxious. Your mind may wander off into fantasy, fear, or obsessive thoughts. Any of those things could happen if you were walking in this deception, not believing that what God says is true about you and your spirit.

What is seen in many people's lives is that in the body, things begin to happen. Headaches appear, ulcers appear, hives, rashes, respiratory ailments, sleep, all kinds of heart problems, eating disorders, etc. Many things show up in the physical body because of the soul not accurately functioning as God has designed it. Now, in the world, there are problems which are called psychosomatic illnesses. These illnesses are based on the *psyche*, the soul, and the *soma*, the body, and these people are not agreeing in their souls with the things that are true about them in their spirits. Consequently, they have physical illnesses that are very real but they are caused by soulistic problems. Many Christians function within that realm. I have a doctor friend who told me that 60 to 80 percent of the people that he treats have psychosomatic illness problems. The problems that they have can be alleviated when they believe the truth of who they are spiritually with their souls. That's an amazing statistic.

"IN" ADAM (Diagram 170-C)

Look with me at your next diagram, 170-C, as we begin to look at the solution. Here you have a diagram that is entitled "'In' Adam." You see that being born in Adam, we are born in sin and separated from God. Romans 5:12 on your diagram says, "Therefore, just as through one man sin entered into the world, and death through sin, and so death spread to all men, because all sinned—" Because you and I were born in Adam (this is the Adam of Eden) we were born in sin. Let me try to illustrate that for you. I have a grandfather who lived during the time of World War I. At that time he was not married to my grandmother. Where was my father during World War I? I have a father who served in World War II. At that time he was not married to my mother. Where was I during World War II? I have a son Kristopher. Kristopher was not yet conceived during the Viet Nam conflict. Where was Kristopher during that war? The answers to all those questions are they were in the loins of their fathers. You and I were in Adam in Eden. All of us came out of Adam, then we came out of Noah, and subsequently we've come out of our ancestors all the way down to the present. So, we could trace our heritage back all the way up this line and all those little boxes to Adam of Eden as our great, great, great . . . grandfather. That was our Adam. You and I were born in him, we were born in sin, and we were born separated from God. This little stick figure in the middle represents us when we were born. Our identity at that time—as man, being mankind, not male, not female, but the whole creation man—was sinner. This is the natural man that we will be talking about as we go through the conference. This natural man, if he does not change course, is on his way to death, that fiery little thing there at the bottom of your diagram. Two deaths. He will die physically and he will die spiritually, eternally in Hell unless he changes his path. See those Scripture verses at the bottom. Romans 6:23 says, "For the wages of sin is death, but the free gift of God is eternal life in Christ Jesus our Lord." Also, Romans 3:23 says, "for all have sinned and fall short of the glory of God." All of us have sinned. All of us have fallen short of the glory of God because of our heritage. **This was our identity when we were born.**

IT'S YOUR CHOICE (Diagram 170-C1)

Look with me at your next diagram, 170-C1. We're going to build on this concept. In this diagram entitled "It's Your Choice" you still see the life in Adam. But something new has been added to the "It's Your Choice" diagram and that is the very life of Christ which is represented by a horizontal line across the page. Now, you have a choice to stay in Adam or to opt for a better deal and enter into the life of Christ. It's your choice. You can choose. This is a salvation presentation. It's your responsibility to make the response to God by faith. You see the little stick figure there. He has to respond to what God has done.

Now, let's talk a little bit about God. This eternal life of Christ that is represented by the horizontal line is Christ's very life. Answer this question for me. When did Christ's eternal life start? It always was. See, the eternal life of Christ is. John 1:1-4, says: "In the beginning was the Word, and the Word was with God, and the Word was God. He was in the beginning with God. All things came into being by Him, and apart from Him nothing came into being that has come into being. In Him was life, and the life was the light of man." Jesus always was in the past, right? He always was. How about in the future? When does the eternal life of Christ end? It never does. It never starts, it never ends, it always is. Jesus always has been. So, when Jesus Christ was born of a virgin, is that when His life began? No, not at all. I believe Jesus walked in the garden with Adam and Eve. When God came and walked with them that was Jesus walking. When I get there and get to talk to Him, I want to ask Him if He wore clothes. I've always wondered that. Have you ever wondered that? But He was there in the beginning. He made them. He has made everything. His life is eternal.

Now then, because of the little cross that is represented there on the life of Christ, the eternal life of Christ, He, through His sacrificial death, has provided for you and me a way to enter into His very life. But man's part is that we must choose to believe. You must choose to receive. You must choose to accept that free gift of God's grace. It takes a volitional choice on your part to get into the life of Christ.

LIFE IN CHRIST (Diagram 170-C2)

Now your next diagram, 170-C2, will develop this a little bit more. This is a **key diagram**, "Life in Christ." Because in this diagram we will begin to see where you are. You are either in Adam or in Christ. If you have exercised faith in what God did on the cross, if like it says in Galatians 2:20, I, Bill, have been crucified with Christ, it is no longer I, Bill, who lives but it is Christ who lives in me, I have been identified with Christ's death. Romans 6:5-6 says, "For if we have become united with Him in the likeness of His death, certainly we shall be also in the likeness of His resurrection, knowing this, that our old self was crucified with Him, that our body of sin might be done away with, that we should no longer be slaves to sin." Now His life, and my life, have become united. His life is my life.

God's part is He transfers us from Adam and plants us into Christ. First Corinthians 1:30 says, "But by His doing you are in Christ Jesus, who became to us wisdom from God, and righteousness and sanctification, and redemption." By God's doing, He has taken us out of Adam and placed us into Christ. Listen to what it says in Colossians 1:13-14, "For He delivered us from the domain of darkness, and transferred us to the kingdom of His beloved Son, in whom we have redemption, the forgiveness of sins." God "relocated" us, changed our life through the act of faith. In John 5:24 Jesus is speaking, "Truly, truly, I say to you, he who hears My word, and believes Him who sent Me, has eternal life, and does not come into judgment, but has passed out of death into life." We have been transferred, transformed, changed completely by entering into this life of Christ.

Christ's very life now becomes our very life as we exercise faith.

So, whose life do you now possess if you are in Christ? Christ's very life has become our life. What kind of life do you have? You have an eternal life, the same identical life as Christ. When did your eternal life begin? It always was, but some people think that when they entered into Christ that's when their life began. But, see, the diagram is very clear. Ephesians 1:4 says, "Just as He [God] chose us in Him before the foundation of the world, that we should be holy and blameless before Him." He has given us a new identity in the past, in the present, in the future, in all ways we have a new identity. Look with me at 2 Cor-inthians 5:17 on the other end of your diagram, "Therefore if any man is in Christ, he is a new creature; the old things passed away; behold, new things have come." What has happened is God has made us new creatures. We are dramatically, totally different because of what God has done. We were dead in sin and trespasses. We are now alive in Christ. We were in darkness, now we're in light. My identity used to be a sinner and I was a very good one when I was one. Now I'm not a sinner anymore. Now I'm a saint, I'm different. I can still sin, but I don't have to. Back here I didn't have any choice, now I have a choice. I don't have to sin anymore. God has set me free because of being a new creature, having a new identity. I'm not the same Bill I used to be. If you've entered into Christ, you're not the same person that you used to be, you are different, you're not the same. That's what I want to help you see in this message. That you and Christ are one, in unity, you and Christ have the very same life.

Back in Illinois I live close to the Mississippi River and oftentimes when people talk about entering into Christ and their life beginning at that time I use the Mississippi River as an illustration. I say, "If you run over and jump into the Mississippi River then you've entered into it,

VCL

VICTORIOUS CHRISTIAN LIVING Conference
Copyright © 1999 Victorious Christian Living International, Inc.

right? They say, "Right." Does the Mississippi River begin when you enter into it? No, it doesn't begin when you enter into it. It actually begins way up in Minnesota. I've been up there. I rode my motorcycle up there and I jumped across the Mississippi River. One giant leap for mankind. It begins way up there. It doesn't begin when you enter into it. You really don't change the Mississippi River by entering into it, but you become a part of it.

Let me try to illustrate what Christ's life in you is like. This happens to be a very nice glass. Let's say that this is a pottery cup. In the Bible, God says that we are earthen vessels and He tells us to go to the potter if we want to understand. If I took this cup and I drained the water down to about there and set this in the river it would just kind of float along just like a boat does. If I fill this cup all the way up to the top with water and set it in the Mississippi River, it will completely sink. See, many Christians just kind of float along, don't they, half in the world and half in Christ, not really submerged. But if I took that all the way full and dropped it into the Mississippi River, put on my scuba gear, and went to the bottom, could I find that mug if I spent enough time down there? Yes, I certainly could, couldn't I? It's a unique vessel, full of Christ and surrounded by Christ. That's kind of like you and I are in Christ. See, when we're full of the Spirit, when we're surrounded by God's Spirit, walking after His Spirit, that makes us available to a totally different experience.

Maybe scuba diving would be a good illustration. I don't know how many of you like to do that. I like to do that. I actually sold my scuba gear in Illinois because I got spoiled one time. God sent me to the Bahamas and I went down there and I never want to scuba dive in Illinois again because the water is too murky. I'm asking God to send me further south in the Bahamas where the water is even better to scuba dive. When you get submerged under the water it's a totally different life. That's like the life of Christ.

Let me try to illustrate for you the transformation, the change, that took place in us. Back when I was in the army, I was in an army unit and I drove a jeep for the company commander. I took a field jacket and secured it underneath the seat of the company commander in case it got cold. Well, also under that seat was the battery. One night we were on a field problem and it got cold and I pulled that field jacket out, put it on, got my gloves out of the pocket, and as I was doing that I noticed that there was something wrong with my field jacket. It had holes eaten in it by the battery acid and I said, "oh, sugar jets" or something like that because I was not a believer at that time. I wore the jacket until the end of the field problem and took it to the supply sergeant at the conclusion of that mission in the wilderness. I took it to Sergeant Smith and held it up and he said, "Sergeant Houck, what did you do to that jacket?" I said, "I stuck it under the CO's seat and it got battery acid on it." He said, "It's not worth anything, throw it in the bin over there." So I wadded it up and did my best Michael Jordan three-pointer and swished it. He went to the back room and brought out a brand new field jacket wrapped in plastic. He said, "Sign here Sergeant Houck." I signed for it and he gave me a brand new field jacket. I went home and had Juli sew the patches on it. We starched it. I could hardly wait until Monday morning formation so I could go profile my new threads. I had a brand new field jacket.

Well, see, that's kind of like my life in Christ. What I had before was worn-out, rotten, good for nothing, holes in it. It was just a filthy rag needing to be thrown away. In the process of being transformed into Christ, He gave me a robe of righteousness. He gave me a brand new life, not just a coat—He transformed me from the inside out. He gave me some nice threads by the way in the process, but He gave me everything new. I traded in old and got new. I exchanged an old, rotten life for a brand new life. He wants to do that for everyone here.

WALK AFTER THE FLESH/SPIRIT
(Diagram 170-D)

Please look with me at your last diagram, 170-D. The top part of this diagram is "Walk After the Flesh," and the bottom half is "Walk After the Spirit." Here again, you see the individual's spirit, soul, and body. The fact is true in both of these that this person is spiritual, this person has been saved, this person is enlightened, this person is indwelt by God's Holy Spirit. So you see that's the same in both diagrams. That's the spiritual fact, but the function is much different isn't it? The function in the soul in the top one is walking after the flesh. This person is believing what he or she thinks is true, how he or she feels, or what other people say, more than what God says. So the person's function is in error, it's not correct. The person's body begins or may cause or may show up problems because of that wrong functioning.

As you look at the bottom diagram, "Walking After God's Spirit," you see this person is spiritually alive. He or she is functioning correctly. This person's soul is complete, has sufficiency and freedom in Christ, and so lives at peace. The person's body is offered up as God's property. He or she is renewed daily, hourly, by the minute, second by second, millisecond by millisecond. The person becomes disciplined and the person's life begins to reveal and demonstrate the very life of Christ. Now it could be said that this top person knows *about* God. The bottom person knows God.

Let me try to illustrate that for you. One of my favorite characters in the Bible is Joe, Joseph. Joseph was engaged to Mary, the Virgin Mary, the mother of our Lord Jesus. Joe found out Mary was PG. He took her home to be his wife, but he did not know her as a husband knows a wife did he? She went the nine months of pregnancy, she went through the delivery, she went through the process of ritualistic purification by the law present at that time, so about a year after Joe took Mary to be his wife, he finally knew her as a husband knows a wife. See, Joe knew her growing up. Joe knew her before he brought her to his house. He knew her while they lived together, but he didn't really know her until he knew her like a husband knows a wife.

I want you to come to know God, not just as someone you live with, someone you've been around, but somebody you're intimately, personally involved with on a daily basis. And you love to get alone with Him. You love to talk to Him about everything, and you love to share with Him what's going on in your life the same way a husband shares with a wife and a wife shares with a husband. That's the way I want you to know God: as your identity, as your very life. That's walking in God's Spirit after God's Spirit. That's functioning in a practical relationship with God.

Now when I'm walking in this relationship, how does it affect sin? You see, I died to sin with Christ Jesus on the cross. Sin no longer has any power or dominion or authority over me. See, I used to have to sin. I didn't have any choice. Now I have a clear choice. It's like some people who have a beeper. You know, I'm not one of those important people that has one but, you have a beeper on and somebody calls your beeper and when you are a natural man, when you're a sinner, you've got to answer the call. You don't have any choice. But after you become a Christian, the beeper goes off "lust, Bill, lust" beep, beep, beep, "sin, Bill, sin" beep, beep, beep. I can look at the beeper and say that call's not for me and put it back on. I don't have to answer that call. I don't have to obey the beeper of the world, the flesh, or the Devil. I don't have to sin any more. I am free not to do that because of my identity in Christ.

I have this identity. I am seated right now with Christ in the heavens. This may be difficult to believe, but I am because of Christ's works. I don't always feel holy, but God says I am, and I

VCL

VICTORIOUS CHRISTIAN LIVING Conference
Copyright © 1999 Victorious Christian Living International, Inc.

am. God says I am righteous, I have the very righteousness of Christ. God says it. I believe it. That's it. Done. I am righteous. I could go on and on and on with the identities that are true about me because of what God has done. I am a spiritual being. I have a soul and I live in a body. The spiritual aspect of me, what Christ has done, is the most important part. That is my identity—who I am in Christ.

Now, here's our choice and function. "Hubba. Hubba. Hubba. Who are you going to believe?" I think that's a line out of Batman, one of the Batman movies the Joker does, "Hubba. Hubba. Hubba. Who are you going to believe?" Are you going to believe others or yourself, or are you going to believe God? Those are your choices. Which one of those three is trustworthy? By golly, it's not me, it's not others, it's not you, God's the only trustworthy one. Believe in what He says about you, who He says you are. That's the most important thing about you. Not what others say, not what you've believed in the past, not how you look, not how you feel. That's all peripheral. What's the most important part? What God has done for you.

REVIEW

Look with me at your review page in conclusion. Number 1, "I am given the life of Christ." God gave it to me by grace.

Number 2, "I am no longer dead, but alive 'in Christ.'" Hallelujah!

Number 3, "I am no longer a slave to sin. It is a choice now."

Number 4, "I am a new creation—God's child!"

The next one. "I am to be transformed by the renewing of my mind." Within my soul, the battleground will be in my mind, the battleground will be in your mind. Think on God. Think on His ways. Memorize the truth. Be involved with His Word. Believe Him and what

He says. Think on these things. Don't be conformed to the world's image anymore. Don't think like the world, think like God. It's totally different.

When I flew out here to do this lesson, I looked down from the airplane at the world below and I was thinking God sees things from a totally different perspective than I do. Look at things from God's perspective, not the world's. Renew your mind. Hang around people who walk in their identity in Christ. Dialogue about this. Read about it. Don't just be dumping in TV all the time. Get into God's Word. Get into some good books that will help you understand who you are.

Lastly, "I am to appropriate His very life." There are bright lights shining on me right now and if I went over and unplugged any of those lights, they'd quit working. They still are lights, but if they're not plugged in they don't work. You and I are lights in the world. Stay plugged into God. Stay attached to Him. Stay involved with Him. You've been grafted into a wonderful olive tree. Enjoy that, allow that sap to flow through your life and become your very life. Paul says, "You are a wild olive branch, Bill, and I've grafted you into the perfect vine." Amen. I was a wild rascal. Now, in Christ Jesus, it's His life flowing through me, He's changing me. Praise God. I am so thankful. My wife says, "Double . . . double bless him, God." Transform him God. Amen. I want to be changed into the likeness of Christ. It's available to you and me.

Remember this fact: meaning and purpose in your life flow from who you believe yourself to be. They flow from your identity. Function out of an identity focused on Christ—God being number one in your life, others being second, and yourself being third. Keep God number one. Look to others, then yourself. An easy way to remember that is JOY, Jesus first, Others second, and Yourself last. If you walk in that identity, if you walk in Jesus being the most important thing in your life, Him being your very life, He will transform you.

Let's pray in closing. "Heavenly Father, thank You for giving us this graceful, wonderful life. Praise be to You, God, You have made it all possible. You have adopted us as children. We can now stand here and say, 'Abba, Father, thank You for blessing us.' Father, I pray that You touch the lives of the people who are listening to this lesson right now, that they would see their identity in relationship to You. Your Holy Spirit can anoint them right where they sit. Reveal to them the truth of who You are and what You have done for them and how they can walk in an intimate, loving, personal, dynamic, powerful, life-changing relationship with You. Oh, Father, thank You. In the presence of Your Holy Spirit and the powerful name of Your Son, Jesus Christ, we pray. Amen." Thank you.

GODSHIP ———————————————————————————

REJECTION ———————————————————————————

EXTERNAL/INTERNAL ———————————————————

PROBLEMS, PROBLEMS, WHY PROBLEMS? ————

MY FLESH—GOD'S ENEMY ——————————————

REPENTANCE ————————————————————————

WHAT'S NEW ABOUT YOU? ———————————————

ACCEPTING YOUR RIGHTEOUSNESS ——————▶

EXTENDING FORGIVENESS ——————————————

SEEKING FORGIVENESS ————————————————

REST, ABIDE, WALK ————————————————————

LOVE ———————————————————————————————

GODSHIP

REJECT

EXT/INT

PROBLEMS

FLESH

REPENT

WHAT'S NEW

ACCEPT RIGHT

EXTEND FORGIVE

SEEK FORGIVE

REST

LOVE

ACCEPTING YOUR RIGHTEOUSNESS

> *He made Him who knew no sin to be sin on our behalf, that we might become the righteousness of God in Him.*
>
> 2 Corinthians 5:21

People who are aimless, disheartened, discouraged, or have given up on life are all around us. One of the saddest things is that all too often these words describe Christians! They "try to live the Christian life" and fail miserably. They allow their behavior to determine their identity. They see the wrong choices they make and then call themselves names like: failure, loser, stupid, sinner, angry person, or liar. Or, they see themselves as addicted to something or someone.

We live in a world that rewards performance. People are promoted at work and given raises commensurate with their performance. Many companies have yearly performance evaluations.

Many sincere people try very hard to gain acceptance from God and others through performance. A believer may say, "I have made some very poor choices, and I know God will love me if I _____." (Fill in the blank with Christian service, sacrifice, or self-denial.) Instead of allowing our actions to determine our identity, we need to see what God says.

Are you accepted right now, today, just as you are?

People are either functioning **for** acceptance or **from** acceptance. Every day we make choices based on our view of ourselves. To see ourselves as unloved, unrighteous, insecure, unstable, and unacceptable is to be deceived and to live in bondage. Sadly, to believe circumstances, past history, emotions, or what other people say, as opposed to what God says, is the norm for Christians. To no longer live under bondage, you must begin by accepting your righteousness in Christ.

WRONG CHOICES

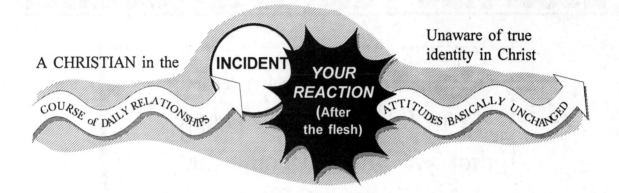

A CHRISTIAN in the

COURSE of DAILY RELATIONSHIPS

INCIDENT

YOUR REACTION (After the flesh)

Unaware of true identity in Christ

ATTITUDES BASICALLY UNCHANGED

2 Peter 1:9

180-A

VCL
VICTORIOUS CHRISTIAN LIVING Conference
Copyright © 1999 Victorious Christian Living International, Inc.

NOTES

Accepting Your Righteousness
STUDY GUIDE

PURPOSE for Diagram **180-A:**

*To illustrate how not knowing who I am in Christ
causes wrong choices.*

? 1. What is a negative incident that has confronted you recently? _____
_____
_____
_____

? 2. Did you react after the flesh? How? _____
_____
_____
_____

> *We are under
> obligation not to
> the flesh . . . .*
>
> Rom. 8:12

? 3. Did the truth of who you are in Christ affect
your reaction? How? _____
_____
_____
_____

📖 4. Study Galatians 5:16 and 2 Peter 1:9.

? 5. What does it mean to carry out the desires of the flesh? _____
_____
_____
_____

ACCEPT RIGHT.

Identity determines behavior.

THE WILL IS THE KEY—WRONG CHOICES

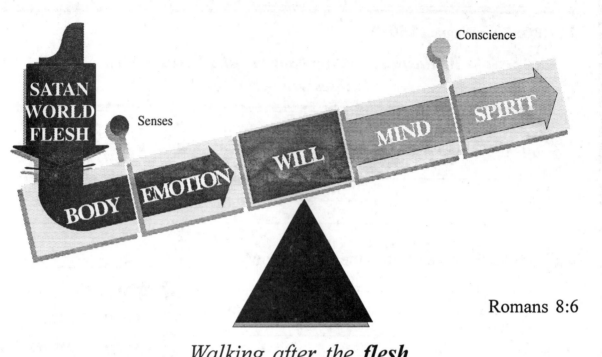

*Walking after the **flesh**.*

Romans 8:6

180-B

NOTES

PURPOSE for Diagram **180-B**:

To illustrate how wrong choices are made through the influence of Satan, the world, and our flesh.

? 1. List some of the identities you have accepted? (such as parent, spouse, employee, employer, friend, athlete, etc.)

_____

_____

_____

? 2. What are you doing to prove your value in the identities you listed? _____

_____

_____

_____

> *Do not be conformed to this world . . . .*
> Rom. 12:2

? 3. How does the world say you should perform if the real you is one of the identities you listed?

_____

_____

📖 4. Study Ephesians 2:2-3.

? 5. Who is it that influences the ways of this world? _____

📖 6. Study Galatians 1:10.

? 7. Are you seeking anyone's acceptance (even your own) rather than God's? _____

My choices are made based on who I think I am.

RIGHT CHOICES

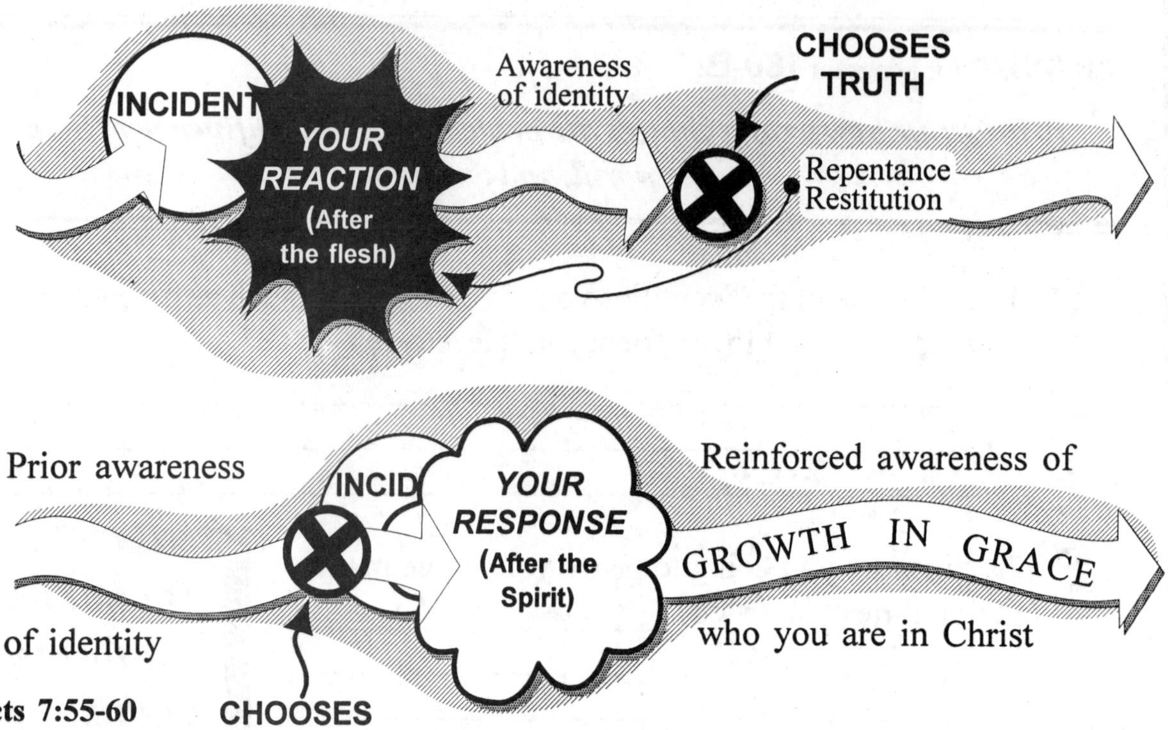

Acts 7:55-60
1 Cor. 4:1-4

180-C

NOTES

VCL
VICTORIOUS CHRISTIAN LIVING Conference
Copyright © 1999 Victorious Christian Living International, Inc.

PURPOSE for Diagram **180-C**:

To illustrate the benefits of choosing to walk in the truth of who I am in Christ.

1. Study 2 Corinthians 5:21.

2. Do you have trouble accepting the **truth** that you are the rightouesness of God in Christ? Why? _____
_____
_____

3. Can you accept that God's word is true regardless of how you feel?
_____

4. Study 2 Corinthians 5:7.

5. If you choose by faith what God says is true about you, how would it affect your responses? _____

> *For as he thinks . . . so is he.*   Prov. 23:7

6. Study John 1:12. Who does this verse say you are? _____

7. If I choose to believe the truth that I am a child of God, then regardless of the incident, I can respond as a child of God (after the Spirit).

Identity is based on birth, not on behavior.

THE WILL IS THE KEY—RIGHT CHOICES

Senses

Conscience

GOD WORD

BODY

EMOTION

WILL

MIND

SPIRIT

Romans 12:2
Hebrews 12:1-2
Deuteronomy 30:19

*Walking after the **Spirit**.*

180-D

VCL
VICTORIOUS CHRISTIAN LIVING Conference
Copyright © 1999 Victorious Christian Living International, Inc.

PURPOSE for Diagram **180-D:**

To illustrate how right choices are made through the influence of God and His Word.

? 1. Why do you want to make right choices? _____

_____

_____

> **. . . be transformed by the renewing of your mind . . .** Rom. 12:2

📖 2. Study 2 Corinthians 5:14-15.

? 3. What does God say should motivate your choices? _____

_____

? 4. Instead of you listening to the one who led you astray, how can you start listening to God? _____

_____

_____

📖 5. Study Psalm 119:11.

? 6. How would you get God's Word in your heart? _____

_____

📖 7. Study Philippians 4:8-9.

? 8. Do these verses characterize your thinking or do you focus on your circumstances? _____

_____

? 9. What other ways can you renew your mind (Romans 12:2)? _____

_____

_____

Read a good book lately—try the Bible.

FAITH IS:

A CHOICE BASED ON GOD'S TRUTH, EVEN THOUGH IT MAY NOT SEEM TO BE TRUE, SO THAT WHAT IS TRUE ABOUT ME ALREADY MAY BECOME TRUE IN MY DAILY EXPERIENCE.

"The assurance of things hoped for, the conviction of things not seen."

Hebrews 11:1

180-E

VCL

VICTORIOUS CHRISTIAN LIVING Conference
Copyright © 1999 Victorious Christian Living International, Inc.

PURPOSE for Diagram **180-E:**

To define "faith" based on biblical truth.

1. Study Ephesians 4:24.

2. Do you feel righteous and holy? _____
   _____

3. Do your feelings negate what God says? _____
   _____
   _____

4. Study Philippians 3:20.

5. If you didn't feel like a citizen of your country, would it change the
   truth of your citizenship? _____
   _____

6. Can you be a citizen of heaven even
   though you don't feel like it? _____

> *Faith is the assurance of things hoped for . . . .*
> Heb. 11:1

ACCEPT RIGHT.

7. Do you want to believe what God says about you? _____
   _____
   _____

8. Check the next diagram to see the truth.

Righteousness is a fact—not a feeling.

The truest things about me are what God says about me (1 Cor. 4:3-4).

> In Christ I am *a child of God—born of God* (John 1:12-13).
> In Christ I am *being saved by His life* (Romans 5:10).
> In Christ I am *free from condemnation* (Romans 8:1).
> In Christ I am *an heir of God, joint heir with Christ* (Romans 8:17).
> In Christ I am *a saint* (Romans 8:27).
> In Christ I am *accepted* (Romans 15:7).
> In Christ I am *a possessor of the mind of Christ* (1 Corinthians 2:16).
> In Christ I am *a new creature* (2 Corinthians 5:17).
> In Christ I am *the righteousness of God* (2 Corinthians 5:21).
> In Christ I am *blessed with every spiritual blessing* (Ephesians 1:3).
> In Christ I am *adopted as God's child* (Ephesians 1:5).
> In Christ I am *God's workmanship created for good works* (Ephesians 2:10).
> In Christ I am *a member of God's household* (Ephesians 2:19).
> In Christ I am *a citizen of heaven* (Philippians 3:20).
> In Christ I am *holy and blameless and beyond reproach* (Colossians 1:22).
> In Christ I am *complete [perfect]* (Colossians 2:10).
> In Christ I am *alive and forgiven of all my transgressions* (Colossians 2:13).
> In Christ I am *a member of a royal priesthood* (1 Peter 2:9).
> In Christ I am *a partaker of God's divine nature* (2 Peter 1:4).
> In Christ I am *given eternal life today* (1 John 5:11-13).
> In Christ I am *released from my sins* (Revelation 1:5).

RENEWING my mind brings about **TRANSFORMATION.**

And do not be conformed to this world, but be transformed by the renewing of your mind, that you may prove what the will of God is, that which is good and acceptable and perfect (Romans 12:2).

1. Read a verse listed above in its context and check cross references.
2. Report to God that I believe (adhere to, trust in, rely on) what He says about me is true.
3. Respond to God in prayer by thanking Him for what He did. "Father, I believe You when Your Word says I am a saint. I may not feel like one, but that's what You call me, so I believe it. Thank You!"—1 Thessalonians 5:18
4. Recognize what this verse teaches me about God and praise Him for who He is!
5. Reject my old view of myself. This would include no longer calling myself names like: failure, dummy, stupid, idiot, and loser. Also, I would stop seeing myself as: sinner, alcoholic, lazy, fornicator, homosexual, or liar. —1 Corinthians 6:9-11
6. Rejoice that my mind is being renewed each time I choose the truth.
7. Receive direction for today as a result of this verse. "Lord, I see what You have done and who You are, now what do You want me to do regarding this truth?"

PURPOSE for Diagram **180-F**:

> *To show how what God says can be used to renew our minds.*

? 1. Are these verses literally true of you? _____
_____

? 2. Can you pick a verse and go through the seven steps now? _____

3. Write out what God shows you.
_____
_____

> *. . . you shall know the truth . . . the truth shall set you free.*
> John 8:32

_____
_____
_____

? 4. Can you choose to believe what God says is true about you even if you don't feel it or have experienced it yet? _____

? 5. What keeps you from believing these truths? _____
_____
_____

? 6. Have you ever received the acceptance God has for you based on what Christ did for you? _____
_____

🙏 7. Would you now, in prayer, like to receive His acceptance of you?
_____

8. You are loved, accepted, holy, blameless, and a saint. Praise God!
Ephesians 1:4-8

God said it.
I believe it.

ACCEPT RIGHT

REVIEW

- I am totally accepted by Christ.

- Christ has made me righteous. I need to believe this truth regardless of how I feel or how I act.

- This truth frees me from trying to gain acceptance from others. I don't have to live a performance-based-acceptance lifestyle.

- Knowing this truth stops the need to compete and makes decision making easier. I am not trying to prove anything.

NOTES

VCL
VICTORIOUS CHRISTIAN LIVING Conference
Copyright © 1999 Victorious Christian Living International, Inc.

ACCEPTING YOUR RIGHTEOUSNESS

Lesson Transcript by Ted Sellers

I'd like to tell you a little bit about myself. A couple of years ago, I had the privilege of pastoring a small church, and I was very pleased to be able to do that, to be serving the Lord as a pastor. I went to Moody Bible Institute and graduated from the Pastor's Course and wanted to study God's Word and teach it to people and see them set free. I found out very quickly that one of the reasons I liked being a pastor was that I liked to study the Word of God and then teach the Word of God. I even counted . . . I like to count things . . . so I counted up that it would normally take me about ten to fourteen hours to prepare for a Sunday morning message. That's a lot of time! And, I put a lot of work into it because I wanted to teach the Word of God.

But there was another underlying motive that I, looking back, didn't even realize that I had learned. That motive was that I wanted peoples' acceptance. I wanted to be accepted by people, and so I would preach the Word. Then, at least in the church where I was pastoring, we had the little routine every Sunday where I would go back to the door and greet people as they left. A lot of churches today don't do that anymore, but this one did; and I was so glad they did because I would be standing there at the door when people would be coming out and leaving. I would be saying things like: "Hi, Mrs. Johnson, it's good to see you today. How was your trip to Michigan?"

But, I had an ulterior motive because I had a little cup that I was holding out. No one ever saw it, of course, but I had my little cup of acceptance . . . had it kind of tucked away . . . so I'd ask her about how her trip to Michigan was, and then I'd stick out my cup. And she would put something in it. And what she would say was: "That was really a good sermon today, Pastor. I learned something that I had never seen before."

"Thank you. Thank you."

And someone else would come up. "Say, Mr. Jones, how you doin'? Oh, you're walkin' really good on that knee. Been prayin' for that knee, that it would recover." And he would say, "Oh, thank you, Pastor. And, by the way . . ."

"Uh huh?"

"I sure liked that sermon today."

"Did you really? Good! Put somethin' in the cup . . . thank you."

Then someone else would come up, and I would make a comment. "Hey! I heard your son isn't feeling well. I'll be over later this afternoon, and I'll be praying for your son."

"Oh, really? Oh, I'd appreciate it if you'd do that. And besides that, Pastor, what a good sermon today."

"Thank you. Put something in the cup."

We even had one lady who was from England, and I loved to see her come in the line because she always said the same thing. As I approached her, I would say, "Hi! How are you doing?" She said, "Oh, I'm doing so well today, and I just want you to know—Good sermon, Vicar!"

"Oohh, I was a vicar!"

I didn't know what that was, but it sounded good and more acceptance than just pastor. I was a vicar! That filled my cup up . . . oh, maybe up to here . . . and I just loved holding my cup out every Sunday. By the end of the line, when the last person left, my cup was pretty full of acceptance. The only trouble was, during the week it drained out and was empty. By next Sunday, I had to start the process all over again: hold it out and hope somebody would put something in my cup.

"Accepting Your Righteousness." Accepting what God says about you. I think we as Christians need to do that because we live in a world that really rewards performance.

Many people that work in industry or even in schools experience a yearly performance evaluation. And those are very serious. They can be very scary. Because if you don't measure up, if you've not performed with the goals that perhaps were set for you, you could lose your job. Even children growing up learn how important it is to perform. A little child comes home, maybe first or second grade, with all A's on his report card. Dad is so impressed. He says: "That's a good job, Son. Here. Here you go. Here's a twenty-dollar bill. Way to go!" What does the boy learn?

"I know. I need to get good grades, and Dad'll like me, and he'll even give me money. I think I understand how this thing works!"

Then we become Christians and we think: "Well, God's probably the same as everybody else. If you do a good job, you get rewarded, and He'll like me." As it says on the introduction page, paragraph 3: "Many sincere people try very hard to gain acceptance from God and others through performance. A believer may say, 'I have made some very poor choices, and I know God will love me if I _____.'" You could fill in the blank with "get involved with Christian service" or if you "sacrifice for Him" or "self-effort." If I just try a little harder, I know that that will mean something to God.

I really believe that everyone is either performing and functioning **for** acceptance or **from** acceptance. I'm trying to get you to accept me by holding out my cup and saying: "Would you put something in my cup? Oh, thank you. Would you put something in my cup? You didn't put anything in my cup. OK, I'll go to someone else. How about you? Would you put something in my cup? Thank you very much." We become like Christian beggars. Then we realize that it doesn't really satisfy, but we don't know any other way.

One man has said this: "Victory, as a Christian [and we call this the Victorious Christian Living Conference] is not a reward. It's a gift." And the gift is a person. That person, Jesus, totally accepts you and me. Bob George, the author of *Classic Christianity* and *Growing in Grace*, said this: "It is my opinion that the average Christian's flimsy understanding of his acceptance and identity in Christ is the major cause of the superficial Christianity that is all around us."

WRONG CHOICES (Diagram 180-A)
Let's go to your first diagram and see how this idea of identity and accepting your righteousness can affect choices. Let me read to you Romans 8:12-13, "So then, brethren, we are under obligation, not to the flesh, to live according to the flesh [or after the flesh]—for if you are living according to the flesh, you must die; but if by the Spirit you are putting to death the deeds of the body, you will live." If I'm living according to the flesh, I need to die to that kind of living. That's wrong living.

Let me read to you the way *The Message* translates this. *The Message* is a fairly new paraphrased translation by Eugene Peterson. I really like the way he translates.

(I just want to say a little footnote here in regard to using other kinds of versions and translations, especially those that are paraphrased. Those of you men that watch sporting events: there are usually two people broadcasting the event. There's the play-by-play guy. He gives you the plays. He calls them out. Then there's the color commentator. The color commentator fills in the blanks, and he tells you a little bit about what's been happening in this player's life and in the past week, or if his wife is expecting a baby. It has nothing to do with the play on the court or on the field. He's just a color commentator. Well, that's the way I think when I think about these other kinds of translations—*The Living Bible, The Message,* Phillips, Good News for Modern Man. They might not be word-for-word translations like the King James or the NIV or the *New American Standard Bible,* but they're color commentators. They bring color and life to it.)

Listen to Romans 8:12-13 from *The Message:* "When God lives and breathes in you (and he does, as surely as he did in Jesus) you are delivered from that dead life. With his Spirit living in you, your body will be as alive as Christ's. So don't you see that we don't owe this old do-it-yourself life one red cent." I always like the way that says, "You don't owe this old do-it-yourself life one red cent." What is that? That's the self-effort kind of life. "There's nothing in it for us, nothing at all. The best thing to do is give it a decent burial and get on with your life. God's Spirit beckons."

So that's what you see as you look at this diagram on this page. The diagram is a person, a Christian going along in the course of daily relationships, and then an incident happens. The person reacts after the flesh. The attitudes are basically unchanged, unaware of the person's true identity in Christ. Identity in Christ has nothing to do with this person.

Let me tell you three words that I'd like you to write on your diagram. Three words: "Depen-

dency determines control." Let me explain that. Whatever I depend on controls me. Let's say, I depend on my job. You'll hear people say: "Well, my job, that's my life. My job is my life." What does that mean? The job controls that person because dependency determines control. Let's say I'm dependent on a person. It could be a spouse, a child, a friend, whoever it is. I'm really dependent on that person. That person has the power to control me because identity determines meaning and purpose in life. Or, meaning and purpose in life flow from identity. If I know who I am, then I know what makes sense in life. You that are listening to this tape are doing so because of your identity. You know who you are, and because you know who you are, you want to find out more about this Christian life. You want to find out about accepting your righteousness. Identity is very important because meaning and purpose in life flow from identity. Whatever I depend on, that thing has the power to control me.

So, let's take a particular incident. We've got a man at work who's got some problems. He's hearing some rumblings through the grapevine. He reacts after the flesh, attitudes unchanged. What he could do is just say, "Eh, that's just the way they are!" and just blow it off. Or he could say, "Management around here—they're so picky, picky!" and become griping or complaining. But, let's say that there's conviction from the Lord. Instead of turning to the Lord, he turns to himself and becomes performance-driven. By self-effort, he tries harder. He realizes: "This job is very important. I'd better hold out my cup. I'd better make sure they like me around here. I'm gonna come in early. I'm gonna take no lunch break. I'm gonna stay late. I'm gonna walk on eggshells. I'm gonna make sure that I'm accepted around here in order to keep this job because this job is my life. I'm depending on it."

Take another incident. How about parents and children, and the children are not obeying. What could the parents, unaware of identity in Christ, do? They could either blow up or they could even beat the children. That would be one way. Or they could say: "Well, what are you gonna do? Kids today . . . ha, ha, ha . . . they just never seem to listen, do they?" But then they may feel convicted and say: "Well, I gotta do something about this. I can't just blow up; I can't beat them up, that's probably wrong. I know what I need to do. I need to live in a relationship with these children so that they will accept me. I really see how important they are. I need to hold up my cup of acceptance and say: 'Let's be friends. Let's all be buddies. Let's be pals.'" And what they're really saying is, "Let's be peers." That's not a parent-child relationship—the parents don't want to be rejected, so they give up control for acceptance.

"We don't want to do anything to make you mad. We don't want to upset you because we have to live with you, and we want you to like us."

Take another incident. Someone criticizes a person or tells the person how horrible he or she is. The person starts getting the identity, "I'm a bad person," and could feel hurt or feel angry and just believe the lies. But if the Spirit convicts and instead of turning to the Lord, the person turns to self-effort, and the person says: "I know what I need to do. I need to try harder to get you to accept me, and I will bend over backwards. I'll do whatever it takes because I want you to like me." If it's a woman, she may be involved in seductive clothing. She may even be involved in sexual promiscuity. Why?

"I need someone to accept me. Would you accept me? Because I have a bad identity I think I'm a bad person, and I want someone to like me." A man, in that kind of an incident, given a title of being a bad person could become mean or hard or even turn to violence and say: "This is the way I am. I'm a bad person, and I'm gonna live that way, and you're gonna like me

because if you don't like me I'll beat you up." It's a different kind of acceptance cup. It's, "You'd better put something in or I'm gonna hit you!" It's that kind of a thing: "Because I know who I am. I'm a bad person."

THE WILL IS THE KEY—WRONG CHOICES (Diagram 180-B)

Let's look at what this looks like when we consider "walking after the flesh." This little teeter-totter here is an illustration of the body, soul, and spirit. The body is the block all the way to the left; the soul is the three blocks in the middle (your emotion, your will, your mind; that could be your feeler, chooser, and thinker), and then the spirit is the block farthest to the right. This is a teetertotter on the fulcrum of the will. As a person listens to Satan and the world and the world's values, they are energized to choose from a false identity. What the false identity could be is: "Hey, I'm only human!" or "My identity is 'worker.' I've gotta really work to gain their acceptance." Or identity: "Parent—I know who I am, I'm a parent. So I've got to make sure that child accepts me." Acceptance is so important! I begin to make decisions based on my identity—my view of who I am.

I heard a story several years ago by Lieutenant Bob Vernon with the Los Angeles Police Department. (Just to show you the power and the need to be accepted.) He said he investigated this incident that had happened with some teenage boys. One boy saw another boy out with his girlfriend. He and a bunch of other guys confronted him about this, and he said, "Yeah, so what?" They got in a scuffle, and they got in a fight. He knocked the boy down who had dated his girlfriend. Out of somewhere came a knife, and he stabbed the boy. Then he handed the knife to one of the other boys.

Lieutenant Vernon said as he interviewed each one of these other boys, they all said the same thing.

"Hey, he handed me the knife, man, and everybody was lookin' at me!"

"Yeah?"

"Well, I didn't want to stab him; but, hey, I gotta live in this project, man, and they're lookin' at me. I need to be accepted by these guys; I need to fit in; I need to hang with these guys. I didn't want to do it . . . the guy was bleeding and crying and . . ."

They eventually stabbed him to death. That's how powerful it is that I must be accepted. That's a wrong choice. Why?

"I want to be accepted; I want to fit in. Would someone please put something in my cup?"

RIGHT CHOICES (Diagram 180-C)
Let's look at the other side of this—the right choices. I think of Paul in 1 Corinthians 4:1-4. This is such a fresh look at the life of Paul. Listen and see if this is a guy who knows who he is. He says this: "Let a man regard us in this manner, as servants of Christ, stewards of the mysteries of God." Did he know who he was? He was a servant of Christ and a steward of the mysteries of God. "In this case, moreover, it is required of stewards that one be found trustworthy. But to me it is a very small thing that I should be examined by you, or by any human court." See, it's a small thing that I should be examined by you. "In fact," he said, "I don't even examine myself. For I am conscious of nothing against myself, yet I am not by this acquitted; but the one who examines me is the Lord."

The Phillips paraphrase puts it this way: "As a matter of fact, it matters very little to me what you, or any man, thinks of me. I don't even value my own opinion of myself. For I might be quite ignorant of any fault in myself, but that doesn't justify me before God. My only true judge is the Lord." Do you see where he was

looking? Just to the Lord. He said: "I don't care what you people think! I don't even spend all day evaluating myself."

Do you know of people that do that? Always checking: "I wonder if I did that correctly? I wonder if I had faith when I was doing that? Was I really doing that in the right way?" It would just get very tiresome. Or, I'm wondering if everybody likes what I've just done.

"Oh, boy. I bet someone was offended. I've got to find out if anybody was offended and go seek their forgiveness."

Paul says, "I don't really care." It's not that he's being rude. He's just not living **for** acceptance; he's living **from** acceptance.

Let's look at the two different tracks on Diagram 180-C. Here we have an incident just like before, reacting after the flesh, but now, an awareness of identity and choosing the truth. Eventually, as the incident occurs, I don't react after the flesh; I respond after the Spirit and grow in grace. Think about the guy who's working. He's got his job, and he hears about some troubles, and now he's been trying hard, remember, walking on eggshells, coming early, staying late? He says this: "I know that God totally accepts me. He loves me. My identity is not just 'worker,' my identity is 'child of God.' I'm accepted by God. And so, I'm going to work not for the boss, not for the pay, I'm going to work for God. He's the one I'm going to work for. There are things that I'm going to do that my boss won't even see, and it doesn't matter because I'm not doing it for him anymore. I'm working as unto the Lord, and I'm doing a better job than when I was walking on eggshells and being fearful of losing my job, because I'm not working for these people. If I even do lose my job, God'll find me another one because I'm gonna be working just for Him. I don't have to work scared. I can work confident in the Lord."

Look up Ephesians 6:5-7. Let me just read those to you. I've shared these verses with many men who found a whole new way of getting up in the morning because they got up in the morning getting ready to do the will of God. Let me ask you something, "Am I doing the will of God sharing the Bible, teaching in a conference like this?" You say, "Oh, yeah."

"Well, how about you, when you get up tomorrow morning to go to work, and you're making widgets or whatever it is you do. Are you doing the will of God?"

"Oh, no, no. I'm not in Christian service."

Well, let's read Ephesians 6:5-7: "Bondservant [slaves]," (maybe that's how you feel) "be obedient to those who are your masters according to the flesh, with fear and trembling, in sincerity of heart, as to Christ; not with eyeservice . . ." (NKJV). That's the way the guy was working before. What is eyeservice? That's being busy when the boss is watching. I remember when I was in the Navy, they said, "You don't have to be busy, just look busy." So you always had a rag nearby, and when the captain or one of the chiefs walked by, "How you doing, Chief?"

"Yeah, how you doing?"

Just look busy. That's eyeservice. That's from the teeth out. "Not by way of eyeservice, as men-pleasers, but as bondservants of Christ, doing the will of God from the heart." Doing what? "The will of God from the heart." What is that? "With goodwill doing service, as to the Lord, and not to men." As I work unto the Lord and not unto men, I'm doing the will of God, no matter what the job is.

Let's say there's trouble at home. You remember that one? What's my identity? What's my identity as "parent"? Meaning and purpose in life flow from identity. Then I've got to get this child to like me. Or I've got to get this child to obey. If he disobeys, my day is ruined. But I have to realize that I've got a deeper identity than "parent." I have an identity as "child of God." "Christian." Because of that, I can correct my child in love. Not overcorrect, not undercorrect—correct. But I do it in love because I know who I am. That child cannot change my identity no matter how he or she may act. Because my identity isn't determined by how good a job I do, even as a parent.

What about verbal rejection? Someone who calls me names. You know, I remember, growing up, they used to say, "Sticks and stones will break my bones, but names will never hurt me." Well, they do hurt sometimes. But what do you do when you hear attacks verbally? It's exciting to know that no human being can change my identity. I know who I am, and you can't change me, no matter what you call me. Because my identity is in Christ, I'm secure in God's love and acceptance.

When we are really, totally loved and accepted by God, then we can love and accept other people. So it doesn't just stop with God and myself. It's not just a vertical thing. It's a horizontal thing, too. Because I know I'm loved and accepted by God, I can love and accept you. We will treat other people the same way we think God treats us. Think about that! If you think that God is always disappointed with you and upset with you, that probably will be the way you treat other people. If you think God is always watching and waiting for you to do it right, then you may be treating people the same way. But if you really believe God loves you, is for you, is on your side, and is encouraging you, then that's probably how you'll treat other people. The way we think we're being treated by God is the way we will treat other people. And we'll make right choices.

THE WILL IS THE KEY—RIGHT CHOICES (Diagram 180-D)
Your next diagram shows this same teetertotter, but now we've teetered in the other direction.

Now, what makes the teetertotter teeter? What makes it go from one side to the other?

I don't know about you, but I never really liked teetertotters. The problem with me was I didn't weigh very much, and I always got on the teetertotter with a chunky guy. He would go down on the teetertotter and I would go up in the air at his mercy. Then you know what he'd do, don't you? He'd jump off and . . . POW! I didn't like that! I didn't like teetertotters because the heavy end is where the teetertotter teeters.

Now, how do you get these teetertotters to teeter? You put rocks on one end or the other. On the other one that we looked at all the rocks are on the world's values—listening to what Satan says, spending a lot of time absorbing things from the world. You don't even have to watch a lot of commercials; you just watch a sports event. Sports events should be safe. Oh no! They have all kinds of commercials that give you the values of the world. What you behold, you will reflect. If I'm beholding the values of the world in whatever way they come, I will start to reflect them, and they will change my values. My teetertotter will teeter toward the world system and toward what Satan would want me to do.

Well, how do I get my teetertotter to teeter the other direction, like this diagram shows? I put rocks on the proper side. In other words, I load up one side of the teetertotter. It's like that chunky guy. I get him on the other side, and it tilts down. If I put enough rocks on the teetertotter and it teeters toward the world, that could even be called an addiction. Because I've done something so many times that it seems to be natural.

I remember a man recently who quit smoking. He didn't quit smoking so God would love him. He quit smoking because he knew God loved him. And that was the difference, see? Many

people quit whatever it is, thinking, "Now the Lord will appreciate and like me." No! He already does, so I don't have to do that and He can give me the power not to. But he said he'd been smoking since he was about twelve years old. He was up to three packs a day. That's a serious habit. That's an addiction; that's a way of life. So many times, trying to make that decision, he honestly didn't think he could ever quit. He said, "I could never see myself on the other side of going over the bridge and being over there and not smoking at all." He said, "I just couldn't believe it. It just couldn't happen." Because he had been putting those little cigarette rocks on that one side of the teetertotter, it teetered, and it felt like an addiction. But by God's power he quit. It only took him about a week, and he called me up and said, "I just want you to know, I've quit."

Now, he was a guy who was a serious smoker. He didn't just buy a pack or even a carton of cigarettes. He bought a lot of cigarettes, and he bought them on the Indian Reservation. I understand they're not real happy about taking cigarettes back, but they said they would even take his cigarettes back. He had over $300 worth of cigarettes that he sold back to the Indians so he could do something else with the money. He thought that was just an added blessing. Because of God's power his teetertotter didn't have to stay stuck.

Well, how do we put rocks on the right side of the teetertotter? What does it say? "God" and "His Word." I need to know what God's Word says about me, and believe it! I need to hang around with people who also understand that truth. Even as Christians, if you hang around with a lot of people who are legalistic, who are into performance, into works, it's going to mess up your teetertotter. You won't know where your rocks are. They'll start rolling back and forth and fall off and you have to find new ones. You want to hang around with people who understand the truth and understand how God thinks about them. Good books, listening to good songs, and having fellowship are also good. I will be putting the rocks on the right side of the teetertotter. Because I am accepted by God and I accept my righteousness my true identity will affect my choices.

See, the enemy wants us to listen to him, even as we want to make right choices, and he comes to us with one of his titles. Revelation 12:10 says he's "the accuser of the brethren." So he comes to you and he says: "Now, listen, who do you think you are? Do you see what you just did, what you just said, or what you just thought? Ha! And you think you're righteous? That's a joke! Come on, get real! Look at you. You can't call yourself a child of God. You can't call yourself righteous. Look at what you just did. You ought to be ashamed of yourself!" And you might say: "You know . . . phew . . . I think you're right. I feel really crummy. Boy!" It's like Satan comes and leads you in a cheer with his little pompoms, and he says, "You're bad, you're rotten, you're no good, you're a loser!" So you say, "You know, I think I'm getting this. Let me have those pompoms!" So you take them out of his hands and then you, without his help, say, "I'm no good, I'm bad, I'm a loser." And he says: "You got it!" And he says, "This guy is set. Let's go on to someone else. He's got the message!" **And then you make choices based on those identities from the accuser that you just gave yourself.**

Do we give ourselves an identity based on our behavior or based on our birth? Let me just ask you this, "Are you an American citizen?" You say, "Sure." Do you always act like an American citizen? Let me ask you, "Did you vote in the last presidential election?" Some of you are saying, "Yes." Some of you are saying, "When was that?" Do you vote on just the local issues, when it's about 8 or 9 percent turnout? Do you vote on those? You mean, you don't always vote and you call yourself an American citizen? How about as you drive home today? Are you

going to watch your speed—that you don't go over the speed limit? The American citizen doesn't go over the speed limit, but if you do and you call yourself an American citizen . . . Do you recycle? That's important! Gotta recycle. If you don't recycle, I'm not really sure you're an American citizen. You say: "Oh, it doesn't matter. I don't even have to recycle. I can speed like a speed demon. It doesn't matter. I know I'm an American citizen."

"How come?"

"Because I was born here!"

"Oh, you mean it's not behavior?"
"No, it's birth. That's the difference."

So **you may not act righteous or feel righteous, but you are if God says you are**. Here's what the Phillips says in Romans 5:17-19: "One act of perfect righteousness presents all men freely acquitted in the sight of God. One man's disobedience placed all men under the threat of condemnation, but one man's obedience has the power to present all men righteous before God." Before you became a Christian, did God just see you as condemned and a sinner? You really weren't. It was just kind of His idea. Or were you really condemned and a sinner? Were you really that way? After you become a child of God, does He just see you as righteous? It's a play. You aren't really! It's Jesus that's righteous; you're not. Or are you really righteous? Yeah, you're really righteous.

FAITH IS (Diagram 180-E)
Let's look at the next diagram: "Faith Is:" What is faith? It's a choice. We are talking about choices throughout this lesson. "A choice based on God's truth, even though it may not seem to be true, so that what is true about me already may become true in my daily experience." "The assurance of things hoped for, the conviction of things not seen" (Hebrews 11:1). A choice based on the truth. Well, what's the truth? The truth is I'm righteous.

VCL
VICTORIOUS CHRISTIAN LIVING Conference
Copyright © 1999 Victorious Christian Living International, Inc.

The key verse for this lesson is 2 Corinthians 5:21. I want us to look at that for just a second. It says, "He made Him who knew no sin to be sin on our behalf." Now, if you look in your Bible, I want you to notice, is there anything unusual about the two words "to be"? You notice those? They should be in italics. Do you know what it means when you see a word in italics? It means the translators inserted that word. It's not found in the original language, and if you take those out, it sometimes sounds a little clumsy, so they've put them in for the flow. But even though they've put them in, they want you to know that. So they put them in italics. So, what's fun to do sometimes is take those out and see how it sounds. Sometimes it's very powerful—like this time: "He made Him who knew no sin, sin." **"He made Him who knew no sin, sin on our behalf, that we might become the righteousness of God in Him."**

Let me ask you a couple of questions about Jesus and sin. Now, Jesus had never sinned. So, did He learn about sin by following the Father's instruction? Did the Father say: "Now, you've never sinned. Let me see if I can explain this to you. You see, sin is being disobedient to your parents, or sin is telling a lie." Is that what happened? Or, did He have sin kind of stuck on Him, like gooey, gobby mud, just kind of plop-plop-plop-plop? He had sin kind of flicked all over Him. Is that what happened? Or did He try to understand sin by self-effort? Just try to think: "What is it? I just can't figure it out." But He tried. Of course not. None of those fit.

Now, let's try you and I and righteousness. Do we learn about righteousness by studying the Bible? By reading the Bible? Do we learn about righteousness? See what the Bible says about righteousness . . . huh! Or maybe we have righteousness kind of flicked on us, like little heavenly sprinkles—little sparkles. Oh, there's a righteous person. See? They, sparkle! Is that what it is? Little sparkles on the outside? Or, maybe we try to be righteous by the way we act and talk.

One of the things that I've heard that can be a little confusing is thinking: "Now, here's what I'm going to do, but I need to think about what would Jesus do? What would Jesus do? And then I'll try to do that." That's living the Christian life by my mind and my will. You know, I don't even always know if Jesus knew what He was going to do ahead of time. He waited for directions from the Father. Yet, you and I try to think, "Now, what would Jesus do?" And then we try to do that in the power of our own self-effort—that's how many people are living the Christian life.

No! The Christian life isn't lived by my body and my soul. It's lived by the Spirit. And there are many times as you even pray about things where you say, "God, do you want me to do this, or this?" As you go to Him and let Him be the authority in your life, He says, "That!"

"Oh, I didn't think of that! Where'd that come from? It must have come from God. I didn't think of it."

Yeah, so let God direct. Now are those the ways we become righteous? Try to learn about it, or have it sprinkled on us or try hard to be righteous? No! **We actually become righteous through salvation.**

Here's a note from the Life Application Version of *The Living Bible*—I really like it. It says: "When we trust in Christ, we make a trade—our sin for His goodness. Our sin was poured into Christ at His crucifixion; His righteousness is poured into us at our conversion." Wow! "His righteousness is poured into us." Justification means to be declared totally righteous by God. It's not an act. It's not a play. It really happened. **If you're a child of God, you are absolutely accepted by God and righteous.**

THE TRUEST THINGS ABOUT ME
(Diagram 180-F)

How do I pile the little rocks on the right side of

the teetertotter so that it teeters in the right direction and even affects my choices? I do what I do because I know I'm already accepted. I need to know what God says about me because the truest things about me are what God says about me. Not what you say about me or not what I think about myself, not what the accuser says about me . . . **the truest things about me are what God says about me**, and I need to know what He says.

What we have listed here are twenty-one verses. There are more, but we picked twenty-one. So, if you take one of these a day and work through this process, this could be three weeks' worth of spiritual retreat into the truth of what God says about you. We call this is our "refrigerator page" because you can get a photocopy of this or make a copy and put it right on your refrigerator and see it as you walk around in your house. The truest things about me are what God says about me. What does He say about me? All of these things. Well, let's see what this says.

By the way, we need to consider Romans 12:2 because that is talking about the wrong side of the teetertotter: "And do not be conformed to this world, but be transformed by the renewing of your mind, that you may prove what the will of God is, that which is good and acceptable and perfect." The Phillips says, "Don't let the world squeeze you into its mold." That's why sometimes you can't tell the players without a program, because the Christians and non-Christians look pretty much alike, because they've all been squeezed into the same mold. And a person who's willing to come out from that mold and be different is a person who knows who he is. Haven't you even heard that when you see a teenager on TV and he says, "You know, what I'm really concerned about is this particular issue." And you say: "Boy, there's a guy who knows who he is. He's willing to stand up and be different. I like that. There's a guy who can think for himself. He's not just allowing the world to squeeze him into a mold!" And, as

Christians, we can do the same thing. We know who we are, so we can act accordingly.

There are seven application steps to use with these verses on 180-F. What do you do to work through these verses? You read a verse listed above in its context and you check the cross references. So we've picked out a single verse or two, but read the verses around them. Get the context. Look up some cross references. Do a little study. And start writing down any ideas or thoughts you have. This is a Bible study. When I assign this to people who come in for ministry, I usually only say, "Do one a day or maybe one every other day, and then bring back your notes and let's talk about it." Sometimes, I've been very surprised. I remember one lady as she did this, she came back and shared her notes. She'd done about the first four. They were totally negative. She had a view of God that He was disappointed with her and He didn't like her. That reflected in how she went through this list. I saw there was a problem. We had her do the thing again according to what the truth is, not the deception that she was believing about God.

First, read the verse. So, in other words, you don't just take this and—pfft!—read it all through. Say: "Yep, read that, no big deal. What's the deal? I don't get it!" No. That's like people who say: "The Christian life. You know what? It doesn't work for me. OK? Works for some people; it doesn't work for me." You know why it doesn't work for you? Because it's not a job, it's a relationship. If it were a job, then you have to work it out by your own performance. But it isn't! It's a relationship with a person, and that person totally accepts you and loves you.

So, number 2. You report to God that you believe what He says about you is true. For example, read the verse. Let's say we're going to do Romans 8:27 which says: "I'm a saint."

"Lord, I report to you, I believe it. You say, I'm a saint, I'm a saint."

VCL

VICTORIOUS CHRISTIAN LIVING Conference
Copyright © 1999 Victorious Christian Living International, Inc.

Number 3. Respond to God. Thank Him.

"Father, I believe you when your Word says I'm a saint. I don't feel like one, but that's what you called me. I believe it. Thank you."

Number 4. Recognize what this verse teaches me about God and praise Him for who He is. What does it teach me about God? It teaches me about His power, that He can take a person who is a sinner and change the person to a saint. They've got to be diametrically opposed to each other. What a powerful God! He just didn't say, "Turn over a new leaf." He didn't say, "Try harder." He said, "I'm gonna change you from the inside out."

"Thank You, Lord, for what this teaches me about You."

Number 5. I reject my old view of myself. That would be no longer calling myself names like failure, dummy, stupid, idiot. I don't know if you do that. I used to do that. I had a men's Bible study one time and I said, "Hey, do you guys do any of this?" Every man there said, "Oh, of course." One guy said, "I wouldn't get nearly as much done every day if I didn't keep beating myself up and calling myself names all day." Ha! How sad! What is that? That's external motivation, isn't it? It's me calling myself names. "Come on, get off your duff you stupid, lazy, no-good . . . ."

"OK, OK."

That's instead of the motivation coming from within. It's like working **for** acceptance, even accepting yourself, instead of working **from** acceptance. I am accepted and God does love me, so let's do a good job for Jesus. I'm working as unto Him. So I reject all my old unbiblical views of myself.

Number 6. I rejoice that my mind is being renewed every time I choose the truth. It's

moving the rocks from the left side to the right side and pretty soon I can teeter the proper direction.

Number 7. Receive direction for today as a result of this verse.

"Lord, I see what You have done and who You are. Now, what do You want me to do regarding this truth? As a saint, what do You want me to do today, Lord? How do You want me to function? [Pause] Oh, You want me to pray for those three people? OK, as a saint, I believe I can do that. I can come into Your presence because of who You've made me."

REVIEW

Well, in review: "I am totally accepted by Christ. Christ has made me righteous. I need to believe it, regardless of how I feel or how I act. This truth frees me from trying to gain acceptance from others. I don't have to live a performance-based-acceptance lifestyle. Knowing this truth stops the need to compete and makes decision-making easier. I am not trying to prove anything." I already know who I am. This decision, this task, won't change my identity. My identity is secure because I know who I am. I can do whatever it is, by His power and for His glory.

Well, I believe we need to tell God that we believe this truth. Do you know what you and I need to do? We need to take our little cups that we've been holding out . . . "Would you put something in my cup? Oh, thank you! Would you put something in my cup?" (And it all drains out the bottom.) We need to hold our cup up to the Lord and say, "Would you fill my cup?" Isn't there a song like that? "Fill my cup, Lord / I lift it up, Lord . . . " We need to lift our cup to Him and say, "Lord, I believe that You have totally accepted me. I've got all that I need in You. Go ahead! Fill it up!" And you know what happens? Pretty soon it's overflowing and you've got so much you say: "Here, you guys take some. I've got so much. Here, you take some more acceptance! I can accept you, I can love you, because I have all this acceptance. I know where to get more acceptance. You rejected me? That's OK. I know where to get my cup filled. Here, take some. I've got plenty. Because I know where to get more. Thank You, Lord, for filling my cup."

Let's pray. And as we pray, I'd like to challenge you to do that, to just say: "Lord, I thank You that You've accepted me, and I believe that You've made me righteous, and I accept the fact that You accept me. Thank You for this truth, Lord. May it set us free. We praise You. In Jesus' name, Amen."

GODSHIP ——————————————————————

REJECTION ——————————————————————

EXTERNAL/INTERNAL ——————————————————

PROBLEMS, PROBLEMS, WHY PROBLEMS? ——————

MY FLESH—GOD'S ENEMY ——————————————

REPENTANCE ——————————————————————

WHAT'S NEW ABOUT YOU? ——————————————

ACCEPTING YOUR RIGHTEOUSNESS ————————

EXTENDING FORGIVENESS ——————————▶

SEEKING FORGIVENESS ————————————————

REST, ABIDE, WALK ————————————————————

LOVE ——————————————————————————

GODSHIP

REJECT

EXT/INT

PROBLEMS

FLESH

REPENT

WHAT'S NEW

ACCEPT RIGHT

EXTEND FORGIVE

SEEK FORGIVE

REST

LOVE

EXTENDING FORGIVENESS

> *Be kind to one another, tenderhearted, **forgiving** each other . . . .*
>
> Ephesians 4:32

Nothing is more practical in Christian living than dealing with conflict in human relations. Roommates, church staff members, married couples, fellow missionaries, co-workers, school friends, family members, business partners—all know the hurt, frustration, and disillusionment that discord brings. Is there a sure route to oneness and harmony? What is forgiveness? How can I make it work? What about repeated offenses?

"I can forgive, but I can't forget. What can I do?" "I can forgive others, but I can't forgive myself." "You're asking me to forgive this person for doing THAT?" These kinds of statements are heard daily in the discipling process.

God wants us to live in harmony and unity in the body of Christ. How can that happen? We must make extending forgiveness a way of life. When someone hurts us, we need to extend forgiveness and not, "Let the sun go down on our wrath."

ACHIEVING ONENESS

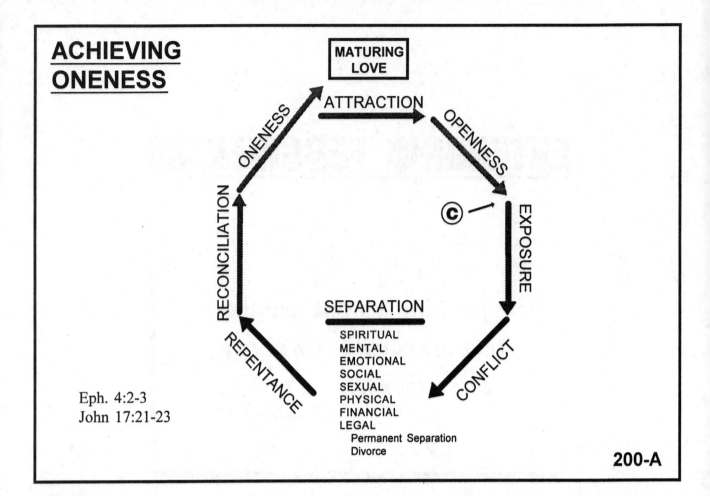

MATURING LOVE

ONENESS → ATTRACTION → OPENNESS → EXPOSURE → CONFLICT

RECONCILIATION ← REPENTANCE

SEPARATION
SPIRITUAL
MENTAL
EMOTIONAL
SOCIAL
SEXUAL
PHYSICAL
FINANCIAL
LEGAL
  Permanent Separation
  Divorce

Eph. 4:2-3
John 17:21-23

©

200-A

NOTES

PURPOSE for Diagram **200-A:**

To illustrate the process of achieving oneness in a relationship.

1. Study John 17:21-23.

2. What was Jesus praying for? _____
   _____

3. Are you experiencing a separation in a relationship now? _____
   _____

4. Since God desires oneness, what area of godship (see Diagram 100-A)
   is keeping you from moving past this separation? _____
   _____

5. Do you withdraw from people to avoid conflict? _____
   _____

> ## . . . *that they may be one.*
> John 17:22

6. Can you see that this withdrawal is another form of separation?
   _____

7. Repentance is the first step back toward oneness. Can you admit to
   God your part in this conflict and separation? _____
   _____

Conflict is inevitable . . . the way to oneness is through it!

VCL _____
VICTORIOUS CHRISTIAN LIVING Conference
Copyright © 1999 Victorious Christian Living International, Inc.

PERSONAL CONFLICT WITHOUT FORGIVENESS

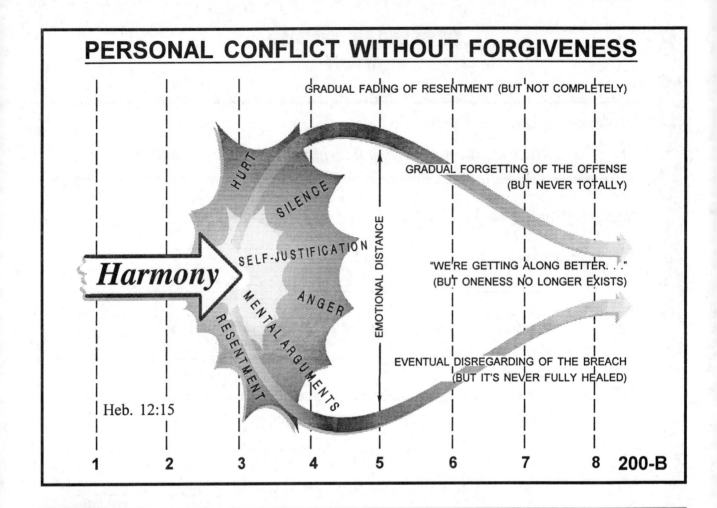

GRADUAL FADING OF RESENTMENT (BUT NOT COMPLETELY)

GRADUAL FORGETTING OF THE OFFENSE
(BUT NEVER TOTALLY)

"WE'RE GETTING ALONG BETTER. . ."
(BUT ONENESS NO LONGER EXISTS)

EVENTUAL DISREGARDING OF THE BREACH
(BUT IT'S NEVER FULLY HEALED)

EMOTIONAL DISTANCE

HURT
SILENCE
SELF-JUSTIFICATION
ANGER
MENTAL ARGUMENTS
RESENTMENT

Harmony

Heb. 12:15

1   2   3   4   5   6   7   8   **200-B**

NOTES

VCL
VICTORIOUS CHRISTIAN LIVING Conference
Copyright © 1999 Victorious Christian Living International, Inc.

PURPOSE for Diagram **200-B**:

To illustrate the effects of unresolved conflicts.

1. Who has hurt you? _____

2. Which of these emotions are you experiencing: anger, bitterness, resentment, desire to seek revenge, or a lack of trust? _____

_____

_____

_____

| **. . . *root of bitterness* . . .** | Heb. 12:15 |

3. Study Hebrews 12:15.

4. Is there a root of bitterness toward anyone in a present or past relationship? _____

5. Are you ready to tear up that root? _____

_____

_____

Time does not heal any wounds!

CONTINUAL CONFLICT WITHOUT FORGIVENESS

Proverbs 16:18
Proverbs 28:25
1 Peter 5:5

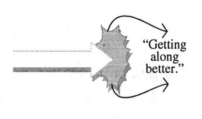

"Getting along better."

"Things are OK now."

"Guess that's just the way life is."

"It's no use."

A
PRETENDING

B
TOLERATING

C
RESIGNED

D
GIVING UP

200-C

NOTES

VCL
VICTORIOUS CHRISTIAN LIVING Conference
Copyright © 1999 Victorious Christian Living International, Inc.

Extending Forgiveness
STUDY GUIDE

PURPOSE for Diagram **200-C**:

To illustrate the effects of unresolved conflict
when time is allowed to pass without forgiveness.

1. Which of the four explosions best describe your relationship with the person who has hurt you?

   A   B   C   D

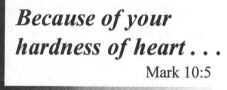

Because of your hardness of heart . . .
Mark 10:5

2. Study Ephesians 4:32.

3. What is commanded in these verses? _____

   _____

   _____

4. What is keeping you from obeying God's command? _____

   _____

   _____

5. Study Proverbs 16:18.

6. Could it be your own pride or self-protection? _____

7. Do those who have hurt you deserve your forgiveness? _____

   _____

8. Study Colossians 1:13-14.

9. Has God forgiven you? Did you deserve it? _____

   _____

No forgiveness, know loneliness.
Know forgiveness, no loneliness.

EXTENDING FORGIVENESS

> **Extending forgiveness is taking the time to consider how a person has hurt me. This would include listing the act, my hurt, the ramifications, and my sinful reactions. Then I depend on the indwelling forgiver, Jesus, as I extend grace to the offender just as Jesus extended grace to me.**

I. WHAT FORGIVING IS NOT

When I endeavor to understand forgiveness—what it is and how it works—much time and effort can be saved and misunderstanding avoided, if I eliminate what forgiveness is NOT. It is not ignoring, disregarding, tolerating, excusing, overlooking, or closing my eyes to the wrong another person has done against me. It is not simply letting time pass after the offense has been committed. It is not forgetting that the offense happened—or pretending that it didn't. It is not just resigning myself to the other person's actions by saying, "Well, that's just the way that person is."

II. WHY FORGIVENESS IS NECESSARY

A. If I don't exercise true forgiveness, I continue to hold the offender responsible (guilty) for the wrong. This can result in an accumulated "treasure" of fault in my mind toward the offender all ready to be "cashed in" when I feel the situation calls for it.

B. Without forgiveness, an attitude of unforgiveness fosters resentment, and this crystalizes into bitterness (Hebrews 12:15). This can make me harsh, critical, cynical, and mistrustful. Forgiveness breaks the bondage of bitterness.

C. Without true forgiveness, I may secretly await the "joy" of seeing the offender punished by God—and be delighted when it happens. This is a form of vengeance which is godship.

D. Not forgiving may cause problems in relating to another person who reminds me of the initial offender.

> *Do not rejoice when your enemy falls, / And do not let your heart be glad when he stumbles; / Lest the Lord see it and be displeased, / And He turn away His anger from him.* Proverbs 24:17-18

> *Never take vengeance into your own hands. Stand back and let God punish, if He will.* Romans 12:19 (PHILLIPS)

III. THE PROCESS OF EXTENDING FORGIVENESS

A. I need to make four lists. First, I list what this person did or didn't do that affected me. Second, I list all the hurt I have felt regarding this offense. I think of all the emotions I've experienced and write them down. These feelings could include being: embarrassed, belittled, devastated, defiled, hustled, cheated, or ridiculed. Third, I list all the ramifications of the offense. How did this action affect me spiritually, psychologically, physically, socially, financially, maritally, or parentally?

200-D (2 pages)

This clarifies HOW the offense has affected me. Another ramification is that I can develop "rotten reasoning" about God, myself, or others. For example: God can't be trusted; all men are horrible; or I will never love anyone again. Fourth, I list my sinful reactions regarding this offense. That would include such things as: bitterness, gossip, revenge, slander, rage, and abusive speech. This could include any grudge I may be holding. This could also include an attitude of unforgiveness.

B. Now I check page 8A and use the keys of forgiveness on Diagram 200-E2.

C. This completes human forgiveness.

D. Destroy the list.

NOTE: Do not tell the offender he/she is forgiven. The forgiving of a person does not require that the person be told. Telling the person may simply create more conflict. Your forgiveness of him/her was between you and God alone.

- Forgiving the offender deals with unforgiveness which was your side of the breach. The offender may never seek your forgiveness. If or when he/she does, all you need to say is, "I am so thankful that you asked me. Yes, I do forgive you."

E. If his/her offense is of a persistent nature that disrupts Christian harmony, God may lead you to confront the person with his/her need—after you have exercised forgiveness toward him/her.

- The first objective of such a confrontation is to purify the church.

- The secondary purpose is to "win" or "restore" the offender.

- The pattern for confrontation is given in Matthew 18:15-17 and Proverbs 25:9.

- The attitude required on the part of the confronter is spelled out in Galatians 6:1-2.

I AM THE OFFENDED

1

OFFENDED

When I am offended, in my mind I see the offender as guilty (James 4:12). Only God has the right to execute judgment (Ps. 9:7-8; Acts 17:31). My attempt to lay guilt on the offender by setting a standard is reacting after the flesh. For example: "This person should not have treated me that way" (Matthew 7:1-5).

200-E

NOTES

VCL

VICTORIOUS CHRISTIAN LIVING Conference
Copyright © 1999 Victorious Christian Living International, Inc.

PURPOSE for Diagram **200-E:**

To describe how an offended person acts like a judge.

? 1. Where do you see yourself in this diagram? _____

📖 2. Study James 4:12.

? 3. What is God's message to you? _____
_____
_____

📖 4. Study Psalm 9:7-8 and Acts 17:31.

? 5. Who is the only One who is qualified to be The Judge? _____

> *. . . who are you to judge your neighbor.*
> James 4:17

? 6. Can you see how you have tried to play god by judging this person? _____

No one made me the judge.

THE RESULT OF MY FLESHLY REACTIONS

2

I may react silently and "stuff" my bitterness or wrath. Or I may express it in abusive speech or actions, slander, or swearing. The result is the same.

Ephesians 4:26-27, 31-32
1 Peter 5:8-9
Ecclesiastes 7:9

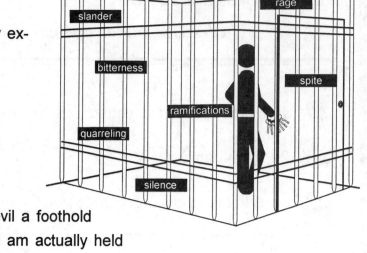

Going to bed angry gives the Devil a foothold to torment me, a child of God. I am actually held prisoner by reacting after the flesh. This control of the flesh and torment by the Devil can only be stopped by extending forgiveness. The offender should ask forgiveness from me, but may never do so. Consequently, I must initiate forgiveness. Notice: I have the keys to freedom in my hand.

200-E1

NOTES

VCL
VICTORIOUS CHRISTIAN LIVING Conference
Copyright © 1999 Victorious Christian Living International, Inc.

PURPOSE for Diagram **200-E1:**

To illustrate the result of judging someone "guilty."

1. Study Ephesians 4:31-32.

2. Which of the jail cell bars apply to you? _____
   _____

3. Study Ephesians 4:26-27.

> *. . . do not let the*
> *sun go down on*
> *your anger . . .*
> Eph. 4:26

4. When do you need to extend forgiveness?
   _____
   Have you done it yet?_____

5. What happens if you don't do it?
   _____

6. Study 1 Peter 5:8-9.

7. What does Satan want to do to you? _____
   _____

8. Do you want to get out of jail? _____

The unjust judge goes to jail.

EXTEND FORGIVE

I CHOOSE TO EXTEND FORGIVENESS

3

I can achieve freedom by extending forgiveness. By using these keys I am set free from the prison and torment. Now the truth about me can be seen and realized.

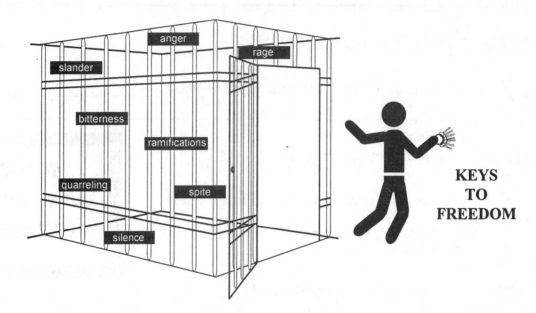

anger
rage
slander
bitterness
ramifications
quarreling
spite
silence

KEYS TO FREEDOM

Key #1 -   I admit to God how I felt regarding this offense (Psalm 62:8).

Key #2 -   I admit to God that I have been holding the person guilty for the act, the hurt, and the ramifications of the offense (Luke 6:37; Rom. 2:1).

Key #3 -   I now extend (give freely) my forgiveness to the person for that action, my hurt, and the ramifications of the action. This forgiveness is extending grace to the offender as Christ extended grace to me (Eph. 4:32; Col. 3:13).

Key #4 -   I now put the offender into God's hands and let go. I will allow God to work in this person's life in His time (1 Peter 5:7).

Key #5 -   I now name and confess (agree with God) that my sinful reactions and attitudes (including holding the offender guilty) were wrong. I ask God to show me areas of godship and repent (1 John 1:9).

Key #6 -   I choose to live as the new creation that I am (2 Cor. 5:17). This means I accept that God has forgiven me, and I lay aside my fleshly reactions (Eph. 4:31; Col. 3:8, 12).

Key #7 -   I tell God I am willing to be reconciled to the offender and allow Him to love the offender through me (2 Cor. 5:18; Col. 3:14; Heb. 12:14).

200-E2

PURPOSE for Diagram **200-E2:**

To give specific steps (keys) to freedom gained only through forgiveness.

1. Write down exactly how the offender has offended you.

   _____

? 2. What are your feelings regarding that offense? _____

   _____

? 3. What are the ramifications (effects) of that offense? _____

   _____

? 4. What were your sinful reactions to the offense? _____

   _____

Now free yourself from the prison of this offense by applying the keys of forgiveness!

✔ 5. Check off each key as you finish it.
   - [ ] #1
   - [ ] #2
   - [ ] #3
   - [ ] #4
   - [ ] #5
   - [ ] #6
   - [ ] #7

> *. . . do not judge . . .*
> *. . . do not condemn . . .*
> *. . . pardon . . . .*
> Luke 6:37

EXTEND
FORGIVE

Freedom to love and live again!

PERSONAL CONFLICT WITH TRUE FORGIVENESS

> "Let all bitterness and wrath and anger and clamor and slander be put away from you, along with all malice. And be kind to one another, tender-hearted, forgiving each other, just as God in Christ also has forgiven you."
>
> Ephesians 4:31-32

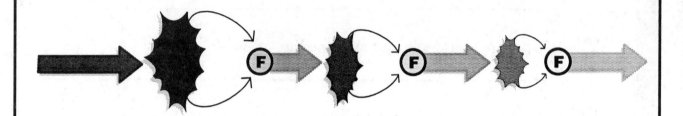

MATTHEW 18:21-22

200-F

VCL
VICTORIOUS CHRISTIAN LIVING Conference

PURPOSE for Diagrams **200-F**:

To illustrate the effects of forgiveness.

---

 1. Study Matthew 18:21-22.

2. What principle regarding forgiveness do you see in these passages?

_____

_____

_____

> ...*I will remember their sins no more.*
>
> Heb. 8:12

3. If this person offends you again will you forgive them? _____

Forgiveness is a lifestyle.

TESTS OF FORGIVENESS

A. Do you see the offender as not guilty?

B. Are you sincerely thanking God for the lessons learned during the pain (Romans 8:28-29)?

C. Can you talk about your hurt without getting angry, without feeling resentful, without the slightest thought of revenge (Ephesians 4:31)?

D. Do you have a willingness to accept your part of the blame for what happened?

E. Can you revisit the scene or the person(s) involved in your hurt without experiencing a negative reaction?

F. Are you rewarding with good those who have hurt you (Romans 12:20-21)?

200-G

NOTES

VCL
VICTORIOUS CHRISTIAN LIVING Conference
Copyright © 1999 Victorious Christian Living International, Inc.

Extending Forgiveness
STUDY GUIDE

PURPOSE for Diagrams **200-G:**

To verify that forgiveness has happened by the use if six tests.

1. Study Matthew 6:12.

2. Go through the tests of forgiveness.

3. Did you pass the test? _____

4. Have you forgiven all the ramifications? _____

5. Study Romans 8:1.

6. How does God see you since you
   became a Christian? _____
   _____
   _____

> *Mercy triumphs over judgment.*
> James 2:13

7. How do you see the person who offended you? _____
   _____

8. How would God want you to love this person now? _____
   _____

*Forgiving is not holding
another guilty.*

REVIEW

- God commands us to forgive others when they hurt or offend us.

- This is essential to live with impossible people.

- Pride will stand in the way of extending forgiveness.

- Extending forgiveness is not a thought or a feeling, it is a definite action.

- If I refuse to forgive someone who hurts me, I can end up in a jail of my own fleshly reactions and be tormented by the enemy.

- It does take time to do this because I need to write out the offense, my hurt, the ramifications, and my sinful reactions. Then I need to use the seven keys of forgiveness.

NOTES

Let's talk about a very, very important subject— the subject of extending forgiveness. As I think about the subject of extending forgiveness, I'm reminded of a story that Paul Harvey told. He told a story about two men who went fishing in central Texas. Bob and George were two good old boys that were retired and just had a lot of free time. They went out fishing 2 or 3 times a week. On one of their fishing trips, while their poles were in the water and they were just relaxing, George did something he really enjoyed doing, he removed his dentures. He could never do that at home, but he could do it out in the boat. It just felt so good. He put them on the back seat of the boat and went on fishing. After a little while Bob noticed these dentures on the seat of the boat and decided to play a practical joke. So he picked them up and put them in his pocket. Then he took his dentures out and put them in place of George's just to see what would happen. Well, a little while later George, who had originally put his dentures there, went to retrieve them. He picked them up, put them in his mouth, and tried to adjust them a little bit and took them right back out. He said, "You know, Bob, these things have never fit right and I'm not going to stand it anymore." And he threw them out into the lake. Now there's Bob with George's dentures in his pocket. What's he going to do? He takes those dentures out and turns around and says, "You know, George, these things have never really fit me that well either." And he threw his dentures out into the lake. Hundreds of dollars worth of dentures settled to the bottom of the lake. If these two guys had ever told what they did that day, they would need to extend forgiveness to each other. I don't know if they ever told.

This is a very, very important subject. In fact, just before I began teaching, one of the lady counselors said this is such an important subject she uses this every week when she counsels with someone, because it is something that comes up again and again. Many times as I begin counseling, I ask people to make 2 lists—on one, list all of the people who have hurt you and on the other, list all of the people that you have hurt. Which list do you think is longer? It's the list of people that have hurt you.

This lesson deals with that list. **What do I do with the people who have hurt me?** Forgiveness is very important in God's work. Think about Joseph in the Old Testament. Joseph was a guy who needed to extend forgiveness. His brothers threw him into a dry well. I don't know if that was good or bad. I don't know if you want water to break your fall or you just want to land on the dirt. But they threw him in a well, then took him out of the well, and sold him to the Ishmaelites who took him to Egypt. He went to work at Potiphar's palace and Potiphar's wife falsely accused him. He went to jail, and while he was in jail a couple of people were sent there from the palace. They told Joseph their dreams and he interpreted their dreams correctly. The baker was killed. The other man, the king's cupbearer, was restored to his work. And Joseph said, "When you get back up there and you're working next to the king, don't forget me down here in the pit." The guy said, "Sure, no problem." Remember how long it was that he forgot him? Two years more Joseph sat in prison. One day the king, Pharaoh, had a dream. Nobody could interpret it. And the king's cupbearer said "Oh, wait a minute. I remember a guy who does dreams. When we were in prison. You remember the baker, the guy that made that bad strudel that time, remember him? Remember how you got rid of him? You killed him and you put me in prison. This guy is good. His name is Joseph."

So they sent for Joseph. Joseph came in before the king and the king said, "I've got a dream and nobody can interpret it." Remember what Joseph said? He said: "You know what king, I really don't want to hear your problems. I want to tell you about some of my problems. I want to talk about my brothers, 11 of them. These guys are real jerks. You know what they did? Let me tell you what they did." Joseph explains about his brothers. "And you remember that woman over there? I never touched that woman and I went to jail. I didn't lay a hand on her. And then, you, you forgot me for 2 years. No, I'm ticked. I'm not going to do dreams." Is that what he said? No. Joseph, I believe, had learned how to forgive all the way along so that when that big moment came, he was right, he was ready and he did do a very important job in interpreting that dream.

This lesson will bring great freedom into your life if it's applied again and again. I've used it many, many times in my life. I've even been able to forgive people and not remember later what it was they did or said to me. It's an amazing thing as you walk through how to extend forgiveness. I've seen it literally set hundreds of people free and it can do the same for you.

ACHIEVING ONENESS
(Diagram 200-A)
Let's turn to your first diagram, 200-A, "Achieving Oneness." This is an octagon. It starts out with the word "attraction." Under the word attraction you can put some pluses on your diagram, because when two people begin to get to know each other there is an attraction. There is a desire to have that relationship grow because they like what they see in that other

person. This could be two people who may end up in marriage, it could be two people who are going to go into business together, or it could be two people who are going to be college roommates. But, as they spend time together, there's an attraction.

Then there's openness. You can put some more pluses under that word "openness" because they begin to share more and talk more and reveal more as they spend time together. That eventually leads to the big "C."

See that "C" on your diagram. Under that "C" you can write the word "commitment." If they're dating, the commitment is getting married or if they're going to be roommates the commitment is signing a lease. If they are going into business together, it's the contract. They are committed. With one's expertise in selling and the other's expertise in organizing the office they ought to make a killing and so they go into business.

Now we have "exposure." Right beside the word exposure you need to put a couple of minus signs. These are negatives. There are two kinds of exposure. There's external exposure, what I see in you that I don't like. There's also internal exposure, what I see in me that I don't like. I remember when I was dating Susan, the girl that I eventually married. She found some external things about me that she didn't like. What she didn't like were my clothes. She said, "I wonder, if it would be possible, if I could look in your closet." We had been dating a while so I felt comfortable with her looking in my closet, because I had some neat suits and clothes. I had little red and white check things, I had some polyester pants that were so sharp you could cut bread on the seam of those pants. I thought I had some good clothes. She looked at my clothes and said, "Oh, this is sad. Everything stretches and it's all polyester and fake and there's nothing here that's breathing and alive." I didn't know what she was talking about. This isn't a zoo, it's a closet. She was talking about

VCL
VICTORIOUS CHRISTIAN LIVING Conference
Copyright © 1999 Victorious Christian Living International, Inc.

cotton and wool. She said, "I hate your clothes. I like you, but I can't stand how you dress." That's external exposure. She was able to throw those things away and now when I walk, I breathe because I have all natural material that she enjoys.

There's also internal exposure. I find out things about myself that I don't like. Obviously, it's your fault because I never acted like that until I met you. I didn't know that I was impatient until I had a child. That is one of the best ways to find out how impatient you are. You can find that out in your relationship.

Business partners get together and they start to have conflicts because they're finding out: yes, he's organized, but he's also meticulous and picky and perfectionistic. I don't like that part. He's coming in every day and redoing my office and straightening out my desk. Everything is all moved around. I don't like that. I'm getting upset. I never used to be this upset. It's his problem. We need to dissolve this relationship. These external and internal exposures cause conflict.

That's the next word, "conflict." Three words you'll want to write next to the word "conflict"— conflicts are normal, conflicts are neutral, and conflicts are natural. They will happen. You can't put two people together without having conflict. The problem is not that there is a conflict. Many people try to prevent conflicts. They say: "Peace at any price; don't rock the boat; let's make sure we're friends, we're not going to have any disagreements because we're Christians and we won't argue; there won't be conflicts, the Lord will protect us from that." No, conflicts will happen.

In the Bible there were many godly, spiritual men who had conflicts. Paul and Peter had a conflict. The problem is not the conflict. It's what I do with it and how I handle it, because the conflict often produces separation. We have a whole list here of separations that occur all the way down to some kind of a permanent separation or even a divorce. Now the separation in itself is not necessarily a bad thing. God permits separation to get our attention, to wake us up to realize something is wrong in this relationship. Something needs to be dealt with.

Many times when people come for counseling they say: "I've just realized I've got a real problem with this other person. Let's talk about how we can fix this other person, because I know this person is the problem, I'm not. This person is a problem. Maybe, you can help me cope with this person." The separation is to get a person's attention to work on himself or herself, not to try to fix the other person, but that's what many people think. If I can fix that person then we're done, we've solved the problem because that person is the problem. Romans 14:12 says, "So then every one of us shall give account of himself to God." When I talk to God he isn't going to say, "Let me talk to you about your wife." He's going to say, " I want to talk to you about you."

That moves us to repentance. When we begin to see what we've done and we want to be reconciled, there needs to be repentance. First, repentance toward God and then, second, repentance toward the people that have been offended. When there is repentance there can be reconciliation.

There are three parts to reconciliation. Somebody has to seek forgiveness. Then the person who has been offended will extend forgiveness and they can rebuild the relationship. We're going to deal with the second part of that today, extending forgiveness. Seeking forgiveness and rebuilding the relationship are covered in the "Seeking Forgiveness" lesson. Once reconciliation happens, then there is oneness and maturing love. Then you can have more attraction and more openness and even more exposure. We go around and around that circle. The more times you go around the deeper the relationship becomes. That's a good thing. However, many people stop at the conflict phase or they stop at the separation phase. Here's what happens if you do.

PERSONAL CONFLICT WITHOUT FORGIVENESS (Diagram 200-B)

The next diagram, 200-B, is "Personal Conflict Without Forgiveness." Here's a question, "What do most people do when there is a conflict?" Nothing. They don't do anything. They just think it will get better. Time heals all wounds. That's a verse out of some book in the Old Testament. Right? No, it's not even in the Bible. Notice the harmony arrow. Then observe the conflict explosion. Then there is hurt, silence, anger, and resentment and there's a big emotional distance between these two people. The vertical lines indicate time passing. Numbers 1 through 8 could be days, weeks, or months. There are four statements there and in each one of them I want you to circle the same word. It's the word "b-u-t, but." There's a gradual fading of resentment, **but** not completely, gradual forgetting of the offense, **but** never totally. We're getting along better, **but** oneness no longer exists. There's eventual disregarding of the breach, **but** it's never fully healed. There needs to be reconciliation. There needs to be the seeking and extending of forgiveness.

CONTINUAL CONFLICT WITHOUT FORGIVENESS (Diagram 200-C)

If you go on to the next diagram, 200-C, "Continual Conflict Without Forgiveness," you'll see what happens if this pattern continues. You see the explosions are getting bigger and a person says: "Well I'm pretending, this is okay I think. I'm tolerating it. I'm resigned—I guess that's the way it is. I give up; it is no use." Many times as I counsel married people and I show them this diagram I say, "Where would you say your relationship is right now?" I have a lot of little pen marks on that letter "d."

"It's no use. We're right here. We're ready to give up this whole thing." I was just thinking today that this diagram is a lot like flossing your teeth. Why do you floss your teeth? You floss your teeth so that tartar doesn't build up on your teeth, because when you go to your dentist he says: "Oh my goodness, look at all this. We're going to have to really grind and scrape to get rid of this." Then you think, "Why didn't I floss for the last six months to stop the buildup." By extending forgiveness as soon as you are offended, you remove that potential buildup so it doesn't get worse. So a new offense isn't built on the last one and pretty soon you just blow up, because there's too much buildup. How do you remove the buildup? By extending forgiveness all the way along—even if it is not requested.

EXTENDING FORGIVENESS (Diagram 200-D)

Let's look at " Extending Forgiveness," 200-D, on the next page. Here's a definition: Extending forgiveness is taking the time to consider how a person has hurt me. This would include listing the act, my hurt, the ramifications, and my sinful reactions. Then I depend on the indwelling forgiver, Jesus, as I extend grace to the offender just as Jesus extended grace to me. That's the important thing to remember. There are times when people hurt you so severely that you do not want to forgive them. Even as you think about it, you say they don't even deserve to be forgiven. That may be true. I don't know about you, but I don't think I deserved to be forgiven by the Lord. Did you? What did we do to get forgiveness from God? What did we do to deserve it?

I remember ministering to a guy one day who was an ex-con. He'd been in jail for twenty-some years, and he said, "the thing that really impresses me about God is that He is not fair." I said, "What?" He said, "If God were fair, I'd be in hell today." I'd never thought about it like that. Here is a guy who has been punished by society by being put in jail, and when he thought about God, he said, "Of all the things I've done,

VCL
VICTORIOUS CHRISTIAN LIVING Conference
Copyright © 1999 Victorious Christian Living International, Inc.

if God were really fair, He'd toast me. This whole thing of forgiveness isn't fair. God shouldn't have forgiven me, but He did." You think: "It isn't fair that I have to forgive this person, because it won't even change the person or it won't change the past." No it won't, but aren't you glad that God wasn't fair to us, that He forgave us and extended grace? What is grace? God giving me what I don't deserve. That's grace.

Next, "What Forgiving Is Not." This is really important, especially, as I try to walk through forgiveness with people who need to forgive their parents. Well, Mom and Dad did the best they could. My dad never showed love to me. I don't ever remember him ever saying "I love you" or hugging me. He never did that. I can remember old Grandpa Sellers. He was the same way. Old Grandpa Sellers died in Cincinnati, Ohio, on skid row. He was a drunk. He was a tough old bird. He never told my dad he loved him, so why would my dad tell me that he loved me. That's not forgiving, that's excusing. Another thing is tolerating or just overlooking or just letting time pass or saying: "Well, that's just the way he is. He's just a cranky old person." That's not forgiving.

So why is it important that I do forgive? Because if I don't exercise forgiveness there are several things that can happen.

I can continue to hold this person guilty and actually treasure up what they have done. I've got a book at my house called *Love, Marriage, and Trading Stamps*. I've never read it and probably never will, but I just love the title. Do you get the picture? Every time there's an offense I put a little trading stamp in it. I fill a page up, go to the next page, fill the whole book up and save it. When an event happens that reminds me of the offenses in the book, I gather them up and cash them in. The person may say, "What did I do to get all that wrath?"

"What you did was that, that, that, that, and that and I haven't forgotten one of them."

Without forgiveness, I can foster resentment and I can become bitter. Hebrews 12:15 talks about a root of bitterness. Don't let a root of bitterness grow in you. Many will be defiled. Who can be defiled? Anybody who is around you who will listen to you. Have you ever talked to any bitter older people? They tell you about all the people who did them wrong and they'll remember all the events: "Yeah, I remember 37 years ago when that man borrowed my lawn mower and when he brought it back it was broken. I'll never forget that." I don't want to be a bitter old man, but if I don't forgive that's what can happen.

I can secretly await the "joy" of seeing this person punished by God. What is that? That is a form of godship. One of the areas of godship is revenge and vengeance. "Vengeance is mine," says the Lord. "Do not rejoice when your enemy falls, / And do not let your heart be glad when he stumbles; / Lest the Lord see it and be displeased, / And He turn away His anger from him" (Proverbs 24:17–18).

"But he deserves something."

Well, let God do the something. Don't you try to mete out the punishment, let God do it. He's got a lot more resources. He's got a lot more power. God can really affect someone's life. We're pretty puny in our attempts to try to do it, so let God do it. And then in Romans 12:19 in the *Phillips*, "Never take vengeance into your own hands. Stand back and let God punish, if He will."

Not forgiving may cause problems with other people who remind you of someone you haven't forgiven. I remember ministering to a man who had an awful time with his boss. His boss was a lady. He would come in and say, "I've got to forgive my boss. Here is what she did." So we talked about what she did. We walked through this very process that I am showing you today. The next week he came in and said, "Well, we've got to do it again." I said, "Man, this is really getting to be repetitious." He said, "Yeah." All of a sudden it dawned on him and he said, "Do you know why?" I said, "Why?" He said, "We're forgiving the wrong woman." I said, "Well, she's the one offending you." He said: "I know, but it's my mother. She's the one I haven't forgiven. She's the one who broke promises to me when I was a little boy about 5 years old. We were having financial problems and she said, 'We're going to have to do something for just a weekend. I'm going to take you to this place and we'll be back Monday to get you.'" It was an orphanage. He stayed there for 14 years. He had never forgiven his mother for that, and now because of his mom, he resented any woman in authority who tries to tell him what to do.

What's the process of extending forgiveness? Whenever I go through this process, I use four, 3 x 5 cards. You can use 4 x 6 or 8½ x 11 depending on the offense, but have four sheets of paper. On the first sheet of paper, I have the person list what the person did or didn't do that was offensive. You can help the person think through it. Just list the facts of the offense.

"But the person meant well."

"I know, but did they do that, did it hurt you?"

"Yes."

"Okay. Write it down."

On the second sheet, the person lists all of the feelings—all of the hurt. For example: embarrassed, belittled, devastated, defiled, hustled, cheated. We have even compiled a list of many "feeling" words that we can use to help people identify with their feelings.

The third list—ramifications. When we get to the ramifications phase, we look at all seven areas of life because, the way I see it, the offense is like a rock. The rock hits the water and that's what the person did. But the ramifications are all the ripples that have gone out from that offense. The offense may have happened 10 years ago, but I'm still living with some of the ramifications. Think about a person going through a divorce, for example. The divorce may be the offense, but what are the ramifications? What are those ramifications with childcare? There are financial problems. There may even be physical problems because of having to work two jobs. There are social problems. The people in my church don't want anything to do with me now because I've been divorced. There are spiritual problems because I'm a little bit ticked with God. Why did God let this happen? You have to look at all those ramifications. Many times when someone forgives another person, the person doesn't consider the ramifications of that offense and that's why it doesn't feel finished.

The last list is the person's sinful reactions regarding this offense. What the other person did was wrong, but did you do anything wrong? Most people are willing to admit, "Yeah, not outwardly, maybe just inwardly."

"What were they?"

"Well there was bitterness and anger and hate and resentment."

There can also be gossip and slander or trying to get even—revenge. Those are all sinful reactions.

Now we go to Diagram E-2 and use the keys of forgiveness. We'll talk about that when we get to Diagram E-2. What do you do after you get done with these lists and you walk through extending forgiveness? You tear up all those lists. I have a great big pickle jar in my office that's about three-quarters full of torn up pieces of paper from people who have walked through extending forgiveness to others. **Don't tell the person they are forgiven.** That could actually make things a little more difficult. **This is just between you and the Lord.** So after you do this lesson, you may forgive your mom or your dad and then call them up tomorrow and say, "Hi, mom, dad, you know what, I just heard a neat teaching about extending forgiveness."

"Oh, really, that's nice."

"And so I forgave you."

"For what? What do you mean you forgave me? You were the one who was ungrateful. I tried the best I could to raise you and you're forgiving me?"

Don't do that. Don't go to work Monday morning and say to your boss "Hey, I went to a neat conference over the weekend. I learned how to forgive people and you were right on top of the list. I feel a lot better now that I have forgiven you." Don't do that. However, if someone that you have forgiven comes to you a week or two after you've forgiven them and they say, "The Holy Spirit has been convicting me. I haven't been treating you right. I remember what I said to you or what I did to you. Would you please forgive me?" Don't say, "Oh, I'm a lot more spiritual than you are. I did that about 2 weeks ago. I'm glad that you're seeing that offense and that you're able to catch up to where I am." Don't do that either. It's trying to be hyperspiritual. Just say, "Sure, I'd be glad to forgive you. Thank you very much."

Now, if this offense is of a persistent nature, and disrupts Christian harmony, then you may need to confront the person, but you have to have already exercised forgiveness toward that person. The objective is not to punish them or get even or anything like that, it's to purify the church and win or restore the offender. You can check Matthew 18 and Proverbs 25:9 for a

pattern of doing that. The attitude is found in Galatians 6:1–2. I remember one man who found his wife reading romance novels and he decided that was wrong and he told her to quit. She said, "I don't want to. I don't get much romance with you so I find it in these books." He decided to bring that before the church. He said, "What if this Sunday I tell our whole Sunday school class what you've been doing?" That's when she hit him. She smacked him right in the mouth. She said, "You'd better not tell the whole Sunday school class." So there are times when you don't want to tell everyone, especially when it's regarding your spouse. He needed to forgive her and tell no one else.

Let's look at the process. We have some pictures that will illustrate what we've just been looking at. The reason we're doing this is because the process of extending forgiveness has been too simple, too quick, too easy. Someone offends you, the person comes to you and says, "You know what I did yesterday, what I said to you?"

"Yeah, that really hurt."

"Well, I was wrong. Will you forgive me?"

And you say, "Okay." Pretty simple. What we are trying to do is stretch out and make this a little longer and a little more detailed so that we really think through what's happening when we extend forgiveness to someone.

I AM THE OFFENDED (Diagram 200-E)
Go to Diagram 200-E, "I Am the Offended." Here we have a little court scene. You are the offended person. In your mind when you think about the fact that you've been offended, you see yourself as the judge. So now you put on the judge's robe. You sit down and pick up the gavel. The offender is standing there, he's got his hands behind his back, handcuffed. You bring down the gavel and say, "You're guilty, buddy, and I'm going to sentence you to 2 weeks of silence or revenge of some kind or

some kind of punishment."

The only problem is we are not equipped to do that. I love what James 4:12 says. It says, "There is only one Lawgiver and Judge, the One who is able to save and to destroy; but who are you who judge your neighbor?" Who do you think you are, God? God can do it. Psalm 9:8 says, " He will judge the world in righteousness." He is the judge. Shall not the judge of all the earth do right? The reason He can be the judge is that He is sinless. You and I are not. You and I don't have the credentials to be a judge. We don't have the spiritual credentials that God does. So, your attempt to lay guilt on this person by setting a standard is reacting after the flesh. For example: "This person should not have treated me that way"—whatever it was. I've written it generically so that it would fit any situation.

THE RESULT OF MY FLESHLY REACTIONS (Diagram 200-E1)

The only problem is that the judge goes to jail, not the offender, not the prisoner. He's out running around, isn't that true? He's out running around and you're the one feeling all beaten up and hurt. You're in jail. Look at the bars of that jail—slander, bitterness, quarreling, silence, ramifications. There are all the ramifications we've talked about. Some of those ramifications can also be unreasonable thinking or "stinking thinking." For example, a ramification could be because a man hurt me, then I think all men will hurt me and I will never trust another man. Another ramification could be because of what that person did, and God permitted it, I'm not sure I can even trust God. That's stinking thinking or "rotten reasoning."

You can silently deal with this or you can deal with it in a noisy manner. You can have abusive speech, even swearing. The result is the same. If I go to bed angry, I can give the Devil a foothold. Ephesians 4:26–27 says, "BE ANGRY, AND yet DO NOT SIN; do not let the sun go down on your anger, and do not give the devil an opportunity." Do not give the Devil an opportunity. That word "opportunity" has a footnote in my Bible that says "a place." The NIV translates it "a foothold." The Greek word is *topos*. It means a geographical location. In other words, as I allow the enemy to affect me by not extending forgiveness, he begins to torment me. Have you ever met people who are really tormented, they're angry? It could be because people have offended them and they have not extended forgiveness. Going to bed angry gives the Devil a foothold to torment me, a child of God, and I'm actually held prisoner by reacting after the flesh. So this control of the flesh, torment by the Devil, can only be stopped by extending forgiveness. Now the offender should ask you to forgive them, but, as my mother used to say, don't hold your breath, they may never do it. But you can initiate forgiveness. Notice, you've got the keys in your hand, the keys to freedom. There are 7, a perfect number.

The interesting thing about this, this jail is a little like the one that used to be on the Andy Griffith Show. Do you remember Otis, the town drunk? Old Otis would come in all lathered up with some kind of liquor and he'd say, "Andy, I have to spend the night in jail." And Andy would say, "That's all right, Otis. The keys are right there." So Otis would pick the keys up and unlock the jail, put himself in, then hang the keys up outside and then when he'd sobered up in the morning, he'd reach out and get the keys and let himself out. Well, that's the exciting thing about this jail. You can let yourself out, you do not have to stay there.

Oswald Chambers said this, "If there is the tiniest grudge in your mind against anyone, from that second your spiritual penetration into the knowledge of God stops." It's very unwise to go around holding grudges. I like what he says, "from that second your spiritual penetration into the knowledge of God stops." Do you want to

VCL

VICTORIOUS CHRISTIAN LIVING Conference
Copyright © 1999 Victorious Christian Living International, Inc.

know more about the Lord, do you want to grow in the Christian life, do you want to live a victorious Christian life? Here are the keys, get out of jail, forgive that person, don't let that grudge stymie your spiritual growth.

I CHOOSE TO EXTEND FORGIVENESS (Diagram 200-E2)

Diagram 200-E2, "I Choose to Extend Forgiveness." See the little guy, he's out of jail, he's holding his keys, and the door is open, he's free! I can achieve freedom by extending forgiveness and using these keys. I am set free from the prison and the torment. There are seven keys. Let's just go through these quickly. The way I use this in ministering to someone is that the person has the four lists we already made. I tell them to use their lists and pray with their eyes open, that's okay. For some people, that's a little scary. It is amazing how it works.

Last Sunday I did this in an adult Sunday school class of about 15 people. I asked for a volunteer. "Who would like to extend forgiveness to someone?" It was really interesting because a man said "I would." So I passed the 3 x 5 cards over to him and said, "All right, what was it that your wife did or didn't do? What was the act?" He said, "Oh no, it's not what she has done, it's what I have done." I said, "Oh, it's what you have done. Hand the list to your wife." So she took the cards and I said, "What did he do?" We went through extending forgiveness. It was really neat to see this played out.

Afterward, one of the men said, "Wow, that was exciting. That was like spiritual surgery. I felt like I had my mask on. There was blood all over the place. There was bad stuff that was taken out. There was healing brought right before our eyes. There was death and then there was life through extending forgiveness." And the man got to see it happen. He sat there and watched it. That's exciting. You can do this even with the other person in the room. I still remember the first time I did that with two people. The

wife was extending forgiveness to her husband and he was sitting there and I was pretty much oblivious to him, I was just watching her and working with her and she prayed through all this. When she got done, he took a big sigh and looked at me and said, "Thank you." I forgot he was there. I said, "What do you mean, thank you?" He said, "This is the first time in my life that I've ever felt genuinely forgiven. I saw it happen right before my eyes."

Key #1—I admit to God how I felt regarding this offense. That's list number 2, the list of feelings. We start there because that's where anybody can start. People know what they felt. Psalm 62:8 says, ". . . Pour out your heart before Him . . . ."

Key #2—Admit to God that you've been holding this person guilty for the act, that's list 1, the hurt, list 2, and ramifications, that's list 3. You just read down through the list. God, I'm holding this person guilty for what he or she did. This person did this and this and I felt this and this and I'm holding him/her guilty for all these ramifications.

Key #3—I now extend my forgiveness to the person for lists 1, 2, and 3. In Ephesians 4:32 it says, "And be kind to one another, tender-hearted, forgiving each other, just as God in Christ also has forgiven you."

Whenever Paul uses the word forgiveness, he uses the same Greek word. It's made up of two words. The first word is *charis*, that's the Greek word for grace. My pastor's daughter is named Charisa. Being a theologian he wanted to name her something theological. He could have called her Grace, but he called her Charisa, a very beautiful name. So that's the first part. It's *charis omai*. *Omai* means to extend or to give. So what is forgiveness? It's giving grace, extending grace to another person. Isn't that how you and I became children of God? That's what it says, forgive each other just as God in

Christ also has given grace to you.

Where is Jesus if I am a child of God? Where is He? He's living in me. He's the forgiver in me who said, "Father forgive them." That same One is living in me, giving me the ability to do what I need to do in extending forgiveness to whomever it is that has hurt me. So, I extend forgiveness. This is giving grace. I like what Charles Hodge had to say about forgiveness. He said, "God in Christ has freely forgiven you. This is the motive which should constrain us to forgive others. God's forgiveness toward us is free. It precedes even our repentance as the cause of it. He forgave us far more than we can ever be called upon to forgive others."

Key #4—I now put the offender into God's hands and let go. I will allow God to work in this person's life and in His time. First Peter 5:7 says, "casting all your anxiety upon Him, because He cares for you."

"And so, Lord, I put this person in your hands. I let go of this person."

Sometimes this is hard for me, because I've got some words of advice I'd like to give to the Lord: "Here's a couple of things I'd like you to do as I forgive this person, Lord. They need a real lesson on sensitivity, okay, and they could do with some manners." But you don't have to do that. Just take your hands off and let God do the adjusting.

Key #5—I now name and confess, that means I agree with God, that I had some sinful reactions and attitudes (that's list 4) including holding this person guilty. So you just admit that to the Lord, that's what I have been doing.

Key #6—I now choose to live in the new creation that I am. That means I accept that God has forgiven me for those sinful reactions and I lay aside my fleshly reactions.

Key #7—I tell God I am willing to be reconciled to the offender and allow God to love the offender through me. When we finish going through this, I always ask the same question, "Well, is this person guilty now?" The person thinks for a moment and says, "Well, no."

"Was this person guilty?"

"Yeah."

"Is this person guilty now?"

"No."

"Why?"

"Because I forgave that person."

I remember one man who forgave his father. His father had really hurt him as a young boy. He would grab him off of his bunk and as he was falling, he would punch him in the chest. Other times he would just pick him up. He can remember being up in the air looking down at this red-faced man who was swearing at him. He became an angry young man, and as he went through this list forgiving his father, he hit the table really hard. I didn't know if he was mad at me or if he was going to attack me, because he had been known to do things like that. But he said, "This is ordained of God. This is fantastic."

"That's good. I'm glad you like it."

He went on to teach it in his church. It was exciting. Look what happens if we can live this way—personal conflict with forgiveness.

PERSONAL CONFLICT WITH TRUE FORGIVENESS (Diagram 200-F)

Notice on "Personal Conflict With True Forgiveness," the little explosions of conflict are getting smaller. There's a shorter time in between when I extend forgiveness and there's a longer harmony line. That's what we do, we clean off the plaque. We deal with it right away by extending forgiveness.

Here are some tests of forgiveness. Are you thanking the Lord for what's happening, even thanking Him during the pain? Why? Because Romans 8:28 says, ". . . God causes all things to work together for good, to those who love God, to those who are called according to His purpose." Even this hurt. Even this pain that you have gone through. God is still using that for His good. So you can thank Him.

Can you talk about this without getting angry?

Are you willing to accept your part? The way that happens often as you extend forgiveness and you get down to the sinful reaction part, you begin to feel convicted by the Holy Spirit that, yeah, I did do some things here, I probably need to go and seek that person's forgiveness too. It doesn't always happen, but many times it can.

Can you revisit the scene or the person without experiencing a negative reaction.

Are you even rewarding with good those that have hurt you?

Some people often say, "Well, I just can't forget about it. Is that one of the tests of forgiveness?" No, it's not. If someone had abused you in a very mean or violent way you probably will never forget. I can remember several times when people said things to me that hurt me, then I went to the Lord, walked through this process, and forgave them. I remember the person, but I forget what they said. I can't remember. The sting and the pain are gone because of extending forgiveness and that's fantastic.

REVIEW

Let's look at the review. "God commands us to forgive others when they hurt us." This is essential to live with impossible people. Pride will stand in the way of extending forgiveness.

Extending forgiveness isn't a thought or a feeling, it's a definite action. If I refuse to forgive someone who hurts me, I can end up in the jail of my own fleshly reactions and be tormented by the enemy. It does take time to do this because I need to write out the offense, my hurt, the ramifications, and my sinful reactions. Then I need to use the seven keys of forgiveness.

It takes time to walk through putting that all together. Who has the Lord brought to your mind as we've gone through this? Is there someone that you've been thinking about that you need to forgive? I would challenge you to consider that.

As you forgive, there's another thought that comes up. That is what about forgiving yourself. Well, you say I can forgive that person, but I'll never forgive myself. Do you ever hear people say that? They say I need help in knowing how to forgive myself or sometimes they say I can forgive that person, but I don't think I'll ever be able to forgive God because He let that happen. There are even people going around helping people forgive God. I have a problem with that because that assumes that God did something wrong. I don't believe God does anything wrong. What do we do when we think of those two things, forgiving God and forgiving ourselves. In the lesson in the VCL Conference on godship we talked about setting standards. If I have a standard for God and He doesn't do things the way I want Him to, then I judge Him and I can reject Him.

I remember one lady telling me, "My only problem I have with God is the fact that He let my husband die of leukemia and I don't think I'll ever be able to forgive Him for that." Well, was it an issue of trying to forgive Him or just recognizing that she had a standard? And she did and she saw it and she was able to say, "God, would You please forgive me. I admit right now to You I've got a standard. The standard was 'You don't take my husband's life. I needed him. We have children to raise.'" But God did. She didn't need to forgive God, she needed to admit the standard and drop it.

What about forgiving ourselves? Do you have standards for yourself? Maybe even today you were upset because you didn't measure up to your own standard. There's not a verse in the Bible that has anything to do with the standards to which you need to measure up. But you didn't measure up to your standard. Even an issue of being offended or hurt or used by someone. How can I be so stupid to let that happen? How can I be so dumb as to buy that from that bad used car salesman or whatever it is? How did that happen? I should have known better. What is that? It's a standard. I should have known better. What's the matter with me? So what do I need to do? Drop the standard. Am I God to go around setting standards? Who am I to judge me and condemn me? I'm not the judge, remember? You don't have the spiritual qualifications to be a judge, so stop judging yourself. Do you have to forgive yourself? No, drop the standard. Admit the godship.

Let's pray. "Lord, I pray now that You would direct those that have thought of someone to whom they need to extend forgiveness. I pray they would do it today using the seven keys of freedom. I pray in Jesus' name. Amen."

VCL

VICTORIOUS CHRISTIAN LIVING Conference
Copyright © 1999 Victorious Christian Living International, Inc.

GODSHIP ——————————————————————————

REJECTION ——————————————————————————

EXTERNAL/INTERNAL ——————————————————

PROBLEMS, PROBLEMS, WHY PROBLEMS? ————

MY FLESH—GOD'S ENEMY ————————————

REPENTANCE ——————————————————————

WHAT'S NEW ABOUT YOU? ——————————————

ACCEPTING YOUR RIGHTEOUSNESS ——————

EXTENDING FORGIVENESS ——————————————

SEEKING FORGIVENESS ⟶

REST, ABIDE, WALK ——————————————————

LOVE ——————————————————————————

GODSHIP

REJECT

EXT/INT

PROBLEMS

FLESH

REPENT

WHAT'S NEW

ACCEPT RIGHT

EXTEND FORGIVE

SEEK FORGIVE

REST

LOVE

SEEKING FORGIVENESS

> ## Leave your offering there before the altar, and go . . . be reconciled to your brother.
>
> Matthew 5:24

Most people are aware of those who offend them. However, there are times when I am the offender. Even as I go through the process of extending forgiveness, I am pricked by the Holy Spirit where I am also at fault. How important is it that I go and make it right? Do I put it off until I see that person again? Do I say, "Well, that happened so long ago, that person probably doesn't even remember"?

What does God's word say about seeking forgiveness? When should I do it? How do I do it without causing more pain for myself or the other person? These are some of the questions to be answered during this lesson.

SEEK
FORGIVE

VCL _____
VICTORIOUS CHRISTIAN LIVING Conference
Copyright © 1999 Victorious Christian Living International, Inc.

SEEKING FORGIVENESS, Page 1

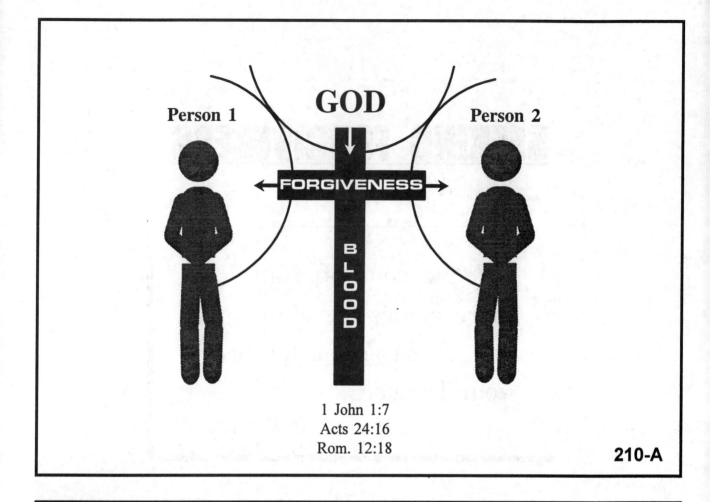

NOTES

Laws of Sowing and Reaping:
1. You reap what you sow (Gal. 6:7).
2. You reap more than you sow (Hosea 8:7).
3. You reap in proportion to what you sow (2 Cor. 9:6).
4. You reap in a different season (Gal. 6:9).

VCL
VICTORIOUS CHRISTIAN LIVING Conference
Copyright © 1999 Victorious Christian Living International, Inc.

Seeking Forgiveness
STUDY GUIDE

PURPOSE for Diagram **210-A:**

To show how God's forgiveness is the foundation for human forgiveness.

? 1. From whom would God want you to seek forgiveness? _____
_____

[book icon] 2. Study 1 John 1:7, Acts 24:16, and Romans 12:18.

? 3. What do these verses say to you? _____
_____

? 4. Check Diagram 200-A. Are you ready to do your part to bring about reconciliation? _____

? 5. Have you forgiven the person you hurt for any wrong-doing toward you?
_____
_____

6. If not, take time to do so now using the keys from the "Extending Forgiveness" lesson.

> **But if we walk in the light . . . we have fellowship one with another . . . .** 1 John 1:7

The foundation for forgiveness is the blood of Christ.

FLESH—SOWING AND REAPING

Galatians 6:7-9

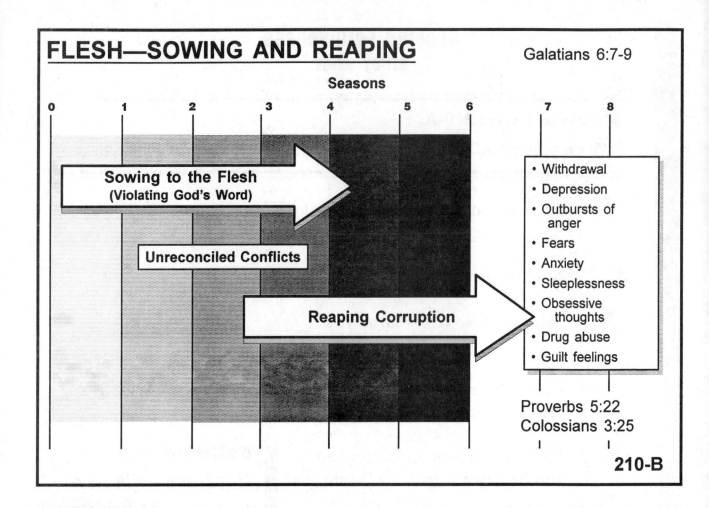

Seasons

0   1   2   3   4   5   6   7   8

Sowing to the Flesh
(Violating God's Word)

Unreconciled Conflicts

Reaping Corruption

- Withdrawal
- Depression
- Outbursts of anger
- Fears
- Anxiety
- Sleeplessness
- Obsessive thoughts
- Drug abuse
- Guilt feelings

Proverbs 5:22
Colossians 3:25

210-B

VCL
VICTORIOUS CHRISTIAN LIVING Conference
Copyright © 1999 Victorious Christian Living International, Inc.

NOTES

PURPOSE for Diagrams **210-B:**

To illustrate the truth that sowing to the flesh reaps corruption.

? 1. How have you chosen to sow to the flesh by violating God's Word? Such as lied, deceived, been sexually immoral, or judged another person? _____

? _____
_____

3. Are you seeing corruption from the fleshly sowing yet? How? _____

> *. . . God is not mocked . . . .*
> Gal. 6:7

? _____
_____

4. What evidences can you check in the box to show the corruption you have reaped? _____

5. Study Colossians 3:25.

📖 6. What does God say will happen when we sow to the flesh? _____

? _____

7. Study Galatians 6:7-9.

📖 8. Are you trying to avoid reaping what you have sown? How?

? _____

I plant it, I harvest it.

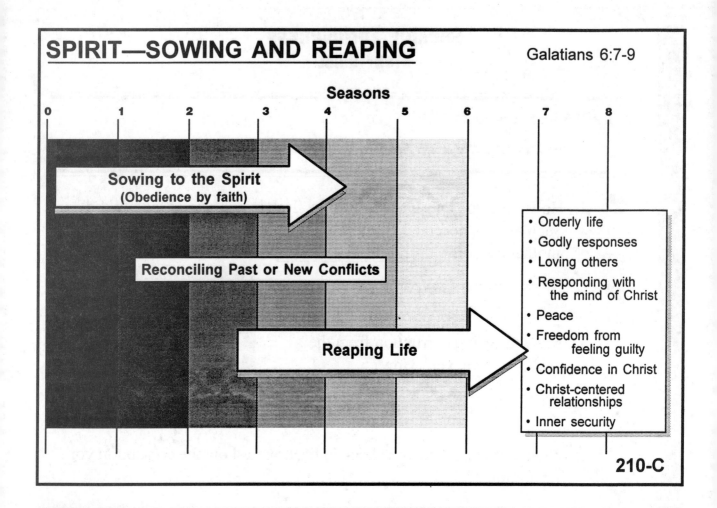

SPIRIT—SOWING AND REAPING

Galatians 6:7-9

Seasons

0 1 2 3 4 5 6 7 8

Sowing to the Spirit
(Obedience by faith)

Reconciling Past or New Conflicts

Reaping Life

- Orderly life
- Godly responses
- Loving others
- Responding with the mind of Christ
- Peace
- Freedom from feeling guilty
- Confidence in Christ
- Christ-centered relationships
- Inner security

210-C

VCL
VICTORIOUS CHRISTIAN LIVING Conference
Copyright © 1999 Victorious Christian Living International, Inc.

PURPOSE for Diagrams **210-C:**

To illustrate the truth that sowing to the Spirit reaps life.

? 1. Are you frustrated because you have sown to the Spirit and not seen positive fruit yet? _____

2. You can start sowing to the Spirit even while you are reaping a bad crop.

? 3. Is seeking forgiveness from someone you have offended something God wants you to do? _____

? 4. What is stopping you from seeking forgiveness? _____
_____
_____

> *. . . let us not lose heart in doing good."* Gal. 6:9

📖 5. Study 2 Samuel 11:1-17, 12:18.

? 6. What should David have done when he saw Uriah? _____
_____
_____

Start sowing to the Spirit even while reaping corruption.

SEEKING FORGIVENESS

1 JOHN 1:9
MATT. 5:23-24

210-D

NOTES

PURPOSE for Diagram **210-D**:

To show the two directions of extending and seeking forgiveness.

1. Study Matthew 5:23-24.

2. What does Jesus say to do when you remember someone has some thing against you? _____

3. Do you see how your worship will be distracted as you think about this person who has been hurt by you? _____

4. If you seek forgiveness from somone, do they have to forgive you?

_____

I can't have a right relationship with God if I have a wrong relationship with others.

> *leave your offering . . .*
> *first be reconciled . . . .*
> Matt. 5:24

SEEK FORGIVE

SEEKING FORGIVENESS PROCESS

"If therefore you are presenting your offering at the altar, and there remember that your brother has something against you, leave your offering there before the altar, and go your way; first be reconciled to your brother, and then come and present your offering."

Matthew 5:23-24

Seeking forgiveness is honestly "seeing" how I hurt another person by my words or actions. Then I go to that person and say I was wrong for what I did and ask that person to forgive me. Before I go I need to forgive anything I am holding against that person.

Twelve Keys to Seeking Forgiveness:

1. Reexamine what seeking forgiveness is NOT.

    It is NOT "apologizing" or "being sorry" for what I have done.
    It is NOT trying to "make up" to someone or be nice to someone I have hurt.

2. Reminded by the Holy Spirit. Don't be continually searching myself.

3. Remembered by the other person.

    Don't seek forgiveness for jealous, lustful, or angry thoughts or feelings.
    Exceptions would be when I have stolen something or slandered someone's name.

4. Respond quickly.

5. Review the offense clearly.

    It may be helpful to have a pastor or counselor help me see how I have offended the other person.

6. Rehearse only as much detail as necessary.

7. Reject any defense, excuses, or blame.

8. Rapidly move to ask, "I was wrong regarding _____, will you forgive me?"

9. Right timing is vital.

10. Request in person.

    Not if I was involved in an immoral relationship.
    Use the telephone if the person lives out of town.

11. Refuse to write a letter.

    It could be kept.
    There is no sense of closure.
    It may fall into the wrong hands.

12. Restitution needs to be offered if something was stolen.

210-E

VCL
VICTORIOUS CHRISTIAN LIVING Conference
Copyright © 1999 Victorious Christian Living International, Inc.

Seeking Forgiveness
STUDY GUIDE

PURPOSE for Diagram **210-E:**

To give a guide for seeking forgiveness.

 1. Study Matthew 5:23-24.

2. Read the definition in the box of seeking forgiveness.

? 3. Who is the person you will go to and seek forgiveness? _____

? 4. How did you hurt this person?

_____

_____

_____

> ## With all humility and gentleness . . . .
> Eph. 4:2

? 4. Does God want you to seek forgiveness?
Yes   No

? 5. When will you go? _____

? 6. Have you forgiven the person for any way he/she has hurt you?

_____

 7. Pray for a good time to go and seek forgiveness.

8. Using these twelve keys, go to the person and seek forgiveness.

Seeking forgiveness should be a way of life.

SEEK FORGIVE

REBUILD RELATIONSHIPS

OFFENDER *needs to*

➤ listen to other person's hurts, needs, and desires.

➤ prayerfully and practically care for the other person's very life.

➤ go out of his/her way to demonstrate I am trustworthy.
  ➤ make restitution and more. *Numbers 5:7*
  ➤ go over and above what would seem to be obvious or expected.

OFFENDED *needs to*

➤ forgive the offender. *2 Cor. 2:7-8*
➤ bless those who curse you.
➤ pray.   ➤ love.   ➤ do good.

➤ turn cheek.   ➤ give.   ➤ do unto them.
  Luke 6:27-32

➤ keep no record of wrong.
➤ always trust God.
➤ always hope.
  ➤ always love. *1 Cor. 13:5-7*

➤ be willing to let the other fail, which could include hurting you again.

Unity

BOTH *need to*

➤ thank the Lord for His ministry of reconciliation.
➤ pray for and/or with the other person.
➤ be willing to have a relationship with the other person.

210-F

NOTES

VCL
VICTORIOUS CHRISTIAN LIVING Conference
Copyright © 1999 Victorious Christian Living International, Inc.

Seeking Forgiveness
STUDY GUIDE

PURPOSE for Diagram **210-F:**

To show how to rebuild a damaged relationship.

1. Study Psalm 133:1.

2. What does God desire in relationships?
_____

> *. . . Come, let us rebuild . . . that we may no longer be a reproach.* Neh. 2:17

3. What do you think is keeping you from rebuilding a relationship? _____
_____

OFFENDER:

4. Are you willing to be inconvenienced to demonstrate that you are trustworthy? Yes No

5. What could you do to restore the offended person's trust? _____
_____

OFFENDED:

6. Have you been offended and told God you would never give that person another chance? Yes No What area of godship is that?
_____

7. Study 1 Peter 2:23.

8. Who is your protector? _____

9. Have you forgiven the one who hurt you? Yes No

10. Are you letting God love the offender through you? Yes No

Rebuilding is harder than building— but well worth it!

SEEK FORGIVE

REVIEW

- It is impossible to live with people and not hurt or offend them.

- As soon as you feel the direction of the Lord to seek forgiveness from another person, it is time to act.

- It is a very humbling thing to go to another person and say, "I was wrong. Will you forgive me?"

- This is essential to live with impossible people.

- Seeking forgiveness from anyone you offend should be a way of life.

- After reconciliation, you need to rebuild the relationship.

NOTES

SEEKING FORGIVENESS

Lesson Transcript by Ted Sellers

I'd like to read an actual transcript of a radio conversation between a United States Naval warship and Canadian authorities off the coast of Newfoundland recorded in October of 1995. Here's the conversation:

U.S. ship: "Please divert your course 5 degrees to the south to avoid a collision."
Canadian reply: "Recommend that you divert your course 15 degrees to the south to avoid a collision."
U.S. ship: "This is the captain of a United States Navy ship. I say again, divert your course."
Canadian reply: "No. I say again, divert your course."
U.S. warship: "We are a large warship of the United States Navy. Divert your course now."
Canadian reply: "This is a lighthouse . . . your call."

Now, that was an actual radio conversation. After the captain of that warship heard that reply I'm wondering if he said, "Oh my goodness! Would you please forgive me, please, Canadian authorities? I am so sorry for being so pompous and pushy. We will definitely divert our course." Do you think he did that? I don't think he did that. No . . . he did not seek that person's forgiveness. Probably what happened after that last communication was just dead silence and the captain, off the air, saying something like, "About hard right rudder, let's get out of here and never tell anyone what we did." But somehow it was recovered and picked up on the internet.

Seeking forgiveness is not something that's a common practice of people who are in the world. In fact, it's not even a common activity for people who are Christians . . . that we quickly go and seek someone's forgiveness as soon as we know that we've hurt another person. I remember one time when an athlete came on the sidelines of a basketball game and kicked a photographer. Afterwards, do you think he sought his forgiveness? Do you think he said, "Oh, how clumsy of me, or how pushy or rude of me to do that. Would you please forgive me?" No. He paid him money, but he didn't seek his forgiveness. It's not something that happens too much in the world. Yet, the Lord is very desirous that we in the church be able to live together in harmony and unity.

Let me read to you from what I call "The Lord's Prayer." The Lord's prayer is not what He taught His disciples in Matthew Chapter 6. The Lord's prayer is found in John 17, and part of that starts with verse 21 and continues for the next couple of verses. Listen to what Jesus says as He prays to His Father: "That all may be one, Father, just as You are in Me and I am in You. May they also be in Us so that the world may believe that You have sent Me. I have given them the glory that You gave Me, that they may be one as We are One. I in them and You in Me. May they be brought to complete unity to let the world know that You sent Me and have loved them even as You have loved Me" (John 17:21-23 NIV). That's the prayer of Jesus, that there would be oneness and unity. The one thing that can divert unity from happening and that can destroy harmony in the church is people offending other people and doing nothing about it. Instead, they just say: "Well, it will blow over" or "I don't know, I don't know what happened. But I'm sure that I don't need to do anything about it." No. We do need to do something about it. When I have hurt another person and harmony is broken, I need to go and seek forgiveness.

If you look at the verse here on page 1 it says, "Leave your offering there before the altar, and go . . . be reconciled to your brother" (Matthew 5:24). That word reconciled means to "unite or bring back into harmony" if there was harmony and it was disrupted. Go and restore that harmony or bring that harmony back. The *Living Bible* says, "Go and apologize and be reconciled to him." Luke 17:4 gives an interesting, almost unbelievable text. It says, "Even if he wrongs you seven times a day and each time turns again and asks forgiveness, forgive him." Seven times in one day. Usually once a day is enough for most people. I can take one abuse or one rejection a day from someone. But imagine, seven times in one day. And if he comes back seven times and asks you to forgive him, forgive him.

It's interesting in this idea of reconciliation that it's always my move. If you have offended me, it's my move to extend forgiveness to you; but if I have offended you, then it's my move to go and seek forgiveness from you. In order to seek forgiveness, I do need to go to you. I cannot do that in my room all by myself. I need to go and talk to you to seek your forgiveness.

THE CROSS OF FORGIVENESS
(Diagram 210-A)
Let's look at our first diagram on page two. As you look at this you see the cross right in the center. As you think about the cross, there's a vertical beam and a horizontal beam. You put those two together and you make the cross. The vertical beam is our reconciliation to God, and God is the initiator of reconciliation. John 3:16 (paraphrase): "For God so loved the world that He initiated the process to bring about our reconciliation with Him." Jesus went to the cross for that purpose. Then the arms that go horizontally represent reconciliation between

people—women to women, man to man, man to woman. I believe that just as God was an initiator of reconciliation to us, we should be initiators of reconciliation with other people.

Have you ever known, or maybe seen in a movie, where two people have hurt each other? You can see that neither one of them is going to budge and, as the movie progresses, they drift farther and farther apart. By the end of the movie they go off in two different directions, the sun sets and they pass the kleenex. You could say, "If I could only get into that movie and tell them, 'Hey, he'll forgive you. He'll forgive you if you would just go and seek forgiveness! WOULD SOMEBODY BREAK THIS STALE-MATE—THIS MEXICAN STANDOFF WITH TWO GUNS NOBODY'S GOING TO SHOOT!! Nobody's going to do anything. Please somebody stop it by going and seeking forgiveness.'"

Many times what stops that is pride. "Well, I'll move if he moves." "I'll move if she moves, but I'm not going to start it. I'll wait to see. They're not doing anything so why should I?" No, that's not what God did. Aren't you glad that He was the initiator. He's the one that took the first step. When it comes to horizontal relationships, why don't you be the one to be the initiator, to take the first steps, so you are committed to being reconciled to each other?

Look at 1 John 1:7. It says, "If we walk in the light as He Himself is in the light, we have fellowship one with another." I always thought it said we'd have fellowship with God, but it doesn't. It says, "If we walk in the light," that's the fellowship, that's the relationship with God. Then we will "have fellowship with one another" as we walk in the light. What does it mean to walk in the light? Walking in the light means not walking in the darkness or hiding in the darkness. How do we do that? By keeping everything open and honest.

VCL
VICTORIOUS CHRISTIAN LIVING Conference

I remember I was counseling a man one time and we were in the last phases of discipleship and I said, "Now, is there anything else that you sense the Lord wants to deal with in your life?" He said, "Well there's one thing but it's . . . it's pretty much already taken care of." I said, "Really, what's that?" He said, "Well I've been smoking for the last couple of months, and I'm pretty sure I'm going to quit. In fact there are a couple of guys at work and we're all quitting together. We're all Christians. You know, as Christians we go out for a smoke break and talk about how we're going to quit smoking, and so we're gonna be doing that probably by the end of the month." I said, "Well that's great that you're quitting. That's neat. Have you told your wife?" "No." "Really! Why, I think she would like to rejoice with you!" "She doesn't know I'm smoking." "Really! You were that good?" "I am that good. I have breath deodorant, I have a spray that I spray on my clothing, I air everything out, I do everything outside, I smoke outside, nothing sticks, I don't do it in the car." I mean this guy was sharp! I said, "Well, why can't you tell your wife? I think that would be important." He said, "Let me explain to you the situation." He said, "When I got married to my wife, she told me in no uncertain terms that she didn't want me to ever, ever, ever smoke and at that time it wasn't a big deal. I said sure. She said, 'The reason that I'm telling you this is that my father died of lung cancer and I watched him die. It was not a pretty picture. I don't want to go through that with you. So buddy, you start smoking and you can kiss me good-bye!' So you can see why I wouldn't tell her." So what do you think his assignment was?

Under God, I did not tell him what to do, but I said, "I think God would want you to share that. That would be walking in the light and not hiding out in the darkness." He said, "Boy, that's the hardest thing I'll ever have to do." He said, "I know it's the right thing to do, God's really going to have to strengthen me." And God did strengthen him and he went and told his

wife. And do you know what she was more upset about than the fact that he was smoking? Yeah, not telling her! She was deceived. He was living a lie and doing a good job at it. She was very hurt that he wouldn't even tell her. And so he had to seek her forgiveness for living a lie and being deceitful, and then, for smoking.

Well, one of the interesting little side notes about this particular couple: they had been married about five years at that point and had really wanted to have a child and for some reason they couldn't. Very soon after he disclosed what he was doing and sought her forgiveness they had a greater degree of unity and oneness. She then became pregnant and had their first child. Since then she's had another one. I think that was somehow connected to walking in the light . . . as we walk in the light by not hiding what's going on in our life and being willing to be reconciled.

Acts 24:16 describes how Paul lived his life: "Herein do I exercise myself, to have a conscience void of offense toward God and toward man" (KJV). That's just a neat way to live—void of offense toward God and toward man. Whenever there was an offense toward someone, Paul would deal with it. He wrote in Romans 12:18, " . . . Be at peace with all men." How can you be at peace? Well, whenever there's not peace, whenever there's turmoil, and I'm the one who has caused it, then I need to go and seek forgiveness so that I can, in fact, be at peace with you.

One of the things that I've thought about recently, when there's conflict between two people and there's no harmony and no unity, is that the people are not really focusing on the most important thing. I've heard it put like this: "We need to major on the majors and minor on the minors." When there's conflict it's because we're majoring on a minor or minoring on a major. What's a major? The major is this relationship. This relationship is too important to let this minor thing destroy it. What happens is we're more committed to being right than we are committed to that relationship.

"I'm right, you're wrong. You're going to lose, I'm going to win and I'm going to show you where you're messed up. Your thinking is way off base or you don't have any concern or feeling for what I care about."

Majoring on the majors, what's important, what's really important. That's what should be considered when you're in a relationship. So don't major on the minors, major on the majors.

When you do sow to the flesh, there are laws of sowing and reaping. How do you sow to the flesh? By having unreconciled relationships and not doing anything about it. If you'll notice, we have four laws of sowing and reaping.

The *first* law is: "You reap what you sow" (Galatians 1:7). For those people here that are farmers, you understand that when you plant wheat you reap wheat.

But when you plant one little kernel of wheat you don't just get one little kernel of wheat. You get a whole stock of wheat. That's the *second* law: You reap more than you sow. So, if you sow the wind, what will you reap? The whirlwind. Yeah, that's a lot more than you sowed.

The *third* law says: You reap in proportion to what you sow. Second Corinthians 9:6 says (paraphrase): "If you sow sparingly you'll reap sparingly. If you sow bountifully, you'll reap bountifully."

The *fourth* law is: You reap in a different season. So you don't plant the seed and overnight it grows up. You plant the seed and you wait for the harvest. Many times we plant bad seeds by not being reconciled with someone and the harvest comes up years later, or months later, and we see a bad harvest. How did that get there? How did that child turn out like that?

Years of bad sowing, years of not being reconciled, then we have a bad harvest over here.

For example, think about King David. Here was a guy who sowed to his flesh. One night, he was alone. Where was his army? Out fighting, protecting him so he could be at home watching videos. After he got tired of doing that he went and looked out on the porch. He looked around and saw someone taking a bath. In fact she did that so much they nicknamed her "Bath-sheba." She's out there and he's looking at her and realizes that she's a very attractive woman, and he wants to explain some Proverbs to her. So he invites her over and they talk about Proverbs, and eventually they have an affair.

Now, what should have happened as soon as the army and her husband, Uriah, got back home? What would be the very first thing King David should have done? He should have gone and said, "Uriah, come here, man. I need to talk to you. You won't believe what I've done. I am so sorry. I feel so guilty. While you were out there defending me, I was messing around with your wife. Would you please forgive me? I don't know what you want me to do to make some kind of amends for this, but I'll do whatever it takes. I am just so embarrassed. I feel horrible about what I've done." Is that what he did? No! He figured out a way that he wouldn't have to do that. Isn't that interesting? Instead of figuring out what the easiest thing would be, we think of something a little more difficult that doesn't hurt our pride. So he figured out a way to get rid of Uriah and you probably know the story. He eliminated the guy instead of seeking his forgiveness. He, in effect, killed him. That's bad sowing! That's bad! That's stinkweed man! That's nasty!

Now what was the crop? What did the crop look like? What happened to the little baby? Oh, that's bad reaping. The harvest came up nine months later—bad harvest. Now what else happened to David's children, even his older

VCL

VICTORIOUS CHRISTIAN LIVING Conference
Copyright © 1999 Victorious Christian Living International, Inc.

children? What happened to some of those? There we had some bad scenes, didn't we? We have a brother raping a daughter, and then Absalom decides he'll fix that. He goes to his brother, Amnon, and kills him. Bad sowing, bad reaping. Then we've got Absalom, trying to replace David as the king. That's a kind of kid you want to have around, right?

"I want to throw you out! I'm going to embarrass you, Dad! I'm going to do the same kinds of things to you. I want to be just like you Dad."

Absalom was also very proud. He had a hang-up with his hair and ended up in a tree. Joab comes along and stabs him and kills him. David is just mortified. That's one more bad crop. All of that happened because of David's bad sowing, when he didn't deal with it.

I remember a man that a pastor told me about. He said this man came and talked to him and said, "Pastor, you gotta pray for me. I am sick." The pastor asked, "What's the matter?" The man said: "I don't know. It's just that my stomach is hurting. It's just gives me so much pain. I'm getting tired of taking Tums." The pastor said, "Well sure, I'll pray for you." So he prayed for the man.

He checked with him a couple weeks later, "How ya doing?" "Oh, I'm not doing good at all," he said, "I'm gonna go see the doctor." So he went and saw the doctor, who gave him a complete physical and said, "I can't find anything wrong with you." This continued for several more weeks and he didn't get any better. Finally, he decided to check into the Mayo Clinic and get all of the high tech testing. They ran all the battery of tests, and you know what they found? Nothing. Nothing was wrong with him.

About a week later he went to see his pastor and said: "I just need to talk with you. I've been really feeling convicted by the Holy Spirit. A while back I started having an affair. My wife

doesn't know about it and I need to seek her forgiveness, but I'm just petrified. I don't know what she's going to do or what she's going to say." And the pastor said, "Okay, we'll set it up." So the pastor got the husband and wife together and they had several sessions and he sought his wife's forgiveness. She was very hurt and wept, but finally was able to forgive him. What do you think happened to his tummy ache? Yeah, it went away . . . it was healed. Well, he was healed because he did what he should have done probably a couple months earlier. Not seeking forgiveness, not being obedient to the Lord, will make you sick.

What to do with an unreconciled relationship? Did you ever wake up in the morning and feel this pit in your stomach because you know there's somebody you need to talk to and you don't want to do it? You know there's someone you've offended and you just try to put it off or just not think about it. "I've got a busy day, I'll think about that later." And the Holy Spirit faithfully reminds you, "Let's deal with it. Let's deal with it so that there can be reconciliation."

FLESH—SOWING AND REAPING
(Diagram 210-B)
Let's go on to the next diagram because it explores more sowing and reaping. Notice the seasons. You have zero through eight and these seasons can refer to years, months, days, or hours. It's just a way of breaking up the time frame from when you began to sow to when you began to reap. If I sow to the flesh by violating God's word, by having unreconciled conflicts, I will reap corruption. You can see it gets pretty dark at the end.

Let's consider some of these violations of God's word. Colossians 3:9 says, "Lie not at all" (paraphrase). Don't tell lies. If I've told a lie to someone, I need to seek the person's forgiveness. I don't need to let that continue any longer. If I do, then I'll start to wait for the harvest. See, when these seeds of disobeying God toward other people happen, when those seeds hit the ground, I want to get down and pick them up quickly before they take root, sprout, and I have a harvest on my hands.

Have you ever played a game called "Alligators"? I've played it with my little boy. Six alligators go in and out in an arcade game and you hit them on the head. When you hit them on the head they back and say, "Oww, oww." My son just loves to do that because he loves to hit things. Then you get so many points, you win tickets and you use them to buy a plastic thing that breaks before you get home. He loves that game and I think that's kind of like seeking forgiveness. As soon as I see that I've offended someone, I deal with it. "Oww!" Let's hit it, let's drive it back, let's not let it take root and grow into a bad harvest. As soon as I'm convicted, I go and deal with an unreconciled conflict.

"For this is the will of God . . . abstain from sexual immorality" (1 Thessalonians 4:3). This uses a key phrase that many Christians get excited about, and that's "the will of God." It is the will of God that you avoid sexual immorality. That's the will of God. But when I do violate someone in that way, I need to go and seek that person's forgiveness.

"Do not judge . . . ." (Matthew 7:1). Don't judge. When I know that I've judged someone, I need to go and seek that person's forgiveness right away. Not long ago, my sister-in-law and brother-in-law from South Dakota visited. They have two daughters. While they were here we were talking about the accident that one daughter had had with her car. In South Dakota you can get a driver's license when you're 14. That's pretty young. Why do you think they do that? South Dakota was a rural area. They needed the boys to drive the trucks and tractors into town to gas up, so they let them have a driver's license at 14. Neither one of these girls are driving tractors, but they still got a driver's license when they were 14. This daughter got a license when she was 14, then her parents got

her a car. Within a couple of weeks she was in a collision, was knocked cold, and really could have been hurt. The car was all mashed up. I said, "I heard about your daughter's accident." She said, "Yeah boy, that was really something." I said, "You know, my daughters didn't get a driver's license until they were 16 because a lot can happen between the time you're 14 and you're 16. People grow up a little more. They also went to Driver's Ed school."

"Yeah, but you know, that really is the law. They can get it when they're 14."

I said, "Another thing, when my daughters did turn 16 and got a driver's license, I didn't buy them a car." She said: "What are you going to do? Everybody's got a car, you know, and she wanted a car and we could afford it, so we did." I went on and said something else and she said, "You know, I don't know if I want to keep talking about this." And so I quit.

The next morning as I was having my devotions and being spiritual, the Lord seemed to speak to me about judging and He said: "Who made you the driver's license cop of the world that you know when people ought to have a driver's license? What is your deal? You see what you're doing? You're judging and you're setting a standard. All you're wanting her to do is do it the right way—the way you did it, the way God does it. Do it like I did it and then you'll do it right." I said, "Ahhh man! That's what I did, didn't I?"

"Hummm."

Then I realized that she was leaving the next day to go back to South Dakota, where they give people a driver's license at 14. So I called her up and I said, "Hello Patty," and she said, "Yeeaah." Like maybe I wasn't done, but had one more dig. I said: "This is Ted. I wanted to talk to you about our conversation yesterday. I was actually very critical and judgmental."

"Oh no! No you weren't."

VCL

VICTORIOUS CHRISTIAN LIVING Conference
Copyright © 1999 Victorious Christian Living International, Inc.

She's very nice so she probably didn't take it badly. I said, "Yeah, I was really trying to make you do things the way I did them."

"Well everybody has their own opinion."

I said, "I know, but I was trying to make my opinion, your opinion. I was trying to change you to believe like I do and that was wrong. Would you please forgive me?" She said, "Oh, of course! I didn't think any more about it."

About a week later I was talking with my mother-in-law, Patty's mother, and she said, "Isn't it wonderful." I said, "What?" She said: "You know, what happened with you and Patty? Everybody's talking about it. You called her and sought her forgiveness. We don't do that. That's neat. I like that. No one's ever done that. We're Norwegian. You know, Norwegian people don't do things like that."

Now I think it just showed me again that this is something that just doesn't happen, especially among families, let alone among people in the church, the family of God.

If I sow unreconciled conflicts, and I don't jerk them up like weeds by seeking forgiveness, then I'm going to reap corruption. As I'm going along, I'm wondering if the Lord brought anyone to your mind that you've hurt or offended? Think about that and ask yourself these questions: "Have I had withdrawal or feelings of depression? Or outbursts of anger and I thought, 'Where'd that outburst of anger come from? Could that have anything to do with the unreconciled relationship I have over here?'" It could. It could definitely be connected. Or fears or anxiety or even sleeplessness. When you can't sleep and you're waking up thinking about that person you've hurt, that could be connected. Obsessive thoughts, drug abuse and even feelings of guilt. I remember one man who was counseling with me and he said, "You know why I use drugs?" He used speed. He said, "I use it very

intelligently." He said, "I use drugs to shut up the Holy Spirit because I can hear what he's telling me. I don't want to hear it and I know how to shut him up." So he used drugs. With him it was being unreconciled with his wife.

It's interesting how Solomon could write these Proverbs. "His own iniquities will capture the wicked, / And he will be held with the cords of his sin" (Proverbs 5:22). Isn't that good. Held with the cords of his own sin. In Colossians 3:25 we read, "For he who does wrong will receive the consequences of the wrong which he has done, and that without partiality." Receive the consequences—yet, many, many times people who know they need to go and seek forgiveness don't do it.

I always remember counseling a man who explained to me how he had called someone up on the telephone. They were having an argument and it got more and more heated, and he began to curse this person, calling him everything in the book. I said, "Do you think that was a godly thing to do?" He said, "Nope, but he had it coming."

"Oh. Okay. Well, when you've hurt someone or offended someone like that, what do you think you ought to do?"

"I don't know."

"Well what do you think God would like you to do?"

"I don't know. But I'll tell you one thing I'm *not* going to do. I'm not going to seek his forgiveness."

I said, "Really?" "Yeah," he said, "He had it coming to him and so I'd probably do it again, and use the same words." I said, "Well, I think that's important." He said, "Yeah, it sure was, it was an important conversation." "No," I said, "The fact that you don't want to do what you

SEEK FORGIVE

know God wants you to do." And he said, "Yeah, so?" I said, "In fact, it's probably so important that, until you do that, we won't really need to meet again." He said, "That's cool." We have never met since. That's how committed he was to not seeking forgiveness. It wasn't a big deal, but he wasn't going to do it, and he didn't. I'd hate to see the crop that comes up in his life.

SPIRIT—SOWING AND REAPING
(Diagram 210-C)
Look at the next diagram "Spirit—Sowing and Reaping,"—being obedient. You see, even when there's a bad crop coming up and we're in this dark area, what do we do? We start sowing to the Spirit. We start reconciling relationships, even when we get bad crops from other relationships. It's never too late to go and seek forgiveness; it's never too late to be reconciled. What can happen as I reap life by reconciling past or even new conflicts by seeking forgiveness? Life gets better. I have an orderly life; there are godly responses. I can love other people. I can respond with the mind of Christ. I have peace and not turmoil. There's freedom from feeling guilty, confidence in Christ, and there's inner security. So I ask you this? Where are you sowing today? Are you sowing to the flesh? Are you sowing to the Spirit in your relationships with other people?

SEEKING FORGIVENESS
(Diagram 210-D)
If you look at the next diagram, you'll see how the process should work. You have the offender and the person who's been offended. The offender seeks forgiveness from the offended and the offended forgives and they are reconciled. There's something I need to add here. Write down Psalm 51:4. Before I even go and seek forgiveness from you, I need to go to the Lord. David said in Psalms 51:4, "Against Thee, Thee only, I have sinned." You know, it's interesting as I read that because David was willing to admit that to God, but he didn't admit

that to Uriah. He did the first step. He did that just fine, but he didn't do the second step. He talked to God, but he didn't talk to the person. Some people are very spiritual and they talk to God. They think that's all they need to do.

"Yep, everything's okay! I talked to God and I asked Him to forgive me because I was really mean to that person."

"But what about that person you offended?"

"Well, that's not a big deal."

No, you have to do that also. That's the next step. So let's look at what that process looks like as we spell it out.

SEEKING FORGIVENESS PROCESS **(Diagram 210-E)**
If you notice on this sheet, there's a definition of seeking forgiveness. What is it? It's honestly seeing how I hurt another person by my words or actions. You may have to have someone help you do that. Many times I've had parents in counseling who know they've hurt their children because their children are alienated from them. I've had to help them see what they did to hurt them. All they know is their children don't want to talk to them. They don't want to have anything to do with them, but they don't know why. They don't have a clue. And it's good to have another person to say: "Is this what happened? Did you do that? Did you not do this?" And they start to see, "Oh my goodness, that's what I've done." So when they go to seek forgiveness it's more than just "Would you forgive me for being a lousy parent?" It's more specific: "Would you forgive me for never encouraging you? Would you forgive me for never going to your games? Would you forgive me for never saying something positive to you? Would you forgive me for never holding you or saying I love you?" That's more specific. So, it's honestly seeing how I hurt another person by my words or actions. Then I go to that person and say I

was wrong for what I did and ask that person to forgive me.

Before I go to seek forgiveness, I need to forgive anything I'm holding against that person. I refer you to the lesson on "Extending Forgiveness" so that you can extend forgiveness first. Then when you go to that person you won't have anything against them. You're not coming to say, "I'm going to seek your forgiveness, but I'm going to wait because you better seek my forgiveness." No, you've already extended forgiveness to them. So Matthew 5:23-24 says, "If therefore you are presenting your offering at the altar, and there remember that your brother has something against you, leave your offering there before the altar, and go your way; first be reconciled to your brother, and then come and present your offering."

Those two words, be reconciled, are in the imperative tense in the original language. In other words, it's a command, do it at once. Make a decisive and effective choice. Don't put it off. Make it happen. Let's look at these 11 keys to seeking forgiveness. Let me ask you again. Has the Lord brought someone to your mind, from whom you need to seek forgiveness? If so, these would be the steps to follow.

1. Reexamine what forgiveness or seeking forgiveness is not. It's not apologizing or just being sorry and it's not trying to make up to someone or be nice to them. It's admitting what you did.

2. You're reminded by the Holy Spirit. You don't have to go on some sort of an archeological dig into your past and think, "I have heard this lesson on seeking forgiveness. I'm sure there's probably lots and lots of people that I've hurt. I don't even know where to start. Probably 4th grade, that's where it all started. I have to think back to Johnny Bumgardner that I hit with my little satchel." No, it is just the people that the Holy Spirit brings to your mind.

3. Remembered by the other person. In other words, the other person should know what you're talking about. Now there are times when you go and seek forgiveness and they remember the incident, but it may not have offended them as much as you thought. And then you think, "Why did I even do that?" I would rather do that than nothing at all. I'd rather go and seek forgiveness and the person say, "Oh yeah, I remember that, but no, I didn't take offense." I'd rather do that than not do anything. I'd rather err on the side of doing it too much than not doing it at all. However, you don't seek forgiveness for jealousy. That's an internal thing, like lustful or angry thoughts or feelings. In other words, let's say that you're a man and and you're at the grocery store and you're at aisle 9 and you go up to a lady and say, "Ma'am, excuse me." And she says, "Yes." You say, "I don't really know you, but we're in aisle 9 and around aisle 2 is when I first noticed you and had lustful thoughts, and for the last 7 aisles I have had these problems. I just wanted you to forgive me, will you please do that?" **You don't do that.**

There are exceptions when you have stolen something or slandered someone. Now, you go to someone and say, "I would like you to forgive me, if you would please, because I stole something from you."

"I didn't know that."

I remember one counselee who actually went back to a U-Haul place that he robbed and sought their forgiveness. That was neat. The Lord used that in his life.

Another possibility is when you slander someone. Now that gets real tricky, but you don't want to go around slandering people and abusing them in the form of gossip or malice. There may be a time, and I've had to do that myself, where I went back and sought someone's forgiveness, because I had talked to another person in a slanderous way. I talked to one of the people on staff here and said, "You know this other guy." And he said, "Yeah, I know him." And I said, "Let me tell you about him." And I said some things that weren't very kind. The next day the Lord convicted me and I went to him and I said, "You know what I said about the other guy yesterday? I shouldn't have done that, would you please forgive me?" He said, "Of course I will. Now why don't you go and seek his forgiveness."

"Oh no, I sought your forgiveness, that's enough isn't it?"

"No, you need to talk to him."

I did. We went out to breakfast and it wasn't comfortable, but it sure put the skids on me doing that kind of thing again.

4. Respond quickly. Don't wait. As soon as you know, what does that verse say? "Leave your gift right there, don't even go through with any kind of religious service, just leave your gift and go do it."

5. Review the offense clearly. We've talked about that.

6. Rehearse only as much detail as necessary. Especially if you're going to seek forgiveness from a teenager, it should last about 42 seconds. You just go and say, "Yesterday when you didn't take out the garbage when I asked you to and I called you a sluggard and a lazy person, I was wrong for that. But you know I don't ask you to do much around here. I try to do as much as I can and the few things that I ask are always met with resistance." Now wait a minute, we've gone into something else and that's next, number 7.

7. Blame and defense. Don't do that, because as you do that with a teenager, after you go over 42 seconds, their eyes glaze over and they know it's

a lecture and it's not seeking forgiveness.

8. Very important. Circle number 8—that's the key one. You rapidly move to ask this question or this statement: "I was wrong regarding (you fill in whatever the offense was), will you forgive me?" You have to use those 3 hardest words in the English language, "I was wrong." It's not "Would you forgive me if what I did offended you? If it was an offense to you, would you please forgive me because, you know, every thing I do offends you. You have your feelings on your sleeve. I can't say or do anything without you being offended." No. Don't do that. Say, "I was wrong, will you please forgive me?"

By the way, can you demand someone to forgive you? "You must forgive me, that's what the guy said, so I'm doing it so you gotta do that." No, this is a humble thing. It's not a demanding thing.

9. Right timing is vital. "Is this a good time to talk?" When I want to talk is a good time, right? It may not be. It may not be at all. This is important. We have to have a good time to talk and then do it in person.

10. Request in person. However, you don't request in person if it was an immoral relationship. I had a man in counseling one time and the Lord finally got through to him and he was convicted about this relationship and he said, "I'll go over to her house tonight and I'll tell her that it's over." I said, "You don't have to that. We can make a phone call." You don't go to the person's house. However, you don't use the telephone if you live in the house. You don't go down to the Circle K and make a phone call. You do that one face to face.

11. But do not write a letter. If you write a letter with today's technology, with e-mail and the internet, your letter could be all over the world in a matter of seconds. Do you want that to hap-

pen? **Don't write a letter.** Plus, there's no sense of closure. The only person you ever really get to know well is your mail carrier, as you wait for an answer. It can fall into the wrong hands.

What if you seek forgiveness and the person does not forgive you? Do you need to keep going back again, again, and again? No, just pray that the Lord would allow the person to forgive you.

What do you do after you seek forgiveness? You work toward reconciliation. There are three parts to reconciliation: seeking forgiveness, extending forgiveness, and rebuilding the relationship.

REBUILD RELATIONSHIPS
(Diagram 210-F)
Doesn't it take longer to rebuild something than to build it? Last year my wife took her fingernail and scratched one of our kitchen cabinets and said: "Oh look. Look at that beautiful wood under that ugly white paint. Wouldn't it be fun to strip all these cabinets and be able to see that wood?" And I said, "Yeah." That was not a good answer. It was not fun. To this day if we walk through Home Depot and we go through the Paint Department and I say, "Look hun, stripper!" AGHHH!!! Stripper!! I hate the sound of that word, I hate that! We bought so much of that stuff we were asphyxiated by that stuff. We stripped all those cabinets. It was a lot of work, but they do look nice. It takes a lot to rebuild something or redo something, but it is worth it. And it's worth it to rebuild the relationship that's been damaged because trust has been broken.

What do you need to do if you're the offender? You need to listen to the other person's hurts and go out of your way to demonstrate that you are trustworthy. You say, "I feel like I'm bending over backwards." You may have to. You were the one that broke the trust. Don't get upset about it. Trust God to give you the pa-

tience to go through it. Remember Zacchaeus? He said, "I'll give back half of all my money to the poor and if I've overcharged anyone four times more goes back." He was willing to reestablish trust with the people that didn't trust him.

If you're the person that's been offended, you need to turn the other cheek. You need to do good to the offender. You need to pray for and love the person. Now, you do not need to be reconciled with some people. If there has been abuse or rape or something like that, you don't need to be reconciled to that person. We're talking about a relationship that already existed. Remember the definition of reconcile? To reunite, to bring harmony again into that relationship.

REVIEW
Let's review. Are you crashing into lighthouses because you refuse to divert your course? Are you refusing to seek forgiveness? Are you damaging relationships by pride? Are you unwilling to say, "I was wrong"? It's time to divert your course. It's time to admit pride or selfishness because it's impossible to live with people without hurting or offending them. But as soon as you feel the Lord's direction to seek forgiveness, it's time to act. It is very humbling to go to another person and say, "I was wrong. Will you forgive me?" It's essential if you're going to live with people who are impossible to live with, and seeking forgiveness should be a way of life, not something that you do once or twice. It's a way of life. Who has God brought to your mind that you need to seek forgiveness? For me it's often the people in my own family. I've had to seek forgiveness from my wife and from my little boy. Who is it that the Lord's speaking to you about today?

Let's pray. "Father, I pray that You would make us ministers of reconciliation, that we would be quick to initiate reconciliation by seeking forgiveness and not waiting for the other person. I pray

SEEK FORGIVE

that You would give each one who's thinking about it now, the courage to go and seek forgiveness. Give them the love, the humility, and the words to say, and the right timing to say those most difficult words, 'I was wrong. Would you please forgive me?' We pray in Jesus' name. Amen."

GODSHIP ——————————————————

REJECTION ——————————————————

EXTERNAL/INTERNAL ——————————————

PROBLEMS, PROBLEMS, WHY PROBLEMS? ———

MY FLESH—GOD'S ENEMY ———————————

REPENTANCE ———————————————————

WHAT'S NEW ABOUT YOU? ——————————

ACCEPTING YOUR RIGHTEOUSNESS ————

EXTENDING FORGIVENESS ———————————

SEEKING FORGIVENESS ——————————————

REST, ABIDE, WALK ━━━━━━━━━━▶

LOVE ————————————————————————

GODSHIP

REJECT

EXT/INT

PROBLEMS

FLESH

REPENT

WHAT'S NEW

ACCEPT RIGHT

EXTEND FORGIVE

SEEK FORGIVE

REST

LOVE

REST, ABIDE, WALK

> ***Let us therefore be diligent to enter that rest, lest anyone fall through following the same example of disobedience.***
>
> Hebrews 4:11

One of the greatest challenges to a believer is to avoid being sidetracked from following Jesus Christ. Life is filled with things that threaten to overwhelm you, things like business affairs, time-pressures, problems, trials, and tragedies. When you are weighted down, when things seem hopeless and the future bleak, the tendency is to look to other people for answers. You may attempt to "fix" the circumstances, or do something other than receiving from Jesus Christ the power to live.

This lesson is designed to help the believer, whether newborn or mature, to know the secret of real power for the drudgery of living day after day after day in grace and triumph. We pray that you will realize that what we call "the process of daily life" is the arena where God's sustaining grace and peace and strength are to be proven. You may tend to think in terms of "what it will be like" when . . . a certain level of spiritual maturity is reached, or a chosen goal attained. But God and His power are for now—not just for the future. Your life can be characterized by either resting or wrestling. Rest is yours when you can shift the focus of your attention from yourself and your problems to God.

REST

REST

Matthew 11:28-30
Philippians 2:3, 5-8
Hebrews 4:9-11
Isaiah 40:28-31

Turn the page to continue on ABIDE & WALK.

ABIDE

John 15:1-11

WALK

Galatians 5:16
Ephesians 5:18
1 John 5:14-15

Action steps to take when I realize I am not resting:

The baby steps are **A**_____ I am not resting and **A**_____ God to take charge of my life. As I mature in Christ, I simply **A**_____ I am not resting as the Spirit reveals it to me, and I thank Him for revealing it to me and once again **A**_____ what is already mine (2 Peter 1:3).

Ask   *Acknowledge*   *Appropriate*   *Admit*

190-A

PURPOSE for Diagram **190-A:**

To describe the Christian's life when he or she is functioning after the Spirit.

REST?

? 1. What does Jesus say in Matthew 11:28 is the first step in resting?

_____

? 2. Rather than coming to Him, how do you respond? Example: worry, struggle for control, retreat to work.

_____

📖 3. Study Philippians 2:3-9 carefully.

? 4. According to verses 6-8, who was Jesus and what was strange about how He lived? _____

? 5. What do you see yourself doing out of selfish interests or lack of regard for others? _____

_____

> *Come to Me, all who are weary and heavy-laden . . . .*
> Matt. 11:28

I must labor to rest.

REST

REST

Matthew 11:28-30
Philippians 2:3, 5-8
Hebrews 4:9-11
Isaiah 40:28-31

Continued from previous page.

ABIDE

John 15:1-11

WALK

Galatians 5:16
Ephesians 5:18
1 John 5:14-15

Action steps to take when I realize I am not resting:

The baby steps are A_____ I am not resting and A_____ God to take charge of my life. As I mature in Christ, I simply A_____ I am not resting as the Spirit reveals it to me, and I thank Him for revealing it to me and once again A_____what is already mine (2 Peter 1:3).

Ask   *Acknowledge*   *Appropriate*   *Admit*

190-A

PURPOSE for Diagram **190-A continued:**

To describe the Christian's life when he or she is functioning after the Spirit.

ABIDE

 1. Study John 15:4-11.

2. Do you enjoy the close, intimate, "abiding" fellowship with the Lord that you desire?_____

3. What will be your experience if you remain in the vine?

_____

4. List some things that indicate that you are living dependently upon the vine.

_____

_____

> *Come to Me, all who are weary and heavy-laden . . . .*
> Matt. 11:28

5. Now list some things that indicate you are living independently of the vine.

_____

_____

WALK

 1. Study Galatians 5:18.

2. Why do you think you are encouraged to be "filled with the Spirit"?

_____

3. How well does a drunk person walk? _____

4. Study Gal. 5:16.

5. What might be some things that hinder your process of walking by the Spirit? _____

Stay connected to the vine.

REST

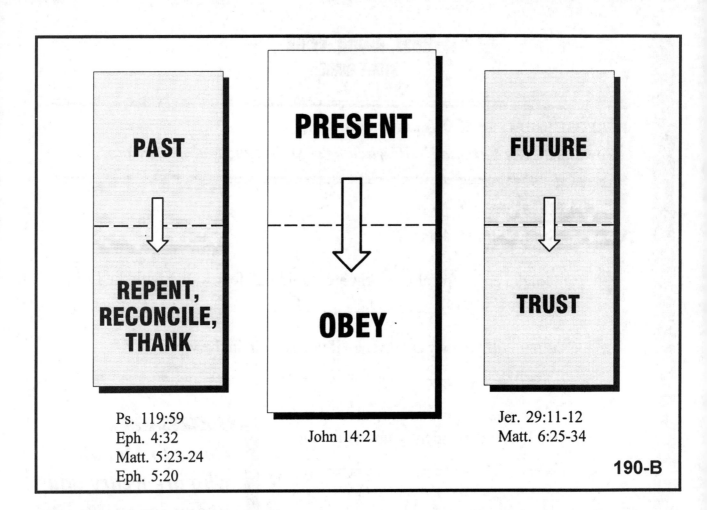

PAST

REPENT,
RECONCILE,
THANK

Ps. 119:59
Eph. 4:32
Matt. 5:23-24
Eph. 5:20

PRESENT

OBEY

John 14:21

FUTURE

TRUST

Jer. 29:11-12
Matt. 6:25-34

190-B

NOTES

PURPOSE for Diagram **190-B:**

To show how to rest regarding the past, present, and future.

1. Study Psalm 119:59.

2. What sin haunts you? Are you ready to repent? _____ _____ _____

> *For I know the plans I have for you . . . .*
> Jer. 29:11

3. Study Ephesians 4:32.

4. Who has hurt you in the past? Are you ready to forgive? _____ _____

5. Study Ephesians 5:20.

6. What circumstances from your past have you not thanked God for? _____ _____

7. Study John 14:21.

8. In what area of your life do you need to obey God now? _____ _____

9. Study Jeremiah 29:11.

10. Can you trust the Creator and Master of the universe with your future? Why? _____ _____

REST

*Today is a gift.
That's why it's called the "present."*

MAN'S VIEW OF LIFE

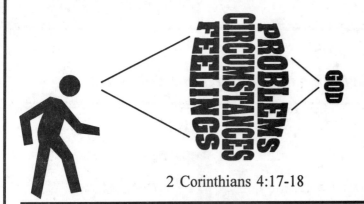

2 Corinthians 4:17-18

Self-Centered
View of Life:

Does your God seem so small you are unable to trust Him and rest? Why? You see most clearly what is closest to you, so God seems small and far away when you concentrate on your problems, circumstances, or feelings. Your prayer might sound like this, "Oh, God, where are you? I'm overwhelmed by what is happening in my life."

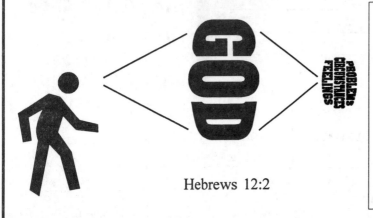

Hebrews 12:2

God-Centered
View of Life:

This is the correct view. God is your focus, not your problems, circumstances, or feelings. You can clearly see Him in all His power, wisdom, and sovereignty. You can rest because you know He is in charge. He is a God of love who can bring you through any issue or problem. Your prayer would sound like this, "Oh, God, I thank you for being in charge of my life. Please show me how you want me to handle this situation."

190-C

NOTES

VCL

VICTORIOUS CHRISTIAN LIVING Conference
Copyright © 1999 Victorious Christian Living International, Inc.

PURPOSE for Diagram **190-C**:

To illustrate how one's focus becomes one's greatest issue.

---

1. Study Hebrews 12:1-3. Which view of life is most often yours? Explain. _____

   _____

2. What problem, circumstance, or feelings are you staring at now?

   _____

   _____

> ### *Fixing our eyes on Jesus . . . .* Heb. 12:2

3. Is your God too small? _____

4. What attribute of God can you think about now? (Omnipotent, omnipresent, all knowing, loving, patient, faithful) _____

   _____

   _____

5. Can you tell Him you are going to focus on Him and stop focusing on the problems that steal your joy? _____

   _____

God is in control!

REST

REVIEW

- God provides a never-failing rest that is the constant, present inheritance of every child of God.

- Self-focus is the first step in the forfeiture of God's rest.

- Jesus calls all who are weary and beaten down to receive His rest and give Him their burdens.

- Abiding in Christ and remaining in intimate contact with Him is the only way to have a fulfilling, fruitful life.

- Walking after the Spirit is a one-step-at-a-time process. Steps are small, manageable movements of progress that both train and prepare for greater strength and ability.

NOTES

VCL

VICTORIOUS CHRISTIAN LIVING Conference
Copyright © 1999 Victorious Christian Living International, Inc.

REST, ABIDE, WALK

Lesson Transcript by David Ritzenthaler

This lesson is entitled "Rest, Abide, Walk." That is resting while you are abiding in Christ walking after the Spirit. This is one of the most popular lessons that we share because there are many people as Christians who find themselves burned-out, stressed-out, and worn-out. This lesson is designed to teach you how to have all the energy every day that you need to live an effective, abundant, dynamic Christian life. So, if you find yourself anxious, depressed, or frustrated with life or people, this is a session that you want to hear.

All of us at times have problems with someone or circumstances. These maladies usually are a result of an issue of godship where we're trying to control life, and it just doesn't work. As you turn to this lesson, "Rest, Abide, Walk," I want you to listen to a letter that I received from the wife of a pastor. This couple had been really going through it while trying to pastor a church. They themselves were having difficulty in their relationship. But even more, she personally was at a point in her life that the pastor was deciding this particular day when he called whether or not to institutionalize her in a mental institution. The church had asked him if he would, one more time, try to help her before institutionalizing her. So he called our center in Illinois and that center called Phoenix. We agreed that they could come for a week and I would spend a week with them, helping them salvage the situation in their marriage and in their lives so that she wouldn't have to go to an institution.

Well this letter that I'm going to read, that she has agreed for me to share, is six months after they were here for a week. During that week's time I shared with her this session. I want you to hear what she has to say. She says: "My husband is still struggling with living the Christian life or appropriating Christ as life. Only God can make it make sense to him. I can model it, explain it, but I can't make him understand. For now, I am content to let God make the changes in both of us. What a relief not to have to do it. What a relief to have God in charge, showing us where the next change has to come and then accepting it and allowing God the freedom to make the changes. What a relief to no longer have to meet standards—my husband's standards, the church's standards, the Bible's standards, or my own standards—only to let God make the changes.

"How restful to lean on Him and to praise Him all day long for the love and care. Such an unbounding joy I'm experiencing. Whenever I slip and try to do it myself again, I quickly fly back to God's hiding place to be hidden in Christ. I am a totally different person than I was six months ago. How I praise Him for the terrible trials and suffering that I went through. I have learned so much and don't ever want to forget it or go back to being that old me.

"Not only am I different, but I have so much compassion for the hurting and wounded and struggling, especially the Christians who can't seem to live this abundant life. I love them and pray for them and can support them with understanding. I have a whole Sunday school class full of them who are struggling. How God loves them and how I love them too. It's fantastic."

What happened with this woman who was going to be institutionalized, to six months later write a letter like this about what is happening in her life, and, interestingly enough, talking about her husband not knowing this yet? This was the husband that was going to institutionalize her. In fact, I have to tell you that that's not the end of that story. A few months after she wrote me this letter, I got a call to find out that he had had an affair and that the church had released him from his responsibilities at the church. She, in the phone conversation, continued to say, "I want you to know it's wonderful to be able to be at peace, to be able to walk through this, to be able to love him, to be able to let God do the work that needs to be done in him." Here she was, at peace in the midst of this terrible circumstance—resting, abiding in Christ, walking after the Spirit.

REST, ABIDE, WALK (Diagram 190-A)

Turn to your outline, Diagram 190-A. You will notice the first word is "rest." In fact, you'll notice the outline is simply made up of the word "rest," the word "abide," and the word "walk." I want to take each one of those words and what I want you to see is that each one of these things, though they're different words and different ways of communicating an idea, they are the same idea scripturally. They're just three different ways that God shows us how to enjoy the abundant life. As this gal began to enjoy that abundant life, she found herself resting while she was abiding in Christ walking after the Spirit. These are all the same thing, just three different ways to say it.

I want to begin to develop this concept of resting. How do you actually rest as a believer? How do you get to the place where anxiety and depression and frustration and all these things are removed from your life? Not the people, not the circumstances, they may be the same, but you and I are able to enjoy in the midst of these things being at peace, being at rest, abiding in Christ, and walking after His Spirit even in the most difficult of circumstances. I would like for us to read Matthew 11:28-30: "Come to Me, all who are weary and heavy-laden, and I will give you rest. Take My yoke upon you, and learn from Me, for I am gentle and humble in heart; and you shall find rest for your souls. For My yoke is easy, and My load is light."

To be able to appreciate what's being said, we need to realize who the speaker is, who is saying this "come to Me." If you have a red letter Bible, you will notice it is in red letters because it's the Lord Jesus saying this. When you and I are depressed, discouraged, frustrated, anxious, burned-out, or worn-out, it is because we are not in the presence of and enjoying the empowering of the Spirit of God. We have walked away. That's why the Lord Jesus says, "Come to Me, all who are weary and heavy-laden." If those are our life experiences, it's not because God isn't supplying, it isn't because God isn't sufficient, it's because you and I have walked away.

In verse 29, He tells us how to practically, specifically, actually come back into His presence to enjoy resting, to be able to be at a place of abiding, and to actually effectively walk after the Spirit. I want us to look at these verses for a few minutes, so we can begin to grasp the idea of how do you rest, how do you come to this place where Jesus truly is empowering you and you are filled with energy today? The Bible says, "In Thy presence [the Lord's] is the fullness of joy" (Psalm 16:11). Another verse of the Bible says, ". . . the joy of the Lord is your strength" (Nehemiah 8:10). So if you want strength, you want joy that is more than you need for yourself. It is in the presence of the Lord, it is enjoying His presence that makes that possible. Let's see what He says here as to how we can make that possible.

You will notice verse 30 says His yoke is easy and His load is light. Now I want you to listen carefully, so that you don't misunderstand what I am saying. What I am saying is this, the Christian life is easy, the Christian life is light. If you've been a Christian for years as many tell me, they say, "Man, for twenty years I've been

VCL

VICTORIOUS CHRISTIAN LIVING Conference
Copyright © 1999 Victorious Christian Living International, Inc.

living the Christian life and it's hard." Well, I have to point out to them that they're not living the Christian life.

The Christian life is not hard. In fact, let me quote what the Bible says, "the way of transgressors is hard" (Proverbs 13:15 KJV). When we transgress, when we walk away from, when we're not coming unto and into the presence of Christ, we've walked away—that is a hard life. Now, it doesn't say that life will be a bed of roses. No. In fact as you watch Paul, he was in the midst of all kinds of difficulties and distresses and problems and beatings and jailings and being lost at sea, I mean floating in the ocean for a day or two. I'm not talking about circumstances all being wonderful and, therefore, everything is wonderful. The reason I read you this letter from this pastor's wife is so you realize that the best place to experience the dynamic of the power of the supernatural life in Christ is in the worst of circumstances. You see, if life was really good and everything was perfect and wonderful around you, would you know if you have the supernatural life? No, you couldn't really know that for sure. The best place to know it is in the worst of circumstances. If you can experience the fullness of joy and be completely thankful in the worst of things, it's probably because you have learned this life of the Christ, the Eternal One living through you and making it possible to live supernaturally.

In verse 29, He tells us two things that actually make that possible, so let's look at these two things and see how you actually come to the place of resting. He has said first in verse 28, "Come to Me" and then in the next verse He says is "Take My yoke upon you." So the first command is to come to Him and the second one is to take His yoke. Notice in verse 30, that His yoke He is asking you to take is light and it is easy. This life of Christ is light, it's easy, so when He says, "Take my yoke," it isn't to take upon yourself a burden. In fact, if you are carrying a burden, what are you going to prob-

ably have to do before you can take His yoke upon you? You are going to have to give your burden or your yoke up and that's no "yoke." How many of you have ever seen somebody carrying a yoke across their shoulders with a couple of buckets carrying water and such? Well, if you are carrying a yoke like that with all that weight, the first thing you have to do is to take that yoke off of you in order to take His yoke on you. He describes here two things that are what you have to do to take His yoke which is light and easy. I want us to see those. Notice the first one. He says, "Take my yoke . . . and learn from Me," and then He tells us two things we need to learn. The first one is, He says, "I am gentle." The word is also translated "meek." The second thing He says is that He is humble in heart. Okay, I've got to learn that He is meek or gentle. What significance does that have to me?

I believe if you will join me, in a few minutes you will see what it actually means to learn of Him and become meek. I'll show you that. In fact, if you just keep something in the place there in Matthew, turn with me to Philippians, the Second chapter. I want to show you what He actually gives as an illustration scripturally to what meekness is. In Philippians, Chapter 2, starting at verse 5, He gives a specific detailed idea of what the thoughts in Jesus were that made him meek. What was it that caused Him to be meek? Look with me starting in verse 5. It is interesting that He actually says that you and I, this is talking to the Philippians here, but also written to every believer, He's telling us in verse 5, "Have this attitude in yourselves which was also in Christ Jesus." In other words, you and I are to have this attitude or this thinking in us. What was this attitude or thinking?

Verse 6 says, "who, although He existed in the form of God, did not regard equality with God a thing to be grasped." Let's stop here for a minute. Let's understand this. Here's Jesus who knew He was God. Now let me ask you a question. Would you view that as a fairly good self-worth, a pretty good view of one's self—viewing yourself as God? Well, that is a pretty high self-worth, but it's more than a high self-worth, it's an appropriate, it's an accurate self-worth because that's actually who He is so there is nothing wrong with it. The Bible doesn't want us to have a low self-worth and it doesn't want us to have a high self-worth, it wants us to have an **accurate** self-worth. He had an accurate one and that was that He was God. Knowing He was God, he made a decision not to hold onto His Godhead.

Notice four things in the next verses. He "emptied Himself, taking the form of a bond-servant, and being made in the likeness of men. And being found in appearance as a man, He humbled Himself by becoming obedient to the point of death, even death on a cross." What I want you to see here is a person who has a very good, accurate view of His self-worth. He wants us to have an accurate self-worth view of who we actually are. He doesn't want us to have a low or a high self-worth. He wants us to be able to face all the positives about ourselves and all the negatives about ourselves. He wants us to be able to accept those totally—recognize and admit this is who we are. I am going to give you four things out of these verses that will show you what it meant when He said, "Have this attitude [thinking] in yourselves," and that thinking was "learn of Me for I am meek." Look at what made Him meek in His thinking.

First, go to verse 7. In verse 7, it says He "emptied Himself." This is point number one of these four things in these verses. When it says He "emptied Himself" it's also translated in other translations He "made Himself of no reputation." Let me ask you a question. How many of you find that something you really look forward to everyday is to be of no reputation? How many of you have found that you have no need to protect your reputation when somebody is maligning you and gossiping about you? Now remember, in verse 5 it says, "Have this attitude [thinking] in yourselves." I want you to see

what would happen when you and I let this thinking become our thinking. When we let the thinking of Christ become our thinking what will happen to us in terms of rest or peace or abiding or walking after the Spirit? Notice what happens. If you truly let this thinking be in you, this meek thinking of being willing to be of no reputation—notice it wasn't that somebody wrecked His reputation—He decided to be of no reputation. When you and I make a decision to become joined with the thinking of Christ and we decide to be of no reputation anymore, can anybody do anything with regard to trying to wreck our reputation that would bug us or upset us or make us depressed or discouraged or frustrated or anxious or whatever? No! If we had no need to protect our reputation anymore, nobody could upset us or make us anxious. Nobody could depress us by the kinds of terrible things that they would say about us, because we don't think that way anymore, we don't think in terms of protecting our reputation.

Notice the second thing He says. Not only are we to have this thinking in us and that is to decide to be of no reputation, but the next thing in that same verse 7, He took upon Himself "the form of a bond-servant." Now let me ask you a question. If you or I decided to be a slave, to be a bond-servant, would there be anything anybody could ask us to do as an employer that would upset us and demean us because it was too lowly a thing to do? Would we have any complaints if someone asked us to do things, if we had decided—now notice it doesn't say someone made Him a servant, it says He decided to be one—to be a servant? Let me ask you a question. Do you think that churches would function more effectively if believers began to be servants to each other? Do you think there would be divisions anymore if they decided to be of no reputation and didn't worry about what somebody's gossip was? In fact, they didn't concern themselves as to what they were requested to do. They were just willing to do whatever because they were living as unto Christ, doing whatever it was as long as it was, of course, moral and legal. I mean we wouldn't have the thinking of Christ and agree to do something that is immoral or illegal. But as long as it isn't, if we decided to become a servant no one could enslave or cause us to feel obligated to do something we didn't want to do, if we had already decided to be a servant.

Notice the third thing. Verse 8 says, "And being found in appearance as a man, He humbled Himself by becoming obedient to the point of death, even death on a cross." Does it say that anybody humiliated Him? No. Come with me for a minute in your imagination when He was taken by the Roman Army before the king and He was being maligned by the things that people were saying about Him. They're punching Him in the face, spitting on Him, crowning Him with thorns, and He says what to them in response? What does He say? He says absolutely nothing. Do you know why He had no need to protect His reputation, no need to respond? Now remember something, here is God. The Bible says that He could call down legions of angels, ten thousands of angels; He could wipe every one of those people out that were spitting on Him, judging Him as the king. He was God, but He said nothing. And the reason is you can't humiliate somebody if they have already decided to humble themselves. Would you be at peace in your life if you had already decided when you got up today to let the thinking that is in Christ Jesus be your thinking—letting the Holy Spirit empower Himself through you with the thinking of Christ which is that you make yourself of no reputation? You are willing to be a servant, you are willing to humble yourself. Do you think it would be possible for marriages to function effectively if more people were willing to humble themselves? So when someone tells you something about yourself that needs to be straightened out, instead of resisting and arguing and fighting, you'd say, "Well, you know, I appreciate your sharing that. In fact, let me tell you a couple other of my flaws so that maybe you

could make note of those, too, and help me with them." Because you already decided to be of no reputation. You already decided to humble yourself so nobody can humiliate you. You see, what we're talking about is a very significant self-worth isn't it? Not a low self-worth. No, a person who you can't humiliate, a person who you can not demean, is a person who has a very strong self-worth.

When I was growing up and I thought of the word "meekness," I thought of the word "meek" and I immediately thought of the word "weak." I thought weak people were meek people. Why would I ever want to be meek? Then I began to realize that meek is actually a person who knows who he is, like Jesus did, but decides not to hold on to it. You see, in a society like ours where our whole commitment is to our personal self-rights, this flies in the face of that. What we're talking about here is giving up our rights and our reputation. Giving up our rights and becoming a servant to another. This is totally different. I realize now, a meek person is one of the most powerful you've ever met, because a meek person is a person who has a good self-worth. Meek people are people who know who they are, but they have chosen to give up their rights. As they give up their self-rights, you no longer can upset them, you no longer can humiliate them, you no longer can enslave them, or cause them to feel a situation of servitude because they have already decided to be a bond-servant.

But there is a fourth thing. Notice in verse 8, He not only made Himself of no reputation, He not only decided to be a servant, he not only humbled Himself, but the last part of that verse 8 he became obedient to death, even the death of the cross. Well, what does that mean? What that means is this: when He was in the garden and He was thinking about the consequences of going to the cross and shedding His blood, He said to His Father, "I don't want to shed My blood, but not My self-will be done, but Your will be done." What He was saying was "I'm

VCL
VICTORIOUS CHRISTIAN LIVING Conference
Copyright © 1999 Victorious Christian Living International, Inc.

giving up My rights. I'm willing to be of no rights and do whatever You want, including to die. Something I can't imagine, because I have lived forever. I'm willing to die. I'm willing to become obedient to You. I'm willing to give up My rights."

Do you realize that if you and I had the thinking in us that was in Christ Jesus which was meekness, there is nothing that could upset us? Meekness is a willingness to be of no reputation. Meekness is a willingness to be a servant. Meekness is a willingness to humble ourselves, admit our wrongs. Meekness is a willingness to give up our rights. Then we would be at peace. There is nothing that could enslave us, nothing that we would have to control because we were the servant. We could actually enjoy rest as we take His yoke which is light and easy, because we had learned of Him, which is to be meek, to let the thinking of meekness be our thinking.

But in Matthew 11:29, you'll notice that there is a second thing He says. He says not only let this thinking be in us of meekness, but He says, "I am humble in heart." What does it mean to be humble in heart? We realize now what meekness is. Meekness is those four things we looked at in Philippians. But what is humble in heart? Well, actually back in Philippians 2:3 you have a description of the second thing as well. Let me read that to you. Philippians 2:3 says, "Do nothing from selfishness or empty conceit, but with humility of mind let each of you regard one another as more important than himself." That's what it means to be humble in heart, not to have a lowly opinion of ourselves, but a high opinion of the other person, to consider the other person more important than yourself.

Do you think there is any marriage that would fail if both parties had meekness and humbleness of heart as their attitudes? I've been counseling for 30 plus years, and I have never seen a marriage to this day that couldn't be healed and transformed and made beautiful if at least just

one person was willing to let Matthew 11:29 and Philippians 2:5–8 become his/her living experience. Because even in the midst of the worst of marriages, married to the most terrible person doing terrible things there can be peace. Like in the letter I read in the beginning. This gal was able to be at peace because she was allowing the thinking of Christ Jesus to be her thinking everyday. She was enjoying resting in the midst of her husband having had an affair. Does that mean that she didn't care? No, that was very hurtful and very painful. Does that mean it isn't important to the integrity of a marriage? No, it's absolutely important to her. But what she had was a supernatural ability beyond human capability of forgiveness. She was able to forgive supernaturally. She was not only able to forgive, but she was able to be free to love him and to pray for him and to live with him and to begin to encourage him and to help him discover this life that she had, because it was greater and more than she needed for herself.

That's the supernatural life of resting in Christ Jesus and that's exactly what God wants. It's not an issue of resting with the idea that you're sitting sleeping or doing nothing. In fact, some of you may have read the new translation called *The Message*. I'll read you Matthew 11:28–30, I want you to read it with me here. It's very interesting the way this man writes this. Here's what he says starting in verse 28, "Are you tired, worn-out, burned-out on religion, come to Me. Get away with Me and you will recover your life. I'll show you how to take a real rest. Walk with me and work with me. Watch how I do it. Learn the unforced rhythms of grace. I won't lay anything heavy or ill-fitting on you. Keep company with me and you'll learn how to live freely and lightly." You see, we're not talking about hiding in the corner and, therefore resting, or laying in your bed. We're talking about living in the midst of the real life circumstances you and I are in, living a dynamic supernatural life. God desires this for each one of His children. This isn't something special for people that are in the pulpit or people that are teachers or people that are pastoring or people that are missionaries or evangelists—this is for every single saint. This is why God wrote these things so that we could understand them.

Look with me in Hebrews as we look at this word "rest." Look in Hebrews 4:9-11. Here's what it says starting in verse 9, "There remains therefore a Sabbath rest for the people of God." This is not for just leadership, this is for all the people of God this Sabbath rest that we're talking about in Hebrews. In verse 10 it says, "For the one who has entered His [Christ's] rest has himself [that's a small 'h' that means you and I] also rested from his works, as God did from His." If we're going to come to the place of enjoying this rest, we're going to have to cease from our own works. In fact, I have to tell you one of the worst works that you and I could become involved with is "religious" work.

When I was in high school I began to have a real desire to have this abundant life Jesus said He came to give. "I came to give life and give it to you abundantly." I wanted it. So while I was in high school I was the president of the Youth for Christ Club and I was leading people to Christ and I was just totally committed to doing everything and anything necessary to live this supernatural life.

From there, I went to a Bible school and I took everything I could take on the studying of the Bible. I went to every conference I could go to. I went to the bookstore and I bought every single book I could read and added them to my library. It's part of why I have such an enormous library today, because I read everything I could read to have this life. In fact, I worked so hard at having this Christian life that I started getting so exhausted that I started sleeping 16 to 18 hours per day. My grandmother, concerned about that, came to the school where I was and took me to a doctor. They put me through all kinds of tests. When I met with the doctor a

couple of weeks later, he said, you know, we have thoroughly examined you and he said, "I want you to understand you are in perfect physical condition, you don't have mono, you don't have any of the things that people would think you have. You are in perfect physical condition. There's not a thing wrong with you." He said, "Dave, I've known your family have for years [Dr. Blumenthal is the name, a Jewish doctor gifted far beyond his medical training]." He said, "I want to tell you something. You come from a very strong-willed German family. If you keep going the way you are going, sleeping 16 to 18 hours a day, Dave, my conclusion after all my evaluation is, you just don't want to live any longer."

Well this was wild. I was now on probation at the school, because, obviously, it's a little hard to do well in school when you're sleeping 16 to 18 hours a day. The only thing I would get up for is to go to the cafeteria to eat lunch and dinner. Now here is somebody who wants life like you can't imagine, was leading people to Christ by the score, was totally committed to living a supernatural Christian life and he is telling me that I don't want to live. In fact, do you know what my response was? At about 20 years of age, kind of a smart aleck that I was, I looked around the room and I said, "Well, now two of us know." Because, you see, he was absolutely correct. I had come to the place I was so frustrated trying to live the Christian life, doing everything I could do to be this supernatural Christian, that I was totally burned-out, exhausted, and fed up with the Christian life.

In fact, after my time with him, I quit school. I said scrap Christianity—it doesn't work. You see, that's what He is saying here. In Hebrews 4:9–10 it says, "There remains therefore a Sabbath rest for the people of God. For the one who has entered His rest has himself also rested from his works, as God did from His." The Lord allowed me to go home, and sleep in the basement of my folks home for another 3 to 4 months for 16, 17, or 18 hours a day and get up to eat. One day I said, "This is stupid, this is a waste of time, I can't seem to die, can't seem to accomplish what Dr. Blumenthal said, I guess I'm not as strong-willed as I thought, because he said, 'if you keep this up you'll be a vegetable.'" I couldn't get to the vegetable state so I decided to go and get a job and go on with living.

God, in His grace, decided just a couple of months later to introduce me to what we're talking about here right now. This is how to come to the place of resting in the Sabbath rest, allowing the Spirit of God to lead and abiding in Him became my living experience, so I didn't have to work at being a Christian anymore. Because I found out God had already done all the work. He'd already accomplished everything and all I had to do was begin to appropriate and enjoy it. In fact, let me read you a quote out of Oswald Chambers, *My Utmost for His Highest*. It says: "'And I will give you rest. That is I will sustain you, causing you to stand firm.' He's not saying I'll put you to bed, hold your hand, or sing you to sleep. In essence He's saying I will get you out of bed, out of your listlessness and exhaustion, and out of your condition of being half-dead while you're still alive. I will penetrate you with the Spirit of life and you will be sustained by the perfection of vital activity." God wanted to produce a supernatural life in me, He didn't want my puny self-accomplished Christian life. He didn't want religion, which is what that is all about, trying to live by laws of the Scriptures. That's why the woman wrote in her letter, "I'm so glad I don't have to meet the standards of my husband, the standards of the Bible, the standards of myself, I don't have to meet any standards anymore." All she had to do was just let this supernatural life of Jesus Christ live in her and through her. That makes it possible for us to go to the next word, the word "abide."

In John Chapter 15, if you'd turn to that, you're probably very familiar with it, it's a familiar passage about the vineyard. In this passage of the vineyard, there are 3 specific people mentioned. The first verse, Jesus again speaking [in red letters], says, "I am the true vine, and My Father is the vinedresser." So here we have the first two. In verse 5 we have the third person. Jesus says again, "I am the vine, you are the branches; he who abides in Me, and I in him, he bears much fruit; for apart from Me you can do nothing." Here we have God the Father, He runs the vineyard. He comes in and waters it and muddies things up. He comes in and prunes away, cuts away on the branches, that's you and I. The only thing we are asked to do is to stay connected to the vine which, by the way, is Jesus. It says He is the vine. God gave us the vineyard to teach us the dimension of supernatural living, of how to abide. You can rest when you are abiding in Christ, when you're simply connected. When we're allowing the flow of the sap of the Holy Spirit through the vine to you and me, the branches, then something wonderful happens.

I'm going to ask you two questions. When I ask you these questions, they are not trick questions, I'm going to ask them both so that you'll realize I'm not trying to trick you, so here they are. Here's the first one. In a vineyard, who produces the grapes or the fruit? Now don't answer it because I want you to think about it, who *produces* it. Here's the second question. Don't answer it. Just think about it. Who *bears* the fruit? You see, you and I are the branches. Where do the grapes come out? They come out on the branch. The fruit, and, by the way, notice that the fruit is the fruit of the Holy Spirit (Galatians 5:22–23). How many of you like me tried to be loving? I tried all the fruit of the Spirit. I tried to do them all when I was in my twenties. I was so exhausted trying to do the fruit of the Holy Spirit, it just wore me out. Those are the fruit not of Dave, those are the fruit of the Holy Spirit. So, all you and I have to do, like the grapes on the branches on the vine, the grapes or the fruit of the Holy Spirit comes out of the branches just because the branches are connected to the vine. And the one who is at work producing that is the vine, of course, because the vine has the branches connected, the vine has the sap coming through it that is producing the grapes. But the other one is the Father. He owns the vineyard. He runs it. He comes in. He pours the water into our lives and muddies them up, and He comes in with the shears and He prunes away on us, the branches. Isn't that exciting? You see, He does that because He wants us to bear more fruit. But who is doing the work here by the way? Is the branch doing the work? I don't know if any of you have ever done this, I took a really sensitive microphone out to my fruit trees and I set it up there. I just wanted to see what kind of sounds fruit trees made. So when I set it up there it was just amazing to listen to the groans and the moanings of the fruit as it was bearing itself. I know you're looking at me like I am weird. Well, if I had done that let me tell you probably it would be weird. There probably is somebody who has done that. No, I didn't do that. The point is, it's not the fruit that is working, it is the Father who is working, pouring the water on, pruning the branches. The branches are doing nothing except staying connected or abiding in the vine. That's all they're doing. The fruit that is coming out of them is something the Father and the vine are producing. If you will look in those verses it says that if you don't stay connected to the vine what will happen is you will wither up and die.

Are you withered up and dying like I was? It was because I wasn't staying connected. I was trying to produce fruit by my own ability. It's an absolutely miserable experience as a Christian. I think there is nothing worse. I think that a Christian trying to live the Christian life is more miserable than a person who isn't a Christian. People who aren't Christians are just caught up with satisfying their flesh, they're having a good time. Sin is pleasant for a season. But a person who has become a Christian and knows all these things that he or she is supposed to do or be and is trying to be all these and is trying to produce

them in his/her own effort, is a miserable person. The most exciting life is the one that we live when we are connected to the vine and we aren't doing anything except enjoying the fruit that is coming from the Spirit through our life. And you're standing back and going "wow, gee," because you know it isn't you. You wouldn't love that person God gives you the power to love. You wouldn't let the person in line because you would rather get through the traffic first yourself, but you go, "Wow, man, I can't believe I let that person in." Because you're just enjoying the Spirit at work because He's doing something you and I humanly wouldn't do.

PAST, PRESENT, FUTURE
(Diagram 190-B)
Look at diagram 190-B. You'll notice there are three categories, three boxes, three things. One says "past," one says "present," and one says "future" at the top. In each of these rectangles, there are words at the bottom under the dotted lines. You can look up all those verses below. Many people, who for the 30 years that I have been counseling, have come for help and they live their lives in the past. When you live your life in the past, what you do is you drag all your baggage with you. What that causes you to be is a very depressed person, because it's a lot of work dragging all your baggage. Or, the other people come in and they're trying to handle and solve and fix all the problems that are going to happen next month, next year, many of which, in fact, most of which, never happen. Those people are filled with anxiety, they're so anxious about what is going to happen that hasn't happened yet and probably isn't going to happen, because most things that we think are going to happen don't. So here you have a person living in the past, depressed, and here you have a person living in the future filled with anxiety and stress. Well, the only place you can live this supernatural life of resting or abiding is in the present. That's the only place you can live it. Because the life of Christ is now, it's not tomorrow, it's not yesterday, it is now. He is an ever-present "I

am" now. So the only thing you and I can do with regard to the past is to repent of things that are not right, any relationships that we are continuing to drag along that are not reconciled through unforgiveness, we need to repent. We need to get reconciled. Or, we need to thank God. "Give thanks in all circumstances; for this is God's will for you in Christ Jesus" (1 Thessalonians 5:18 NIV). In the future, the only thing we can do about the future is trust ourselves to the Lord. If you read Matthew 6:34 He simply says, "Therefore do not be anxious for tomorrow; for tomorrow will care for itself. Each day has enough trouble of its own." Why worry about tomorrow's troubles when you have some today? And of course in Jeremiah 29:11 He says, "'For I know the plans that I have for you,' declares the Lord, 'plans for welfare and not for calamity to give you a future and a hope.'" They're for our best interest, so why waste our time trying to solve them and fix them. They haven't happened yet. The only place you can live this life of resting and abiding is in the present.

REST, ABIDE, WALK (Diagram 190-A)

Look at that last word, the word "walk." This is just one more way of describing the same thing. You see, we're resting, abiding in Christ when we are walking after the Spirit. Walking after the Spirit is the same thing as abiding in Christ, it is the same thing as resting. They're all the same idea three different ways that God shows it to us. But I want us to take the word walk for a minute because, you see, everyone here is familiar with walking. The reason God gives us certain words like He gave us the vineyard, He gave us a physical illustration of the vineyard to teach us about supernatural, spiritual things. He gave us physical walking the same way. He gave us physical breathing the same way. They're all designed to teach us about life. Let me illustrate it to you. Walking has left, right, left, right, etc., it has a twofold dimension. You step with your left then your right, left, right and that moves you—it's a process. Resting is a process. Abid-

ing is a process. Walking is a process. They're all the same.

Well, I'm going to show you in very simple terms how you can start walking after the Spirit or abiding in Christ or resting. Down at the bottom of your page, Diagram 190-A, you'll notice you have four words across the bottom of the page and you have some blanks there. What I want you to see is that walking is twofold. As a baby, when you first started to learn how to walk, you got right up and walked away, right? No, you probably got up, fell on your face, while you were still bawling that wonderful loving parent of yours couldn't wait to stand you up again so you'd fall again. No, they stood you up again because they wanted to see you walk again, they were so excited about your walking. Do you know that eventually, what happened by them continuing to put you up to walk, what did you learn to do? You learned to walk. Falling is a part of getting started oftentimes in walking or abiding, because you don't really know how to do it yet. As a baby, you took one step and then another one and eventually you were walking. Physical breathing is just like physical walking, it's twofold. You exhale, you inhale. What do you exhale for, what is the purpose of exhaling? It's to exhaust the poisonous gases, the used up good quality air that you took in. What do you inhale for? It's to get oxygen in. Where does oxygen go? It goes into the blood. And the blood is the life source of the human being. Well, that's just like spiritual walking. You see, exhaling is just like this. First John 1:9 (paraphrased) says, "If we admit where we're not walking, we're not resting, we're not abiding, He says if we admit that, He will forgive us and cleanse us just like exhaling is a cleansing process, admitting we're not walking in the cleansing process. [You don't have to ask God to forgive you.] He says if we admit we aren't, He will forgive us and cleanse us from all unrighteousness."

The baby steps are, first, **admit.** The second step, if I am not resting is to **ask** God to take charge of my life. So I ask Him to empower me with His Holy Spirit. So when you first get started it's a conscious thing, it's kind of like when you are driving, when you first started driving you did it consciously. Were you any good at it? No. Now when you're driving you enjoy beautiful music, sit and talk to a good friend, look at the beautiful scenery all while driving. You get to the intersection, you stop at the light, you go through the intersection, you get to the other side and you go "Oh my goodness, was that a red light, did I stop?" You aren't even thinking about it. Now I know that with some of the drivers out there it does seem that way, but the point is it's an unconscious thing. It's just automatic. Well, when you mature in your resting or your abiding or your walking in the Christian life, it's the same way, it's unconscious.

There are two more words down there. I'm not resting, as the Spirit reveals it to me I thank Him for revealing it to me again, and once again, first of all, I simply **acknowledge** that I'm not resting. So when I am a mature believer I don't dig around trying to look for anything wrong. I wait for the Holy Spirit to convict and convince me of sin, of judgment, of unrighteousness, and when He does I say, "Thank you Lord. Thank you for showing me." And then secondly, I simply **appropriate** what is already mine. When I was made a brand new person in Christ Jesus, I was indwelt by the Holy Spirit, God gave me everything necessary. I just needed to say thank you and begin to once again stand up instead of laying there on the ground bawling, get up, start walking again and what happens, I'm eventually resting. I'm eventually consistently giving up my rights. I'm consistently letting the thinking be in me which is in Christ Jesus, being willing to be of no reputation, being willing to humble myself, being willing to be a servant, those things begin to become my automatic normal everyday living experience.

SELF-CENTERED/GOD-CENTERED
(Diagram 190-C)
Turn to your last diagram, 190-C. This is just

one more summary for us to see how this works. In the first diagram, notice a person who is focused on the problems or circumstances or feelings. If that is the person's focus, it's hard to see God. It's hard to come to Him because you can't see Him, because all you can see are the problems or circumstances or your feelings, everything is so big that God is small. Notice in the bottom of the diagram Hebrews 12:2. It says, "looking unto Jesus . . . ." Consider what happens when we start coming to the Lord Jesus, we start looking to Him for our life everyday, we let His thinking become our thinking. What happens is the problems and the circumstances become small, they become insignificant, they don't rule anymore, they're not overwhelming to us anymore, we're actually at peace, we're at rest, we're not burned-out, we're not distressed; in fact, we're filled with energy of the Spirit because of the joy of the Lord. Joy is very energizing by the way, and when we're walking in the presence of the Lord, the joy of the Lord is overflowing on us. Life is exciting no matter what the circumstances are, no matter how terrible the people are in our life, we're filled with peace because we're at rest. The life of Christ is abiding in us because we're walking after the Spirit; we're living in a state of rest, and that's what God designed for every one of His children.

REVIEW
Look at the summary there in our review. See what we've said, "God provides a never-failing rest that is constant, a present inheritance of every single child of God." Secondly, we said, "Self-focus is the first step in the forfeiture of God's rest." When we start becoming focused on our rights, we forfeit this rest that God has planned. Third, "Jesus calls all who are weary and beaten down to receive His rest and give Him their burdens." He wants all of us to come back to Him, dump our burdens on Him and let Him once again empower our lives. Next one, "Abiding in Christ and remaining in intimate contact with Him is the only way to a fulfilling, fruitful [Christian] life." The only way to enjoy

the strength that comes from joy is to be in the presence of the One who is joy. In His presence, in this fullness of joy, is all the energy, all the power to be able to live in the midst of the worst of circumstances with the worst of people. Lastly, "Walking after the Spirit is a one-step-at-a-time process. Steps are small, manageable movements of progress that both train and prepare for greater strength and ability."

Would you pray silently with me? As you do I want you to ask yourself a question. Who is the person, what's the circumstance, what is it that's keeping you from enjoying the supernatural abundant rest, abiding in Christ, walking after His Spirit?

GODSHIP ——————————————————————

REJECTION ————————————————————

EXTERNAL/INTERNAL —————————————

PROBLEMS, PROBLEMS, WHY PROBLEMS? ———

MY FLESH—GOD'S ENEMY ————————

REPENTANCE ——————————————————

WHAT'S NEW ABOUT YOU? ————————

ACCEPTING YOUR RIGHTEOUSNESS ————

EXTENDING FORGIVENESS ————————

SEEKING FORGIVENESS ——————————

REST, ABIDE, WALK ————————————

LOVE ⟶

GODSHIP

REJECT

EXT/INT PROBLEMS

FLESH

REPENT

WHAT'S NEW

ACCEPT RIGHT

EXTEND FORGIVE

SEEK FORGIVE

REST

LOVE

LOVE

> *The ultimate aim of the Christian ministry after all, is to produce . . . love.*
>
> 1 Timothy 1:5 (PHILLIPS)
>
> *But now abide faith, hope, love, these three; but the greatest of these is love.*
>
> 1 Corinthians 13:13

The apostle John, inspired by the Spirit of God, sums up all of God's being into one supreme quality and says, "GOD IS LOVE." It follows then that the key characteristic of the life of the Son of God within the believer is love expressed toward God Himself, toward the members of God's family here on earth, toward those outside the family, and incredibly, toward those who make themselves our enemies.

How do I love God whom I cannot see? How do I love my brother whom I can see? Is this love a feeling, an impulse, a sweeping emotional wave that makes the other person's weaknesses, habits, failures, and inconsistencies suddenly of no consequence?

Someone wittily expressed the feelings I may have:

> To live above with saints I love, that surely will be glory!
> But to live below with saints I know—well that's a different story!!

This lesson is designed to show the fruit of the Spirit (which is love) in its practical applications toward both God and man. Never lose sight of the fact that this is none other than THE CHRIST-LIFE in its ultimate expression.

This is not a lesson on how to love. Rather, it is what a life of love looks like in the life of a Christian—both toward God and man.

VICTORIOUS CHRISTIAN LIVING Conference
Copyright © 1999 Victorious Christian Living International, Inc.

LOVE

I. THE PINNACLE OF LOVE.

A. As a goal

1. Matt. 22:36-40
2. Romans 13:8
3. Gal. 5:14
4. 1 John 4:7-13

B. As the end result

1. Eph. 4:11-16
2. Col. 3:14
3. 1 Tim. 1:5

II. LOVE'S TWOFOLD DIMENSION.

A. Toward God: ☐☐☐☐

1. John 14:23-24
2. John 15:9-11, 14
3. 1 John 3:21-22
4. 1 John 5:1-3

220-A

NOTES

VCL
VICTORIOUS CHRISTIAN LIVING Conference
Copyright © 1999 Victorious Christian Living International, Inc.

PURPOSE for Diagram **220-A:**

To show the importance of love and that loving God is obeying Him.

1. Study Matthew 22:36-40.

2. Why is loving God the most important thing to do? _____

3. Study 1 John 5:7-13.

4. What is the goal of the Christian life?
   _____
   _____

> *. . . the greatest of these is love.*
> 1 Cor. 13:13

5. How have you shown your love for God by obedience?
   _____
   _____

6. What area of disobedience is preventing you from loving God?
   _____

7. Study John 14:21.

8. What does Christ promise when you obey? _____
   _____

Let love motivate me in everything!

LOVE

THE EXPERIENCE OF THE OBEDIENCE CYCLE

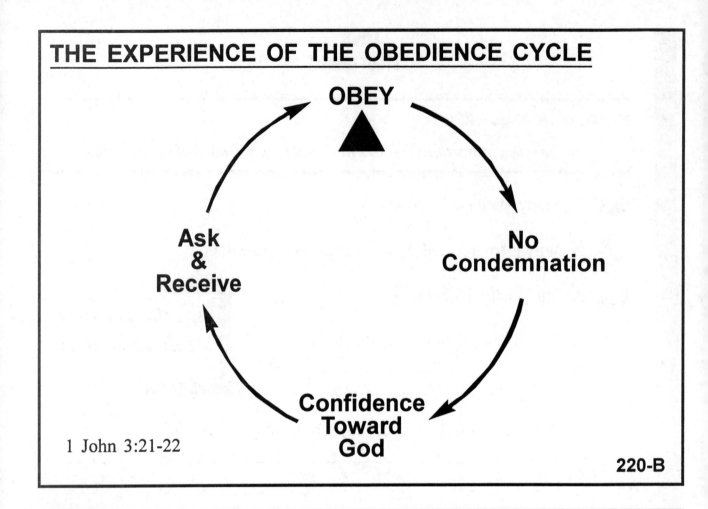

OBEY

No Condemnation

Confidence Toward God

Ask & Receive

1 John 3:21-22

220-B

VCL

VICTORIOUS CHRISTIAN LIVING Conference
Copyright © 1999 Victorious Christian Living International, Inc.

PURPOSE for Diagram **220-B:**

To show how obedience affects our prayer life.

---

1. Study 1 John 3:21-22.

2. Are you asking God for anything specific? _____

3. Are you receiving specific answers? _____

4. If not, do you have confidence before God when you ask?   Yes   No

5. If not, does your heart condemn you in any way? _____
   _____

6. If so, what is the area of disobedience that causes you to feel
   condemned? _____

Obey, then pray.

B. **Toward Mankind:** ☐ ☐ ☐ ☐
1. John 3:16
2. John 13:34-35
3. John 15:12-13, 17
4. 1 John 3:10, 14, 16-18

III. WHAT IS LOVE?

A. A MOTIVE that is _____.

B. A DECISION of the _____.

C. A DEED of present _____ and _____.

220-C

NOTES

VCL
VICTORIOUS CHRISTIAN LIVING Conference
Copyright © 1999 Victorious Christian Living International, Inc.

PURPOSE for Diagram **220-C:**

To show that loving people is expressed by giving.

1. Study John 15:12-13.

2. Who has God brought to you for whom you can lay down your life to meet that person's needs? _____

3. Study Luke 9:23.

4. Do you see that your self-life doesn't want to lay down and die to love others?

> *. . . do not have love, I am nothing.*
> 1 Cor. 13:2

5. Which of the following do you have a hard time giving up for the sake of another: consider your rights, your time, your money, your abilities, your desire to protect yourself from any pain or hurt?

6. Do you love others out of pure motives, or do you want something in return? _____

7. Are you choosing to love others, or do you seek a "feeling" of love first? _____

Love gives.

REVIEW

- Love has a twofold dimension. One is vertical toward God and the other is horizontal toward people.

- Love for God is demonstrated by a life of OBEDIENCE to all He commands.

- Love for our neighbor is demonstrated by GIVING our time, money, and life away to those in need.

- When Christ's life of love rules us, we don't live for ourselves any longer, but for Him and others.

- We don't try to love. Love flows from a relationship with a loving God.

NOTES

VCL
VICTORIOUS CHRISTIAN LIVING Conference
Copyright © 1999 Victorious Christian Living International, Inc.

LOVE

Lesson Transcript by David Ritzenthaler

Love. Big subject. Everybody's talking about it. But what is it that most people are talking about? We hear consistently about falling in love. But if you understand what love is, you know you can't "fall" into it. Love is a decision of the will. In fact, **love is considering what's important for someone else and doing what is in that person's best interest without expecting anything in return**. One of the best examples of that was Mother Theresa. She lived her life without expecting anything in return for giving her life for the many that were in need.

Turn with me to the lesson on love. There is a cute little quote on the introduction page. Someone wittily expressed feelings I have. "To live above with saints I love, that surely will be glory! But to live below with saints I know— well, that's a different story!!" One of the things we see consistently in ministry to people is a lack of love. People really don't know how to love.

One of the things I want to point out before we begin this session is that this lesson is not like any of the other lessons in the VCL. All the other lessons were about causes that bring about effects. This lesson is about the effect. This is the result. This is what happens when you learn issues with regard to godship or you learn issues with regard to identity or you learn issues with regard to problems and their purpose. All the other things we teach about in the VCL Conference cause things to happen. This lesson is different. We're not telling you in this lesson that you need to love. Remember, love is a fruit of the Holy Spirit, the effect of being connected to the vine of Jesus Christ. And it's produced by the Father doing things in our life to produce

love. So, when we talk together in the next few minutes, I don't want you to think that we are saying that you need to love. No. Love is an effect. It is the result of the life of Christ being your living experience.

LOVE (Diagram 220-A)

Turn with me to your outline. Roman numeral one is "The Pinnacle of Love." I would like you to get your Bibles out, because I want us to see some things about love in the Scriptures. First of all, I want us to see that love is God's goal in the life of a believer. Secondly, I want us to see that love is actually the end result of a work that God does in the life of a believer. This is not something that we do. It's something that happens when we do certain things. In other words, love is the result, and it is God's goal. It is what God wants to see happen in the life of a believer. It is, in fact, among believers, the end result of what happens when believers minister to each other. They build each other up in love.

Look with me, if you would, at Matthew 22:36-40. You remember this little discourse where they were talking to Jesus and someone said, "Teacher, which is the great commandment in the Law?" In verse thirty seven: "And He [Jesus] said to him, 'You shall love the Lord your God with all your heart, with all your soul, with all your mind.' This is the great and foremost commandment. The second is like it. 'You shall love your neighbor as yourself.' On these two commandments depend the whole Law and Prophets." I emphasize that, because, the New Testament starts right here, and back here is the Law and Prophets. [Illustrated by holding up the Bible showing the size of the different portions.]

LOVE

It says that the Law and Prophets—all that stuff back there—depends on these two commandments.

You will notice one of those commandments is a vertical commandment. It's loving God. It's a vertical issue. The other one, you will notice, is a horizontal commandment. It is a horizontal issue dealing with loving other human beings, other people. So, you'll see there is a twofold dimension: vertically loving God and horizontally loving our neighbor or other people. The result of loving God and loving others comes from the many things that we teach in the VCL. So, if you haven't had a chance to listen to all the other lessons, I would encourage you to do that because this lesson is the result. This is what should happen in your life. A life of love should be your life experience, if you understand how to let Christ live His life through you.

Notice Romans 13:8 says, "Owe nothing to anyone except to love one another; for he who loves his neighbor has fulfilled the law." In other words, all these books on the law are accomplished simply by loving our neighbor. [Show size of first five books of the Bible.] We don't have to learn all those books. All we have to do is let the Christ of heaven live in us so that we love our neighbor; and then, we fulfill the Law. Also, Galatians 5:14 says, " For the whole Law is fulfilled in one word, in the statement, 'You shall love your neighbor as yourself.'" That's the horizontal dimension. So, we read here that God's whole goal, in all that He wrote in the Law, was that we would love our neighbor.

Also, in 1 John 4:7-13, again notice, it says that love is the very essence of who God really is. Listen as I read verses 7-11. "Beloved, let us love one another, for love is from God; and everyone who loves is born of God and knows God. The one who does not love does not know God, for God is love. By this the love of God was manifested in us, that God has sent His only

begotten Son into the world so that we might live through Him. In this is love, not that we loved God, but that He loved us and sent His son to be the propitiation for our sins. Beloved, if God so loved us, we also ought to love one another." So we see a vertical picture of God loving us, causing us to love Him, and causing us to love other people. It is a result of a work God does in our lives. "B" in the outline also says that it is the end result. In other words, it is not only God's goal, it is the final thing that God accomplishes in the believer.

Turn with me to Ephesians the fourth Chapter. This is a fairly long section, but I want us to read it so we can see that love is actually the end result of the life in the community of believers. You are probably already familiar with some of the verses. We're going to start with verse eleven: "And He gave some as apostles, and some as prophets, and some as evangelists, and some as pastors and teachers." All these people, the Word of God says were given, "for the equipping of the saints for the work of service, to the building up of the body of Christ; until we all attain to the unity of the faith, and of the knowledge of the Son of God, to a mature man, to the measure of the stature which belongs to the fullness of Christ."

Let me ask you a question. If God's goal in the measure of fullness is that we would measure up to the fullness which belongs to Jesus Christ, how complete, how perfect, how full is the measure? That's a fairly mature measure. Notice in Ephesians 4:14-16 how He says this happens: "As a result, we are no longer to be children, tossed here and there by waves, and carried about by every wind of doctrine, by the trickery of men, by craftiness and deceitful scheming; but speaking the truth in love, we are to grow up in all aspects into Him, who is the head, even Christ, from whom the whole body, being fitted and held together by that which every joint supplies, according to the proper working of every individual part, causes the growth of the body for the building up of itself in love." In other words, each one is contributing his or her part. So, we are all functioning effectively together, properly, the way God designed. That's how the body of Christ is grown.

God's goal and end result in the life of believers and in the body of Christ is a life of love. Well, why is that? What's the purpose of all that? We will see that the reason God wants to grow us up is so the whole world can see that we're His children. In fact, the real evidence of the completing work of Christ's life, which is love horizontally to others, is what demonstrates that we are actually His children. Notice with me also in Colossians 3:14 what it says love is. "And beyond all these things" [he's just described various characteristics of the Christian life] "put on love, which is the perfect bond of unity." It's the end result of perfection—a life of love in a believer.

In 1 Timothy 1:5, we see that same thing. Paul in teaching Timothy says, "But the goal of our instruction is love from a pure heart and a good conscience and a sincere faith." The goal—of the teaching, the end work, the end objective of all that God is doing in the life of believers and in the body of Christ—is love. You say: "Well, how do I love? How do I make that happen?" I am truly convinced by my own personal experience and by that of hundreds of others whom I have had an opportunity to watch, that love is not something that you and I can produce. It's not something that we can make happen in our lives. It is truly a work of Christ—Him dwelling in us and His life flowing through us. Love is an effect. It's a result.

Martin Luther said, "I would rather obey than work miracles." And you say, "OK, well, so what?" Well, look at this next section, Roman numeral two, "Love's Twofold Dimension." I want you to see something. First of all, let's look at the vertical aspect of what God calls loving Him and how He describes it. He actually uses other words that are absolutely synonymous with the word love. These words will fit into the four boxes. Let's read some of those together. In John 14:23-24, Jesus says: "If anyone loves Me, he will keep My word; and My Father will love him, and We will come to him, and make Our abode with him. He who does not love Me does not keep My words; and the word which you hear is not Mine, but the Father's who sent Me."

When you think about the idea of loving God, what other word do you see here that could be used to mean the same as loving God? It would be to **obey** Him. The word is "keep" in this particular section, but God says that to love Him is to obey Him. That is why Martin Luther said he'd rather obey than work miracles. Look at John 15:9-11, 14, starting at verse nine: "Just as the Father has loved Me, I have also loved you; abide in My love. If you keep [or obey] My commandments, you will abide in My love; just as I have kept My Father's commandments, and abide in His love. These things I have spoken to you, that My joy may be in you, and that your joy may be made full." Verse fourteen says, "You are My friends, if you do what I command you." Let me ask you a question. How many of you as believers in Christ Jesus would like to enjoy being completely at home with God? How many of you would like God to make Himself at home with you? Did you notice what it says the conditions are? God will make Himself at home with us, and we will have the privilege of being at home with Him, if you and I obey vertically. To love God is to obey Him.

George McDonald says, "I find the obeying of the will of God leaves me no time for disputing about His plans." There are many who, instead of obeying and doing what God says, spend their time arguing in their minds about what God wants. I know. I have been there myself. I remember a situation not too long ago when the Lord was speaking to me. It regarded giving a Suburban I had to a couple with four kids. They had come into the center and I saw their need. Their boys were good-sized and they had a little two-door, hatchback Toyota that barely held them all. In fact, when they all got in, they were packed so tightly that they could hardly breathe. That's how it looked. At the time, I was driving a nice nine-passenger Suburban. I was the only one that rode in it every day. So the Lord spoke His Spirit to my heart and said, "You should give them the Suburban." I did the normal process so many of us do. I argued with the Lord over issues: I didn't have any money to buy another one. I did remind Him, it was painted to match my boat. I went through various discussions with Him. In fact, I put it off. I didn't really like the idea very well. About a week later they came into the center, and, wouldn't you know it, that is when I came into the lobby to get my mail. The Lord said again: "Well David, I want to remind you that I have asked you to give them the Suburban. They need it. You don't need it."

So, I went through the mental gyrations again trying to explain to the Lord the various reasons why that wasn't a very reasonable consideration. Forgetting, of course, that the Lord owns all the Suburbans. Though the name on the title may be mine, it was only a matter of stewardship. He could take me out tomorrow and I wouldn't own the Suburban.

About a month later I was going to work a different way than I would normally go when I came to a four-way stop. I stopped, and I noticed the car on the other side. I waved for them to go on through. As they got into the intersection, I noticed these people were trying to wave at me. It was difficult because it was the people with their four boys in their little two-door, hatchback Toyota. They were having trouble waving because there wasn't much room. I was sitting in my nice, big Suburban, with my stereo blaring. I was enjoying this nine-passenger vehicle, but the Lord convicted my heart. I couldn't wait for the day to be finished, so I could take the car over to their place and give it to them. I figured I would trade them for

the little two-door. So, I'd just drop mine off, and I'd pick up their Toyota.

I got there and presented the fact that the Lord had spoken to me telling me I should give this Suburban to them. They looked at me a little puzzled, then took the title I had in my hand. I said, "I'll just drive yours home then," and they said, "No, we need our other car." There I stood, trying to figure out what God had forgotten in this whole deal. I asked them if they might just be willing to take me home. They were more than glad to do that. They agreed to drive me home in the Suburban.

They dropped me off, and I began to ask the Lord, "Well, what do you have in mind here?" About a day later a guy called me up and said: "Hey, I have an old, old Chevy station wagon. It is about to die. The engine is about shot in it, but I'd like to give it to you. I know you need a car." I said: "Now wait a minute, Lord! This is not a very fair deal here." When the man brought it over, he explained the situation to me. He said: "I want you to understand, I do have another motor for it and I'll change it out when it is necessary. But I'll tell you what, because of the condition it is in, if it needs to be repaired I want you to take it to the shop where I have my other cars and trucks repaired. It won't cost you anything. You just take it there and have it repaired."

I thought, "Well Lord, okay. Now you're getting started here and this is good." As we stood there talking he said: "Well, I'll tell you what. I'll pay for the gas and the oil for it for this next year, too, so it really doesn't cost you anything to drive it." And I thought, "Lord, now you're really getting down to business here." The Lord is amazing and He is gracious. I did enjoy, for over a year, driving that car all over the place. One day I went out the front entrance of the office, and it decided it wasn't going to go anymore. Do you know what the Lord wanted to do? The Lord wanted to give me a new

VCL

VICTORIOUS CHRISTIAN LIVING Conference
Copyright © 1999 Victorious Christian Living International, Inc.

Suburban. That was why He wanted that one to quit. It was just a couple days later a guy called me up and said, "Hey, I understand you're driving an old wagon and you need a car. I know you like Suburbans. Go out and look for what you want, then I'll go and buy it for you." So, I enjoyed that one for years. Just recently, another man came along and said, "I think you need a new Suburban." He bought me a new Suburban. I now drive a brand new one. The Lord is amazing.

There is a key thing He wants to get through to us, so we can enjoy His supernatural provision. If I hadn't obeyed and given the first Suburban away, I never would have enjoyed all the Suburbans since or His supernatural provision. I would have been caught up in trying to provide them for myself. The Lord wants us to obey. The key way that God says He experiences us loving Him is by obeying Him. Notice some of these in John 15:9-10: "Just as the Father has loved Me, I have also loved you; abide in My love. If you keep my commandments, you will abide in My love; just as I have kept my Father's commandments, and abide in His love." Read verses 12 and 14: "This is My commandment, that you love one another, just as I have loved you. You are my friends, if you do what I command you." Would you like to be a friend? Would you like to be in this situation? "If anyone loves Me, he will keep My word; and My Father will love him, and We will come to him and make Our home with him" (John 14:23 NKJV). Would you like to experience the Lord's presence, of Him being at home with you? It comes through practical, actual steps of obedience when He speaks to your heart. When His word tells you to do things, you do what He says, you don't—as George McDonald says—dispute about His plans.

THE EXPERIENCE OF THE OBEDIENCE CYCLE (Diagram 220-B)
Only in those moments when we find ourselves in an impossible situation and choose to obey what God told us to do, do we begin to experience the supernatural working of His life. We experience the incredible enjoyment of His presence because we become friends. In 1 John 3, I'd like to illustrate Diagram 220-B. This diagram is designed to take chapter three of 1 John and simply lay it out for you to see what it says. Turn to 1 John 3:21-22 and let's look at what the Word says with regard to how to experience the presence of God, and how to actually enjoy the results of obedience. This particular Scripture is designed to help us see that. Starting at verse twenty one: "Beloved, if our heart does not condemn us, we have confidence before God; and whatever we ask we receive from Him." This next word "because" is key. Because what? What is "the cause" that causes your heart not to condemn you, for you to have confidence or faith, and therefore ask and receive? What is it? "Because we keep [obey] His commandments and do the things that are pleasing in His sight." Experientially what begins to happen? If you look at your diagram, there is a little triangle under the word obey— because we obey or keep His commandments, that's point number one. It causes the effect that brings the rest of the results. So, when we obey God, what happens? In obeying, we actually, experientially have no sense of condemnation. We begin to experientially know God as our personal experience. Because we have no sense of condemnation, it gives us experientially the faith or the confidence to believe that if we ask we will receive. That is exactly what you see is the next issue.

Well, what do you think asking and receiving from God would cause us to want to do? Obey more, so that we would have less condemnation. Now I understand that when you were born again spiritually you were made completely perfect in spirit—God has already accomplished that. If you listen to other lessons, you'll realize God is in the process of sanctifying in your soul—mind, will, and emotions—what's already accomplished in perfection in your spirit. He's

LOVE

in the process of doing this. I'm not talking about being perfect spiritually in position. I'm talking about practice, by your experience, of what is true in position. You're already in a place of no condemnation. God's already forgiven all your sins. Everything is cleansed, but experiencing that positional reality comes through obeying. Vertically, to love God is to obey God.

One last thing: If you turn to 1 John 5 and read the first three verses of that chapter it says: "Whoever believes that Jesus is the Christ is born of God; and whoever loves the Father loves the child born of Him. By this we know that we love the children of God, when we love God and observe His commandments. For this is the love of God, that we keep His commandments; and His commandments are not burdensome [grievous]." Obeying God's commandments, loving God, is not grievous. It's not a burden; it's not difficult; it's not a hard thing. It's a wonderful thing, because when we do, we begin to experience the manifestation of His presence. We begin to enjoy being at home with Him, and He begins being at home with us. We experience what it is to be His friend.

This effect of living the Christ-life rule doesn't only produce a life of obedience to Christ. Oswald Chambers says of obedience: "The golden rule for spiritual understanding is not in love, but obedience. If a man wants scientific knowledge, intellectual curiosity is his guide; but if he wants insight into Jesus he can only get it by obedience. If things are dark to us then we may be sure there is something we will not do. Intellectual darkness comes through ignorance. Spiritual darkness comes because of something we do not intend to obey. All God's revelations are sealed until they are open to us by obedience. We will never get them open by philosophy or thinking. Immediately when we obey, the light comes on, the promises of God are of no value to us until by obedience we understand the nature of God. We read something in the Bible

three hundred sixty five times and it means nothing to us. Then all of a sudden, we see what God means because in some particular way we've obeyed God, and instantly His life and His word is opened up to us."

Obedience is a wonderful thing. Because obedience is what causes us to actually, experientially, experience God. Yet this whole issue of loving God or obeying God can only be accomplished when we let the Holy Spirit of God, when we let the Christ of heaven through all of His supernatural power, live in and through us. By abiding in Him, by walking after His Spirit, by resting in His presence, there is fullness of joy.

TOWARD MANKIND (Diagram 220-C)

Along with this twofold dimension of vertically obeying God, God says there are two commandments. The second commandment is the horizontal one of loving mankind. You notice here in the outline are four little boxes. The word love has four letters. There is another word that has four letters that describes love. It is synonymous with loving mankind. God says if you love, this is what you will do. It's the same as the word love. It's just a word that helps us better understand what love actually means. Most of you probably learned the first verse there, John 3:16, "For God so loved the world that He gave His only begotten Son . . . ." You see, loving horizontally has to do with another dimension. Vertically has to do with obeying. Turn with me again to John and let's look at what He says the horizontal process is. John 13:34-35: "A new commandment I give to you, that you love one another, even as I have loved you, that you also love one another. By this all men will know that you are My disciples, if you have love for one another."

The way God demonstrates love actually exists in us, the way God demonstrated that His life actually dwells in us, is through the horizontal process of loving other people. In other words, a believer who is abiding in Christ, who is resting, who is walking after the Spirit—the result of that person's life is a life of love toward other people. If you are struggling with loving other people, if you're struggling with Christ's life being expressed in love, it's probably because you haven't learned how to let Christ be your life. God wants us to be where we are totally incapable, so that we will in fact depend on Him to produce His life.

Look at John 15 again. Starting at verse twelve, it says: "This is My commandment, that you love one another, just as I have loved you." Then He begins to give us greater detail, "Greater love has no one than this, that one lay down his life for his friends." Then He says again, "You are My friends, if you do what I command you."

So what does this horizontal life look like when we love others? What are we actually doing? What would be another word just like the word love that we could put in these four little boxes with four letters that's the same as loving? What would it be? If love is to **give**, giving is the same as loving horizontally. When the life of Christ dwells in us the effect or the result of what happened in our life is that we give our life away. We give our time, we give our money, we give our very life for our friends. In fact, the Lord Jesus even gave His life for those of us that were enemies. The life of Christ is so supernatural and powerful that it gives itself away for those that are even enemies.

I had a young man come a number of years ago who had tried to commit suicide a number of times. His aunt called and arranged for him to see me, and when he came he began to tell a story. I can appreciate why he was at this place. You see, he grew up in this family where his father was a doctor. When he was a young boy, his father took him to a psychologist because at ten years of age he wasn't doing very well in school. As is true in the psychological world there are various theories that people are devel-

oping. (That means a theory is something that they can't prove that it works; but it's a good idea, so they include it as one of the many theories of how to help people.)

At that particular time there was a theory around in education that if you put a bunch of chairs on the floor and you had this kid crawl through these chairs, it would help him in learning. So Neil's dad set up these chairs and had Neil doing this. After a period of time Neil thought this was kind of ridiculous. He didn't really want, at ten years of age, to do this anymore. So his father took him back to the psychologist.

Neil gave me a letter which said, "You are welcome to share this with anyone." What happened, I was told, was this psychologist told his father he needed to get a cattle prod and use it, and that would insure that Neil would go through the chairs. So he got a cattle prod, and Neil informed me that at times he found himself even with bloody knees crawling through these chairs to try to make himself learn better. That was just the beginning of things.

At 18, Neil was a senior in high school, graduating that year. He went home one day from school and went into the house looking for his mom, but he couldn't find her. Well, he did find her in her closet. She had taken a shotgun and blown her head off. That's the way he found her.

So by the time I met Neil at nineteen years of age, he informed me he had tried drugs, he had tried all kinds of things to mask the pain of his home, his family, and his life experience. He tried sex; he tried rock music; he tried everything he could try—as much as he could get of it, to try to get rid of the pain. The only thing left was to kill himself. He really wanted to die because he felt he would finally be at peace.

I remember meeting with Neil that one day and I remember saying to Neil: "What you need to do is die. That's exactly what you need to do." He

LOVE

said he thought, "Oh man, this guy understands." I said, "Neil, what I want you to understand is that you don't need to die physically. Your conviction is if you die physically then you'll be at peace. I want to show you how you'll be at peace by dying to your self-life."

As I began to explain these things and show him how Christ could be his life and he began to discover this life, he then wrote this letter and I want to read what he said: "I just want to write and tell you thanks for showing me to Christ. He has shown me so much and He still shows me more and more. I am so excited to see what He has done and, also, has in store for me. If you ever need any help in anything, I give you my life. You can call on me anytime! My heart is open to you and anyone else who comes into my life. It is so neat to see how far I've come. I'm so glad my aunt found you because I know I would be dead today. I wouldn't be able to share God's love with anyone. Since I'm alive, I've watched so many people grow in Christ. You see when a person discovers this life and Christ becomes his life, what happens is his life becomes consumed with someone other than himself."

You can hear it happening right here in the letter. He says: "It is so exciting to see my family come closer together since my mother took her life and we got so far apart. I have a lot of teenagers who come up and ask me if I want to get high on drugs, but I say, 'no.' I tell them I can get high without drugs and it doesn't cost me a thing. They're always so curious and ask, 'Well, how can you get high without any drugs?' I tell them that God gives me a high to where I feel like my head is going to burst with all the love that is locked up inside me. It is so neat to share the Word of God. Each day gets more exciting. Now when I cry, it's a happy cry. You know I used to give to myself and I didn't love myself, and now I give to others and I love myself. I feel happier giving to others than I do giving to myself. So, I want to tell you

thanks. I love you so much, don't be surprised if I hug you the next time I see you."

You see the life of Christ produces automatically the result of vertically wanting to obey God and horizontally wanting to give your life away to someone else. It isn't something you have to teach or command or motivate someone to do. The person can't help it, because the love of Christ constrains him to begin to give his life away to others.

On your outline, Roman numeral number three, it says, "What Is love?" You know we went all this way through this to finally define what is love. We hear people saying all the time, "I love you." In fact, many times I have had a young woman come in for counseling and tell the sad story of some man, who even called himself a Christian, meeting her in a bar, telling her he loved her, and she went home with him. Now she lives with the tragedy of having had an abortion or whatever else. You see this word is thrown around all the time, this word "love."

The Bible says, "God is love." Yet, God is not a part of any of that kind of corrupt immorality. That isn't love, that's lust. When a young man says, "I fall into love," what he is really saying in most cases is I fall into lust. I give myself over to lust. You see as we describe love: "What is love?" A. **It is a motive that is always right or righteous.** It's never, never considering what is for my own pleasure and benefit. It's always considering what is best for someone else, giving to that person the very lifetime energy that I have, without considering anything in return for myself. Love is always right; it's motive is righteous. B. **It's a decision of the will; it isn't something you fall into.** It's because you decided to let the Christ of heaven rule your life and as a result of Him ruling your life, you can't help but be filled with an overflowing dimension of life that's greater than what you need for yourself. **Love is a decision and a commitment for someone else's benefit and not for**

VCL

VICTORIOUS CHRISTIAN LIVING Conference
Copyright © 1999 Victorious Christian Living International, Inc.

yourself. C. It's a deed of present attitude and action. It isn't just thinking good thoughts; it's action on those good thoughts. It isn't someday "pie in the sky wanting to do something." It's when God speaks, and all of His Holy Spirit in all of His grace and mercy work in your heart to not only think the thought, but take the action to do it. **Love is a deed of present attitude and action.**

I would just ask you, as we conclude this lesson: Is love your living experience? Could you truly put your arms around any human being in the world and tell that person genuinely, "I love you"? Would you at this point in time be willing to give of everything that you have, because God might ask it of you, because you are only a temporary steward of it anyway? It isn't yours and it isn't mine you see. Are you enjoying this supernatural life? If you're not, I would encourage you to go back and listen to the rest of the series of tapes in the VCL that speak to how you have the supernatural life. Jesus said, "I came that they might have life, and might have it abundantly" (John 10:10). That's more than you need for yourself. This life of love is the result of having that life. It's the effect you can't help. It just happens through you because it is Christ Himself living through you and me.

If that's not your life experience, I would pray that, today, you would make a decision to discover the answer how to have that supernatural life. Would you join with me as we conclude and as we pray.

"Heavenly Father, I pray right now that the life of love would be the living experience of everyone who listens to this video. I pray, heavenly Father, that Your Spirit would enjoy the freedom and the privilege of dwelling in, and flowing through, the lives of every believer in obedience to You—to the giving away of everything—their life, their time, their energy, and their money to those that need to know You. Even to those that know You who have never discovered You as the fullness of their life. Heavenly Father, we just thank You for the privilege of being Your children. We thank You that You loved us first. You gave Yourself without any limitations, so that You could produce that same kind of life in us. In Your gracious and wonderful name, Lord Jesus, we give thanks. Amen"

CONGRATULATIONS!
You just completed the first level of training at Victorious Christian Living!

We have three levels of training:
1. Victorious Christian Living Conference
2. Life Ministry Training
3. Training In Discipleship

Would you like to be trained to use this Victorious Christian Living Conference material to help someone else?
You can by taking the second level of training, Life Ministry Training.

This is a 36-hour training workshop that will teach you:

1. How to obey the great commission to disciple others.
2. How to minister the Victorious Christian Living messages to another person.
3. How to apply the Victorious Christian Living messages to yourself and others in all seven areas of life.
4. How to use God's Word in ministering to others.
5. Ministry principles to guide you in ministering to others.

Check with your church to see when the next Life Ministry Training Workshop will start or call Victorious Christian Living International at 602-482-2164.

ISBN 0-7392-0015-1 $30.00

5 3 0 0 0>

EAN

9 780739 200155